RECREATIONAL RAILROADS

RECREATIONAL RAILROADS

THE WORLD'S
FINEST RAILROADS RESTORED
TO THEIR FORMER GLORY

Arthur Tayler

CHARTWELL
BOOKS, INC.

A QUINTET BOOK

Published by Chartwell Books
A Division of Book Sales, Inc.
114 Northfield Avenue
Edison, New Jersey 08837

This edition produced for sale in the U.S.A., its
territories and dependencies only.

ISBN 0-7858-0654-7

Reprinted 1997

This book was designed and produced by
Quintet Publishing Limited
6 Blundell Street
London N7 9BH

Creative Director: Richard Dewing
Designer: Peter Laws
Project Editor: Diana Steedman
Editor: Philip de St Croix
Cartography: Julian Baker

Typeset in Great Britain by
Central Southern Typesetters, Eastbourne
Manufactured in Singapore by
Eray Scan Pte Ltd
Printed in China by
Leefung-Asco Printers Limited

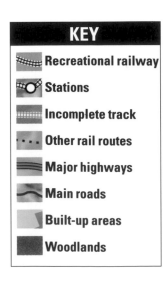

Contents

Introduction

Until the 1950s, railroads were an everyday part of life in countries throughout the world. Since then, the pace of change has accelerated, with familiar institutions being rapidly destroyed. The once-familiar steam locomotive was fast disappearing, and it has been left to a few individuals to save it from extinction. Parts of the railroad systems of many countries have also been rescued, often lines that have special scenic or historical attractions but that were no longer profitable to operate. Some have been preserved and turned into working museums, and others have become pure tourist attractions. Many such lines are operated by steam locomotives, but by no means all of them: there is also a growing interest in first-generation diesels and early electric railroads. Whatever the type of motive power, the preservers strive to maintain the unique character of each individual line.

There are a number of countries around the world where railroad preservation is growing, motivated both by enthusiasm for railroads and by a wish to support tourism. It is not big business, and these lines are operated mainly by unpaid volunteers who give many hours of their valuable time to make their lines successful.

During the golden age of rail transport, it was accepted that most railroads lost money, and in many countries they were subsidized by government, if not government-owned. The Depression of the 1930s affected railroads' fortunes, and many could not afford new

rolling stock. With the start of World War II, railroads needed every piece of rolling stock they could lay their hands on—but new locomotives and freight vehicles could only be built if they were needed for the War effort.

Many European railroads were severely damaged during the War; locomotives, carriages and wagons were destroyed, and most could not be replaced at the time. Many miles of track were also destroyed or seriously damaged. When the War ended, there was a huge backlog of repairs and maintenance, and much rebuilding work to be done. In many cases, where railroads had been under temporary government control, there was little or no funding available. American railroads were the exception: they had learned from their experience in World War I, and had remained in control of their own affairs.

With the end of the War, railroads found themselves ill-equipped and unable to make a quick recovery. The automobile, for which the public had hungered for five or six years, was suddenly made widely available, and many smaller railroad lines lost their traffic. Ten years after the end of the War in Europe, many country branch lines that could not pay their way were closed, their tracks removed and rights-of-way sold. At the same time governments were pouring money into building new roads, and the remaining railroads were left without support.

In Great Britain Dr Richard Beeching, appointed Chairman of the British Railways Board on 1 September 1963 by Ernest Marples, then Transport Minister, is synonymous with the closure of many thousands of miles of railroad, both main and branch lines. His single-minded approach was dictated by the need to end the mounting financial losses that were crippling British Railways. To this end he had to close many lines; in consequence the process was dubbed "wielding The Beeching Axe" by dismayed railroad supporters and enthusiasts.

The process had begun before the Beeching regime, but he accelerated the closure process. Railroad preservation really came into being in the middle-1950s, certainly in Great Britain. Railroad enthusiasts, and others who saw their dependable local railroads about to disappear, bitterly contested the closures at first. In the end, railroad supporters had to accept economic realities, but groups were formed to preserve something of the more remarkable lines that were disappearing, and to open them to tourist traffic.

In the USA, meanwhile, new highways were being built, and internal airlines grew to take much of the passenger traffic, and later freight, from the railroads. Here, preservation was motivated mostly by people who suddenly realized trains were interesting in themselves and "fun to ride," and by groups who saw that preserved lines could boost the tourist industry while holding on to something of the past. Tourist railroads grew up, offering people the opportunity simply to enjoy the experience of riding a train.

Recreational Railroads highlights some of the world's finest preserved or museum railroads. Out of the many lines now operating, some of the longest, most scenic or most interesting have been chosen. Preserved, tourist and museum lines, and railroad museums, exist in many countries around the world. In addition to preserved lines, all of these countries operate special trains for groups or individual owners of locomotives, often over considerable distances, on main-line routes. The book includes 23 lines and museums in the USA and Canada (where altogether there are over 350 lines and museums), 12 lines in the British Isles (over 90 lines and museums), 12 in western Europe (over 80 lines and museums), and seven in the southern hemisphere (over 30 lines and museums). There are maps showing locations and, where applicable, former connections with the main-line system; a brief history of origins; and date lines showing important points in history. Each line's extensions, rolling stock future plans and visitor facilities are listed.

This selection of preserved, tourist and museum railroads is far from exhaustive, and the list continues to grow. The object of this book is to give some idea of what each country offers and, it is hoped, to whet the reader's appetite to visit and ride more lines.

NORTH AMERICA

Royal Hudson Steam Train

BRITISH COLUMBIA, CANADA

USEFUL DATA

Headquarters BC Rail Passenger Depot: 1311 West First Street, North Vancouver, BC.

Phone (604) 631 3500/ (604) 986 2012.

Fax (604) 984 5505.

Mail to PO Box 8770, Vancouver, BC V6B 4X6.

Public Stations BC Rail passenger station, Pemberton Street, Vancouver & Squamish.

Reservations, Timetables & Tickets 800 663 8238.

Public access
BC Transit Shuttle; North Vancouver Seabus (521 0400).
Car park at BC Rail Passenger Station (free).

Facilities
Snack bar on train; picnics at Squamish, meals on boat.

RIGHT *"Royal Hudson" 4-6-4 No 2860 carrying the Royal crest on the Capilano Bridge North Vancouver.*

BRITISH
COLUMBIA

PRINCE GEORGE

QUESNEL

WILLIAMS LAKE

EXETER
100 MILE HOUSE

CLINTON

SETON PORTAGE
D'ARCY
PEMBERTON
WHISTLER

LILLOOET
SHALALTH

SQUAMISH

NORTH VANCOUVER

ROYAL HUDSON
STEAM TRAIN

ABOVE *The "Royal Hudson" crest conferred by King George VI of England on No 2850.*

The Royal Hudson Steam Train is not a preserved railroad, but rather a chance to experience rail travel on beautifully restored coaches hauled by a preserved steam locomotive, traveling through magnificent scenery. The excursion is run by the Royal Hudson Steam Train Society, in conjunction with Harbour Ferries Limited, over British Columbia Rail's tracks from Vancouver north along the shore of Howe Sound to Squamish —a distance of about 40 miles.

BC Rail is a Class I Railroad. It was founded on 27 February 1912, and opened in 1914 as the Pacific Great Eastern Railway, to link the Grand Trunk Pacific from Edmonton, Alberta, at Prince George with the Port of Vancouver. The line was soon built from Squamish to the Cariboo, but the final stretch south to Vancouver was not completed until

1956. The name was changed to BC Rail by the owner, the Province of British Columbia. The line's revenue is derived mainly from the transport of forestry products, coal and other minerals.

When King George VI of England visited Canada with Queen Elizabeth in 1939, the train that carried them was drawn by Canadian Pacific "Hudson" engine No. 2850. To commemorate the journey, the King conferred the title of "Royal" on the class of engine hauling the train. The engine used today is No. 2860, actually built by Montreal Locomotive Works in 1940, but still of the same class. There were 45 "Royal Hudson" semi-streamlined locomotives altogether, and each carried a cast-metal replica crown on its running-board skirting.

The trip from Vancouver is full of scenic

provincial Marine Park, the line passes the site of what was once Canada's largest copper mine at Britannia Sound, which closed in 1979. At the entrance to the Squamish Valley is The Stawamus Chief, a 2,138-foot rock face renowned for the number of climbers who come from all over the world to face its challenge; it was scaled for the very first time in 1957.

The train then reaches Squamish, originally called Newport until the officials of the Pacific Great Eastern decided the name ought to be changed. A contest among school children in 1912 decided the town should be called after the native Squamish people. Here the steam train terminates, and travelers have the choice of returning to Vancouver either by train or by a cruise through Howe Sound on board the MV *Britannia*. On occasion, the train may be hauled by BC Rail's other restored steam locomotive, a "Consolidation" 2-8-0 No. 3716.

The Royal Hudson runs from May to September, Wednesday to Sunday. The round trip by train, or out by train and back by boat, takes about 5½ hours. The coaches are air-conditioned and the train has a snack bar, while a salmon dinner is available on the boat return journey.

In addition to the Royal Hudson, BC Rail operates two other passenger services. One of them, the Whistler Explorer—a Rail Diesel Car (RDC) train—runs Monday to Friday from May to mid-October, in conjunction with buses from Whistler north to Clinton, through some of the most spectacular mountain scenery in Canada. Another passenger train (also RDC) service, the Cariboo Prospector, covers the whole of the 462½ miles from Vancouver to Prince George, through picturesque scenery and an area packed with history. One can travel the whole or part of the distance, and spend days and nights in the fascinating towns on the route.

ABOVE *"Royal Hudson" 4-6-4 No 2860 leaving the tunnel cutting off Whytecliff on today's Royal Hudson special.*

DATE LINE

Pacific & Great Eastern Rly founded	**27 February 1912**
First train ran	**1914**
Completed from Squamish-Vancouver	**1956**

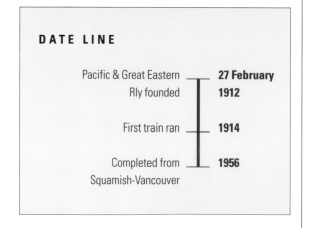

interest. The journey starts at BC Rail's Vancouver passenger station at the foot of Pemberton Street. The line passes under the Lions Gate Bridge, opened by King George VI in 1939, and then through Ambleside and residential West Vancouver to Horseshoe Bay, where the original 1914 line ended at a station called Whytecliff. This is now avoided by a 1,500-yard tunnel, the longest on BC Rail. Having reached Howe Sound, now a

Salem & Hillsborough Railroad

N E W   B R U N S W I C K ,   C A N A D A

LEFT *Canadian Pacific No 29 & Canadian National 1009 double head a train arriving at Salem. No 29 was severely damaged in the fire of 16 September 1994.*

USEFUL DATA

Headquarters Salem & Hillsborough Railroad, PO Box 70, Hillsborough, New Brunswick E0A 1X0.

Phone (506) 386 1346

Public Station Hillsborough.

Timetables phone Headquarters.

Tickets Hillsborough.

Reservations & Charters (506) 734 3100 or 3195.

Public access from route 114 halfway between Moncton (via rail and air) and Fundy National Park.

Facilities Museum open daily July-August. Gift shop with Ticket Office.

Special features Dinner Train (reservations through Railroad Office).

The Salem & Hillsborough Railroad Inc. in New Brunswick, Canada, operates a stretch of just over 11 miles through rural country on what was the Albert Subdivision of the Canadian National Railway, a branch from the line that runs from St John on the Bay of Fundy to Moncton on the Quebec-Halifax line.

The Albert Railway Company was incorporated on 13 April 1864, to run from Salisbury as a feeder to the St John-Moncton-Shediac line—formerly the European & North American Railway—for the transport of timber and minerals. Due to difficulty in raising the money, it was ten years before the first sod was turned in 1874. A local contractor built the line and it was opened on 30 June 1877. Construction was not simple, as the line had to negotiate high ground between Salisbury and the gypsum mill at Hillsborough, which was near to sea level.

Traffic was heavy at first, mainly of gypsum from the huge deposits around Hillsborough, but by 1884 the bondholders had foreclosed. In 1888 the railway was extended to Harvey Bank, and the operating company was renamed the Salisbury & Harvey Railway. With further government subsidies and money from the parishes, the line was extended a further 16 miles on 15 June 1892, and the Albert Southern Railway reached Alma. Traffic was mainly freight, with some passenger services. In 1901 the line was declared unsafe and closed between Harvey and Alma.

NEW BRUNSWICK

Moncton

BALTIMORE

SALEM

HILLSBOROUGH

Albert

Alma

Bay of Fundy

St John

By 1909 the Salisbury & Harvey had passed to a new owner, who renamed it the Salisbury & Albert Railway. Operations were fairly profitable until the middle of World War I, but a decline set in when the gypsum mines closed in 1920. The line had been bought by the Federal Government in 1918 (Intercolonial Railway), and incorporated into the Canadian National Railways.

In 1955, CNR decided to abandon the 20 miles from Hillsborough to Albert, but because there was still traffic from the plaster mill at Hillsborough, it remained in use until 1982. The CNR abandoned the section to Hillsborough, with a power plant at the Salisbury end taking 3 miles, on 10 March 1983. This was subsequently sold to the power company, but the track to Hillsborough has since been lifted.

The Salem & Hillsborough Railway Inc. is owned by the New Brunswick Division of the Canadian Railroad Historical Association. They purchased the 10 miles of line from

ABOVE *Railman Mike White checks on the readiness of No 1009 on 16 September 1994.*

Hillsborough to Baltimore in 1983 for $1.00 because that section offered good scenery.

The original line was laid with relatively light track, and runs in part over marshland with some curvature, so the normal motive power was not very large. Trains were mostly mixed passenger and freight.

Hillsborough was first established in 1692. By the middle of the 19th century it had become a gypsum-producing town. The Salem & Hillsborough yard occupies part of the site of one of the largest gypsum-mining operations in Canada. Between Hillsborough and Salem is the scenic portion of the line, crossing Weldon Creek Bridge, used to film a small part of the "Anne of Green Gables" series. There are dykes and terraced lagoons, but the highlight of the trip is Hiram Creek trestle bridge, built entirely of large square timbers and the last of its kind in New Brunswick. It is 209 feet long and, unusually, curved, and is 44 feet above the road below. The section of line beyond Salem to Baltimore is through wood-

DATE LINE

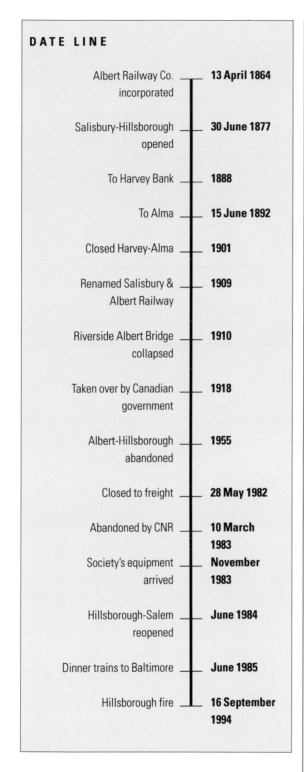

Albert Railway Co. incorporated	**13 April 1864**
Salisbury-Hillsborough opened	**30 June 1877**
To Harvey Bank	**1888**
To Alma	**15 June 1892**
Closed Harvey-Alma	**1901**
Renamed Salisbury & Albert Railway	**1909**
Riverside Albert Bridge collapsed	**1910**
Taken over by Canadian government	**1918**
Albert-Hillsborough abandoned	**1955**
Closed to freight	**28 May 1982**
Abandoned by CNR	**10 March 1983**
Society's equipment arrived	**November 1983**
Hillsborough-Salem reopened	**June 1984**
Dinner trains to Baltimore	**June 1985**
Hillsborough fire	**16 September 1994**

Alco RS1 diesel was completely destroyed, while another RS1, held for spares, is of no further use. The other steam locomotive, an ex-CNR 4-6-0, was parked outside and suffered little damage. Three passenger cars and a boxcar had to be scrapped, along with all of the offices, workshops, machine tools, office equipment, and many historical papers.

In spite of all this, the railroad operated throughout 1995. At present it is confined to diesel haulage, although the 4-6-0 is serviceable. It has taken a great deal of time and dedication to recover from this major setback. Money has to be raised to begin reconstruction of the buildings, which are badly needed again for maintenance work and winter storage. Nonetheless, the railroad managed to organize 12 special events for 1995. At present there are two operational diesel-electric locomotives; one steam locomotive is serviceable but stored, and one is unserviceable and needing restoration. There are eight passenger cars in service.

In 1995, trains were operated between 11 June and 2 September. Excursion trains run on Sundays. Three-hour Dinner Trains are run with bar facilities and entertainment—details available on request.

ABOVE *Fire damage sustained by No 29 on 19 September 1994, although with much hard work No 29 is restorable.*

land, and is not really suited to operation by steam locomotives.

Disaster occurred on 16 September 1994 when fire completely destroyed the main building at Hillsborough, which housed the offices, workshops and some of the rolling stock. One steam locomotive, an ex-Canadian Pacific 4-4-0 built in 1887, was badly damaged, but fully restorable. An operational

White Pass & Yukon Route

A L A S K A

The White Pass & Yukon Route is a 3-foot-gauge line covering 28 miles of a railroad that was originally opened in 1900, running from the US at Skagway on the Gulf of Alaska through a small part of British Columbia to Whitehorse in Yukon Territory, Canada. It resumed excursion-train operation on 12 May 1988, and is now owned by Russel Metals. Tourist passenger trains run as far as Fraser, BC.

The line had its origins in the gold rush of 1898, when a railroad was needed to transport machinery and supplies from the coast at Skagway, Alaska, over the Coast Mountains to the Yukon River in Yukon Territory, Canada. Construction began in 1898 with gangs working both from Skagway and from Whitehorse in the Yukon. They met at Carcross in the Yukon on 29 July 1900. The line's ultimate destination at one time was Fort Selkirk, Yukon, at the junction of the

Pelly and Lewes (Upper Yukon) rivers. In fact, there were three railroads—the Pacific and Arctic Railway & Navigation Co. with 20 miles in Alaska; the British Columbia–Yukon Railway with 32 miles in British Columbia; and the British Yukon Railway with 58 miles in Yukon territory—all operated by the White Pass and Yukon.

As gold mining eased off, the railroad reorganized, but it continued to carry supplies into the Yukon and to bring out silver, lead, and zinc. The economy of the Yukon was revived by the threat from Japan and the approach of World War II, which increased the railroad's business. The bombing of Pearl Harbor in 1941 resulted in the building of the Alaska Highway, with Whitehorse the construction base. Suddenly the WP&Y was overloaded with traffic and had to be rescued by the US Army's Military Railway Service.

ABOVE *A diesel-hauled excursion crosses a wooden trestle on the White Pass & Yukon.*

DATE LINE

Construction commenced	**1898**
Construction gangs meet Carcross	**29 July 1900**
Opened Whitehorse-Skagway	**August 1900**
Operated by US Army	**1941**
Operated reverted to WP&YRR	**1945**
Formed corporation of three lines	**1951**
Suspended operations	**1983**
Reopened as tourist line	**12 May 1988**

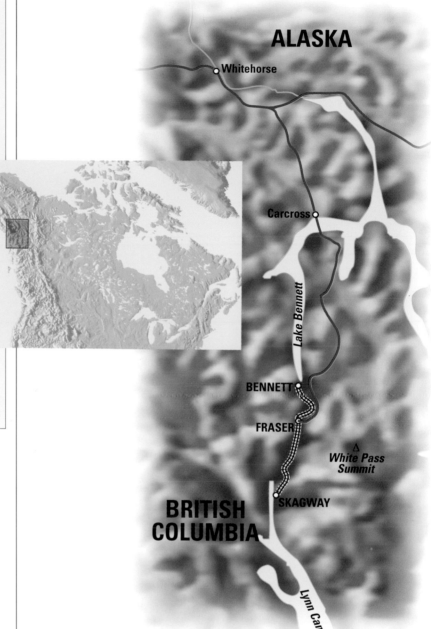

ALASKA

Whitehorse

Carcross

Lake Bennett

BENNETT

FRASER

△ White Pass Summit

SKAGWAY

BRITISH COLUMBIA

Lynn Canal

ABOVE *A trestle and tunnel under construction in 1899 on the White Pass & Yukon route in Alaska.*

WHITE PASS & YUKON ROUTE

USEFUL DATA

Headquarters
White Pass & Yukon Route,
PO Box 435, Skagway,
AK 99840.
Phone (907) 983 2217;
(800) 343 7373.
From British Columbia,
Northwest Territories, and
Yukon (800) 478 7373.
Fax (907) 983 2734.
Public Stations Skagway,
AK, White Pass Summit and
Fraser, BC.

Timetables & Tickets
details by phone, fax, or mail
from Skagway.
Public access
by ship and express bus and
car. Car park.
Facilities
Restaurants & lodging at
Skagway and Whitehorse.
Klondike Gold Rush National
Historical Park. Sightseeing
by helicopter. Locomotive

To handle the extra traffic, the Army purchased narrow-gauge locomotives from several US lines. In 1943, the railroad handled the equivalent of 10 years of pre-war tonnage. This could not last, and when the War ended the railroad returned to the mundane tasks of moving supplies in and minerals out. The railroad also developed a tourist business in connection with cruise ships calling at Skagway. In 1951 the WP&Y became a corporation to acquire ownership of the subsidiary companies.

The mines gradually closed down, and in 1983 the railroad suspended operations. A new highway between Skagway and Whitehorse took the remaining mineral traffic. There was still some revenue from a pipeline paralleling the railroad, with its own large trucking operation.

In 1988 the railroad decided to resume tourist business. Trains now make the round trip from Skagway over the summit of White Pass to Fraser, British Columbia, with buses connecting to and from Whitehorse.

There are some 110 miles of line in all, but only 28 miles are operated for tourist trains. Currently there is one steam locomotive, a Baldwin 2-8-2 built as late as 1947 for the WP&Y, and 13 diesel-electrics built between 1954 and 1966. Seven more from Alco were delivered in 1969 and a further three in 1971. Two of the former were destroyed by fire and the remainder have now moved elsewhere. There are 40 passenger cars, a mixture of coaches and parlor cars. Some are originals which have been restored, while some were built new in the Skagway shops.

Trains are operated between mid-May and mid-September. The round trip to White Pass takes about 4½ hours. Usually there are two round trips each day. The excursion to Whitehorse, with bus north of Fraser, requires an overnight stay. Reservations are recommended 30 days in advance. They can be made direct with the WP&Y headquarters or through a travel agent. Skagway can be reached by air or water from Juneau, Alaska, or by highway from Whitehorse, Yukon.

Grand Canyon Railway

A R I Z O N A

On 17 September 1989 Max Biegert announced, "The Grand Canyon Railway is for real." A century earlier, in the early 1890s, Arizona politician and promoter William O. "Buckley" O'Neill had promoted the idea of a railroad to serve the mines in the Canyon region. His efforts led to the creation of the Sante Fe & Grand Canyon Railroad Company, which began operation on 15 March 1900 between Anita (20 miles south of the Canyon) and Williams, where connection was made with the Sante Fe Pacific Railroad, now part of the Burlington Northern Sante Fe Corporation (Sante Fe division).

Several months later, bankruptcy forced the SF&GC into the control of the Sante Fe Pacific, which completed the line to the rim of the Grand Canyon in 1901. It was the railroad that introduced tourism to the Grand Canyon. Together with the Fred Harvey

USEFUL DATA

Headquarters
Grand Canyon Rly Business Office, 123 N San Francisco, Suite 210, Flagstaff, AZ 86110.
Phone (520) 773 1976.
Fax (520) 773 1610.

Timetables & Tickets
518 East Bill Williams Avenue, Williams, AZ 86046-1704.
Phone (602) 635 4000, (800) THE TRAIN.
Reservations (800) 843 8724.

Public access
Williams is on I-40. Take exit 163 and follow Grand Canyon Boulevard ½ mile to Williams Depot and Fray Marcos Hotel.

Facilities
Grand Canyon Museum, Depot Gift Shop, Depot Cafe, Espresso Bar, Concession stand. Refreshments available on trains.

LEFT *A passenger train of the Grand Canyon Railway with a restored Alco 2-8-0 hauling a train of former Southern Pacific commuter cars.*

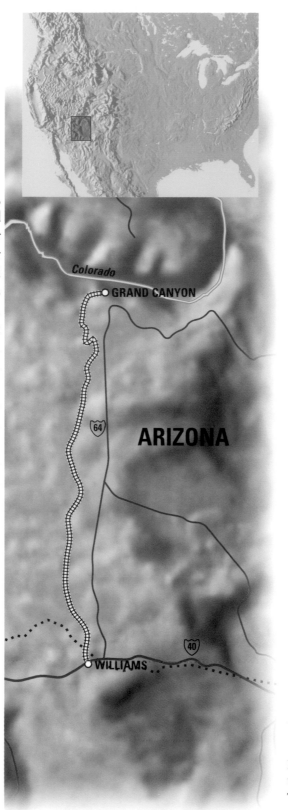

Company, it built hotels, shops, restaurants, a hospital, steam and electric power stations, a water reclamation plant, a fresh water pipeline, a railroad yard and structures, etc. Sante Fe crews erected most of the 600 buildings, many still existing today, that comprise the majority of the Grand Canyon Village National Historic District.

The railroad enjoyed success until the mid-1920s when the road from Williams was paved and the automobiles started to come. From a peak of 70,382 passengers in 1927, the decline began, and in 1954 the Sante Fe pulled out of the hotel business, selling its commercial buildings to the Harvey Company and donating the power stations and utilities to the National Park Service. In 1956 the passenger service was reduced to summer months only, and by 1960 the annual number of passengers had fallen below 10,000. Sante Fe filed for discontinuance in 1968 with only three passengers on the last passenger train. The line was abandoned in 1974.

Sante Fe received permission to take up the tracks in 1980, and contracted Railroad Resources Inc. to do the work. Railroad Resources chose to purchase the right-of-way in order to revive the Grand Canyon Railway as a tourist railroad. The project died in 1987 due to a lack of resources. Then in 1989 along came Max Biegert, a successful Arizona businessman, who had invested in Railroad Resources and now found himself with 22 miles of right-of-way, complete with track.

Rather than selling the track for scrap, Biegert decided to buy the rest of the property and revive the railroad himself. Biegert's aim was to re-inaugurate the railroad on the 88th anniversary of the line's first passenger train to the Canyon in 1901. In only six months, not only was the track restored, but a huge amount of work was done on depots (stations) and buildings, including the Fray Marcos Hotel. The Williams depot is listed on the National Register of Historic Places as the largest and oldest poured-concrete structure in Arizona.

The acquisition of suitable locomotives and rolling stock was a major problem. Eventually, four 2-8-0s, built by Alco for hauling ore trains on the Lake Superior & Ishpeming Railroad and retired in 1960, were purchased, three from a company in Wisconsin and the fourth from a private owner in Iowa. Earlier negotiations with China to purchase four American-built Baldwins were ended by the events in Tiananmen Square. Seven Southern Pacific passenger cars formerly used on commuter services in the San Francisco Bay Area were purchased and restored by GCR at the Pacific Fruit Express car yards in Tucson. Six more have been restored subsequently and the railroad has also rented an elegant heavyweight Pullman Parlor Car, "Chief Keokuck," built in 1927.

At a press conference in 1989, Max Biegert made the declaration quoted above, and went on to say, "Operations will begin with a steam train from Williams to the Grand Canyon on September 17, the 88th anniversary of the first passenger train to the Canyon in 1901." The inaugural train was operated by 2-8-0 No. 18, which had been restored in less than a month by a team of more than 30 people.

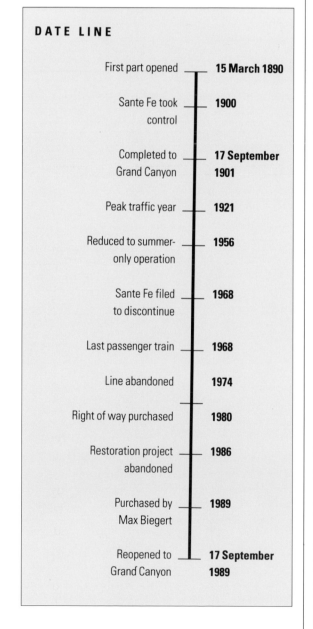

DATE LINE

First part opened	**15 March 1890**
Sante Fe took control	**1900**
Completed to Grand Canyon	**17 September 1901**
Peak traffic year	**1921**
Reduced to summer-only operation	**1956**
Sante Fe filed to discontinue	**1968**
Last passenger train	**1968**
Line abandoned	**1974**
Right of way purchased	**1980**
Restoration project abandoned	**1986**
Purchased by Max Biegert	**1989**
Reopened to Grand Canyon	**17 September 1989**

The line has a severe profile with many sharp curves and, in places, 3% (1 in 33.3) gradients. The 128-mile round trip is the longest regular scheduled steam duty in the USA today. At present two of the four steam locomotives are usable, with the other two under restoration. Recently a much larger ex-Chicago, Burlington & Quincy 2-8-2, No. 4960, has been purchased from the Mid-Continent Railway Museum and has been restored. Also, ex-Southern Pacific 4-6-2, No. 2472, has been rented from the Golden Gate Railroad Museum.

Long-term plans include more tourist facilities in Williams and other points along the line—there were five intermediate stations. A new 80-room hotel is being built in Williams. Perhaps more importantly, there is a proposal for a new 4-mile rail line from the Canyon's South Rim to Grand Canyon Airport in the village of Tusayan, 8 miles to the south.

ABOVE *A busy day with two trains lined up at Williams for the journey to Grand Canyon.*

Railtown 1897 State Historic Park

C A L I F O R N I A

USEFUL DATA

Headquarters Railtown, PO Box 1250, End of 5th Avenue, Jamestown, CA 95327.

Phone (209) 984 3953.

Public Station Jamestown.

Timetables & Reservations phone headquarters daily 9.30 am to 4.30 pm, or by mail.

Tickets Jamestown depot.

Public access

by rail: Amtrak to Riverbank and connecting Amtrak bus. By road: Three blocks off Highway 108 in Jamestown. Access for wheelchairs & baby strollers.

Facilities

Museum complex with roundhouse, gift shop, picnic grounds, refreshments. Restaurants & lodging in Jamestown.

Railtown 1897 Historic Park, in Jamestown, California, is owned by the state of California and runs steam excursion trains over tracks of the former Sierra Railway. The present-day Sierra Railroad is possibly one of the world's best-known railroads: its line and trains have featured in more than 50 movies, as well as countless TV shows and commercials. It is often known as Hollywood's railroad.

Construction of the Sierra Railway line began in 1897. The original sponsors were Thomas S. Bullock, William Crocker and Prince André Poniatowski of France, Crocker's brother-in-law. Fifty-seven miles of standard-gauge line between Oakdale and Tuolumne, California, were completed in 1900, in California's famed Mother Lode Gold Country, to the southeast of Sacramento. Running into California's Gold Rush Country, the railroad was built to connect the mines and lumber mills of Tuolumne County with the outside world. Early business was both passenger and freight. Not long after opening, the railroad passed into the sole ownership of the Charles Crocker family.

Freight was always the most important commodity and still continues to be the major source of revenue. The freight railroad and

RIGHT Former Sierra Railroad 2-8-0 No 28 on an afternoon trip from Jamestown in July 1978.

ABOVE *A rare appearance for the Rodgers 4-6-0, built in 1891. This characterful train is occasionally used in filmwork, as shown here.*

business is now owned and operated by Coast Enterprises as the Sierra Railroad. It has changed to diesel locomotives—the Railroad Company has three diesel locomotives of its own—and continues to feed traffic into the Southern Pacific system. Today there is one main route of 50 miles from Oakdale to Sonora.

Passenger traffic ceased in 1939, but freight, particularly mineral traffic, continued. In 1971, a steam passenger service was inaugurated as a tourist attraction—Jamestown lies on the route to the Yosemite National Park—by Charles Crocker Associates, using steam locomotives from the former Sierra Railroad. The steam locomotives, and historic passenger and freight cars, were purchased in 1979 and given to the state of California. The state purchased the roundhouse and workshops in 1982.

While the Sierra Railroad has its own head-quarters at Sonora, the eastern end of the line, the state of California set up Railtown 1897 in historic Jamestown in 1983, on a 26-acre site that includes the roundhouse and workshops complex. This is one of only two shortlines in the nation to preserve its own working facilities; the other is in Strasburg, Pennsylvania (*see under* STRASBURG RAILROAD). The aim has been to set up a "living museum," and the working facility still rebuilds and maintains steam locomotives. Steam trains are run on a regular basis; all originate from Jamestown, running in both directions and to varying distances along the line. Steam passenger trains are operated by former Sierra Railway locomotives: a Rogers 4-6-0 of 1898, a Baldwin 2-8-0 of 1922 or a Lima 3-truck Shay. There are also three diesel-electric locomotives. There is a good selection of passenger and

ABOVE *Over 100 years old! A former Sierra railroad Rogers 10-wheeler, 4-6-0 No 3 of 1891 with vintage rolling stock near Chinese Camp.*

freight cars, while historic vehicles are kept and used for filming.

Operation is from April to the end of September on weekends and holidays. The Mother Lode Cannonball and the Twilight Limited are the two most popular trains, the latter being a barbecue dinner train, while there is also a Beer and Pretzel Run and a murder mystery train, the Wine and Cheese Zephyr. Guaranteed advance reservations are required for the Twilight Limited, and reservations are suggested for the other special trains. Tours of the roundhouse are available daily for groups by reservation, and a place for one person to ride on the locomotive is available on every Mother Lode Cannonball —advance reservations required. The Caboose Birthday Party is a complete package for up to 12 children, which includes a ride on the Mother Lode Cannonball—phone for prices and information.

Railtown 1897 State Historic Park is administered by the California State Railroad Museum at Sacramento, CA, and is located in Jamestown, CA, at 5th Avenue and Reservoir Road, three blocks south of Highways 108 and 49, about 120 miles from San Francisco and 80 miles from Sacramento. The grounds are

accessible to handicapped people. There is a shop complex and a museum store; the gift shop, roundhouse and picnic grounds are open daily year-round, except Thanksgiving, Christmas and New Years Day.

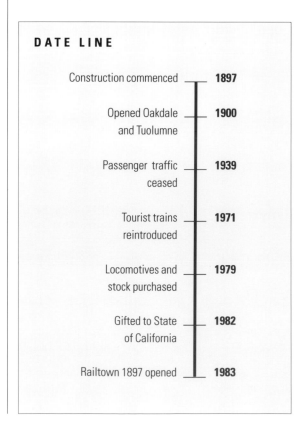

DATE LINE

Construction commenced	**1897**
Opened Oakdale and Tuolumne	**1900**
Passenger traffic ceased	**1939**
Tourist trains reintroduced	**1971**
Locomotives and stock purchased	**1979**
Gifted to State of California	**1982**
Railtown 1897 opened	**1983**

Durango & Silverton Narrow Gauge Railroad

C O L O R A D O

USEFUL DATA

Headquarters 479 Main
Avenue, Durango, CO 81301.
Phone (303) 247 2733.
Public Stations Durango,
Silverton.

Timetables & Tickets

from Headquarters at
Durango Depot.
Reservations required, by
phone or mail. Train seating
availability on local radio:
KIQX-FM 101.3.

Public access

by car to Durango, ample
parking. Durango is at the
intersection of US 160 and
US 550; Denver, CO 332
miles, Albuquerque, NM 220
miles, Flagstaff, AZ (for
Grand Canyon RR) 315 miles.

Facilities

Gift shop at Durango.
Concession cars on all
trains. Beverages & light
snacks on all trains. No pets
carried. Ticket office manned
all year.

The railroad from Durango to Silverton was a branch of the once-extensive network of narrow-gauge lines run by the Denver & Rio Grande Western Railroad. Most of the original D&RG was built to 3-foot gauge for reasons of economy. Smaller locomotives and rolling stock cost less, the curvature could be made to sharper radii, and the smaller rolling stock required smaller tunnels and cuttings.

The Denver & Rio Grande Railway was founded by General William Jackson Palmer and incorporated in 1870, but it was 1881 before the rails reached Durango in the extreme southwest of Colorado. The first passenger train arrived from Denver on 1 August 1881. Durango was created by the railroad, and from it a branch was pushed some 45 miles, rising 2,780 feet to Silverton. Silverton was settled in 1873 and incorporated in 1876. Although gold had first brought prospectors to the San Juan mountains, it was silver that made the town boom. Lead, copper, and zinc have also been mined here.

To get the ore out, the only practical means of transport was by mule train. In 1879 a good toll-road was completed to the upper Rio Grande via Stony Pass, giving reasonable access to Alamosa. Also in 1879, D&RG engineers were mapping possible routes, and by October of that year a surveying party was

RIGHT Former Denver & Rio Grande 2-8-2 No 482 approaches a water stop near Hermosa on the Durango & Silverton Scenic Railroad.

SILVERTON

ELK PARK

NEEDLETON

ARIZONA

160

TEFT

TALL TIMBER

TACOMA

Turning
Triangle

ROCKWOOD

HERMOSA

DURANGO

Millian Dollar Highway

DURANGO & SILVERTON

478

working on locating a line in Animas Canyon. The rails finally reached Silverton in July 1882, and it is reasonably certain that the first train, a work train, arrived on 8 July.

From the mid-1880s, the D&RG created some standard-gauge lines: either by adding a third rail, as between Denver & Pueblo, to accommodate trains of another railroad; or by conversion of an existing line, as from Pueblo to Ogden, Utah, between 1887 and 1890. From 1899 many lines were converted to standard gauge, but the branch from Durango to Silverton, with its mainly ore traffic from the mines, remained narrow-gauge, as did most secondary routes.

In 1889 another railroad, the Rio Grande Southern, was incorporated and built a line from Dallas, north of Ridgeway, to Durango. This was completed in 1891. Durango now had two outlets for the products of the Silverton mines. The Silver Purchase Act of 1890 brought brief prosperity to both the DRS and the D&RG, but the Act was repealed in 1893. The DRS went bankrupt and the D&RG acquired control in 1894. It was finally abandoned in 1953.

D&RG constructed another branch from Durango south to Farmington in 1909, this time on standard gauge, to head off a proposed Southern Pacific line. It was converted to narrow gauge in 1923, and carried traffic in pipeline materials and oil-drilling equipment until 1956. It was abandoned in 1968.

By 1921 two major narrow-gauge routes remained: the original main line between Salida and Montrose via the Marshall Pass, and the line from Alamosa west to Durango and its branches to Silverton and Farmington, with a branch south from Antonito to Santa Fe. The circle of narrow-gauge lines was completed by the Rio Grande Southern.

There were no major abandonments until the 1940s. The narrow-gauge circle was broken in 1949 when the Marshall Pass route was abandoned. The Salida Monarch line was standard-gauged in 1956, and in 1967 the D&RGW ceased all narrow-gauge operations except for the Silverton branch. The remaining line from Antonito, CO, to Chama,

ABOVE *Durango &*
Silverton 2-8-2 No 478
stokes up in preparation
for the steep climb up
through the Animas
River Canyon.

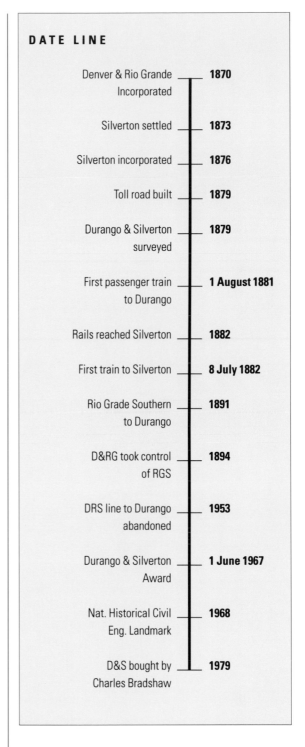

DATE LINE

Denver & Rio Grande Incorporated	**1870**
Silverton settled	**1873**
Silverton incorporated	**1876**
Toll road built	**1879**
Durango & Silverton surveyed	**1879**
First passenger train to Durango	**1 August 1881**
Rails reached Silverton	**1882**
First train to Silverton	**8 July 1882**
Rio Grade Southern to Durango	**1891**
D&RG took control of RGS	**1894**
DRS line to Durango abandoned	**1953**
Durango & Silverton Award	**1 June 1967**
Nat. Historical Civil Eng. Landmark	**1968**
D&S bought by Charles Bradshaw	**1979**

NM, over the Cumbres Pass was sold in 1970 to the states of Colorado and New Mexico.

The Silverton branch was strikingly successful. The train named San Juan from Salida was discontinued in 1951, but the Rio Grande continued to run a weekly mixed train from Durango to Silverton. Tourists began to use the line for its many scenic features: operated entirely by steam locomotives, the trains hug the mountainside through the Animas River

Canyon, with its sheer drops. Train frequency had to be increased; weekend operation began in the mid-1950s, and by the summer of 1964 the railroad had to schedule two trains each way every day. New cars had to be built, and the D&RG continued to operate the line until 1979. On 1 June 1967, the National Park Service honored the Durango & Silverton railroad, officially designating it a Registered National Historical Landmark. It received another honor in March 1968, when the American Society of Civil Engineers designated it a National Historic Civil Engineering Landmark. In 1979 the D&RG sold the Durango & Silverton Narrow Gauge branch to Charles Bradshaw jr., a Florida citrus grower and railroad enthusiast, who continues to operate it to this day.

The distance from Durango to Silverton is 45.18 miles, and much of this is climbing the San Juan mountain range. In the first 11 miles to Hermosa, the line rises only 125 feet and the gradients are mainly 1% (1 in 100) up or

down, with one piece of 1.2% (1 in 83). From Hermosa the climbing starts, and the gradient is almost continuously 2.5% (1 in 40) except for a stretch of three miles of down grade at 1.42% (1 in 70) between Rockwood and Tacoma. At Cascade Canyon, 26 miles from Durango, a "wye" was built in 1981, where trains are turned on winter trips. Durango is 6,520 feet above sea level, and the line takes the traveler through magnificent scenery along what was the Animas Glacier to Silverton, at an altitude of 9,320 feet.

The line owns 10 steam locomotives, six working and four others. There is one ex-D&RG and DRS 2-8-0 built in 1887, nine 2-8-2s, three Alcos and six Baldwins built between 1902 and 1925, and some 41 passenger coaches. Up to four trains daily are operated in the summer season, and charter trips may also be run. In the winter period, trains continue to run, but only as far as Cascade Canyon, 26 miles. Some freight trains are also operated.

Shoreline Trolley Museum

C O N N E C T I C U T

Trolley lines were part of the American scene from early in the 20th century, but they died out quickly once the automobile and bus appeared. In 1945 the Branford Railway Association was incorporated to preserve and operate trolley cars, as a reminder of a clean and quick means of urban travel. The Association purchased a short piece of track in East Haven and Branford, Connecticut, and began bringing cars in from New Haven in March 1947. The Museum opened to the public in 1953.

The Sprague Memorial Visitors Center commemorates Frank Julian Sprague, a native of nearby Milford, who is considered the father of electric traction and transportation. Sprague was the first engineer to place the driving motors in the bogies, inventing the Nose-Suspended Traction Motor that is widely used today. He also invented multiple-unit control, which enabled a number of cars to be controlled from one driving position. This arrangement, first used on the South Side Elevated Railway of Chicago, was known

USEFUL DATA

Headquarters Shoreline Trolley Museum, East Haven, CT. Mailing address: 17 River Street, East Haven, CT 06512.

Phone (203) 467 6927.

Public Stations East Haven Sprague Station, Farm River Road, Car Barn Yards, Short Beach.

Tickets to Ride, from East Haven.

Charters (203) 467 7635.

Public access
by car: from exit 52 of Connecticut Turnpike or from US-1.

Special features
Gift shop & displays.

Nearby attractions
Valley Railroad, Connecticut Trolley Museum, Yale University, Peabody Museum, Mystic Seaport, Fort Nathan Hale.

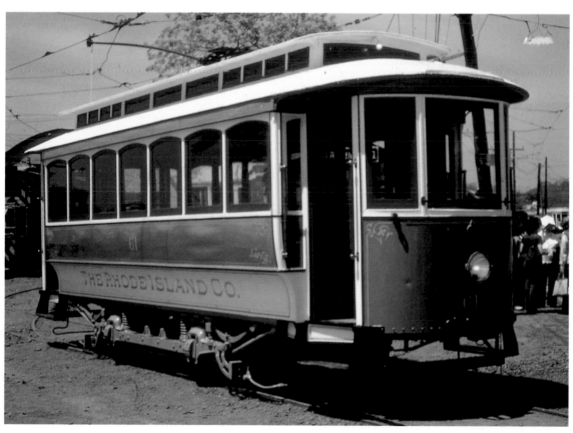

ABOVE *A former Rhode Island trolley car on the Shoreline Trolley Museum at Branford Connecticut.*

RIGHT *A very early car of the New York & Harlem street car line.*

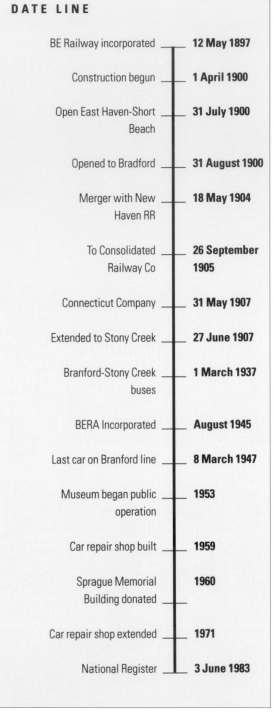

DATE LINE

BE Railway incorporated	**12 May 1897**
Construction begun	**1 April 1900**
Open East Haven-Short Beach	**31 July 1900**
Opened to Bradford	**31 August 1900**
Merger with New Haven RR	**18 May 1904**
To Consolidated Railway Co	**26 September 1905**
Connecticut Company	**31 May 1907**
Extended to Stony Creek	**27 June 1907**
Branford-Stony Creek buses	**1 March 1937**
BERA Incorporated	**August 1945**
Last car on Branford line	**8 March 1947**
Museum began public operation	**1953**
Car repair shop built	**1959**
Sprague Memorial Building donated	**1960**
Car repair shop extended	**1971**
National Register	**3 June 1983**

ABOVE *A Lynchburg open platform car of 1905.*

as the Sprague-General Electric System. His firm, Edison-Sprague, became one of the principal constituents of General Electric when that company was formed in 1893.

Trolley cars were introduced in Branford, CT, on 31 July 1900, by the Branford Electric Railway Co. They were dependent on the Fair Haven & Westville Railroad for access to the extensive street railroad system serving the city of New Haven and surrounding towns. By the end of the 19th century, Branford was not only a major summer resort but also a dormitory town for New Haven. The single railroad line no longer served the town's needs, so the trolley became the chief means of transport to the city for shopping and employment.

The BER ran from Branford to East Haven, but soon the New Haven & Hartford Railroad began buying up the trolley lines to control competition. The BER was one of them, and on 31 May 1907 became the Connecticut Co., a division of the New York, New Haven & Hartford Railroad. By the time of World War II, trolleys had been abandoned in all but New Haven and its suburbs, and only the heaviest-density lines remained, most routes being converted to bus operation. Fortunately for the BER, government regulations prohibited conversion to buses for the duration of the War. It was this delay that gave the Branford Electric Railway Association the chance to acquire

the complete operating trolley line from East Haven to Short Beach when it closed on 8 March 1947.

The Shoreline Trolley Museum is a working museum. Over the years it has not only amassed a large collection of historic trolley and interurban cars, but also built up and restored a 1½-mile section of the former BER. This is now the oldest suburban trolley line in continuous operation in the USA, and is

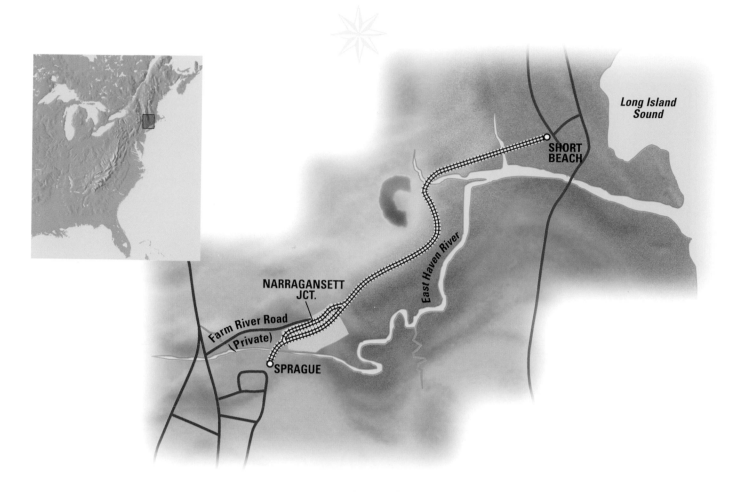

typical of many thousands of miles of line once in existence. It is also one of the most scenic of the (now numerous) museum lines. The main aim of the museum is to keep the line operating, enabling future generations to learn about trolley cars and enjoy an old-fashioned trolley car ride. The Museum was placed on the National Register of Historic Places in 1983.

Trolleys operate over 1½ miles of track from Sprague Station in East Haven to Short Beach, Branford, CT. The line passes through woodlands and over salt marshes, and includes two major trestle bridges. The round trip takes about 55 minutes and includes a guided tour of the depot (the "carbarn").

A trip to the museum provides a great and authentic experience of the trolley car era between 1904 and 1947. The collection includes cars of many different types, from places as far away as St Louis and Montreal, with a few from New York City and the Connecticut Company; there are street cars, rapid transit cars and even interurbans, as well as work cars of various kinds. Building the collection was not an easy task, as many types had disappeared. Altogether there are around 95 streetcars and interurbans, and most

operating days there are seven cars working with trolleys running about every 30 minutes.

Special events include New York Transit Days, Old-Time Music Days, Oktoberfest, Halloween, and Santa Days. The line is open Sundays in April, Saturdays and Sundays in May, every day from Memorial Day to Labor Day, Saturdays and Sundays in September and October (plus Columbus Day), Sundays only in November, and Saturdays and Sundays for Santa specials in December.

ABOVE *A restored car of the former Connecticut Company from around 1911 now in use in the trolley museum and popular for fine day outings.*

Valley Railroad

C O N N E C T I C U T

Valley Railroad runs steam trains from Essex, about six miles from the mouth of the Connecticut River, northeast along the west bank of the river through Deep River to Chester, Connecticut, a distance of about six miles in all. Essex lies about 30 miles east of New Haven and 40 miles southeast of Hartford, CT.

The New York, New Haven & Hartford Railroad branch, running south along the Connecticut River, served a number of small towns. It joined the coast line from New Haven to Providence, Rhode Island and Boston, MA, close to the mouth of the Connecticut River. It was opened originally in 1854 as the New Haven & New London Railroad, and was later part of the Hartford & Connecticut Valley Railroad. Trains crossed

the Connecticut River at Saybrook by ferry until a bridge was built in 1870.

The New York, New Haven & Hartford Railroad was formed in 1872 and bought the Hartford & Connecticut Valley Railroad in 1882. By the turn of the century, the New Haven had a virtual monopoly of all the railroads and steamboat lines in Connecticut, Rhode Island, and much of Massachusetts. Following the Depression in the 1930s, the New Haven cut out most of its branch lines, but the Connecticut Valley Line to Old Saybrook kept going as a rural branch line until 1968, when the owners, Penn Central, abandoned the southern part.

Almost immediately, the Valley Railroad was chartered: the state purchased the track from Penn Central in 1969 with the idea of

RIGHT Locomotive 1647, a 2-8-2 built by the Tang-Shan works in China in 1989 heads a train into Chester from Essex, CT in October 1990.

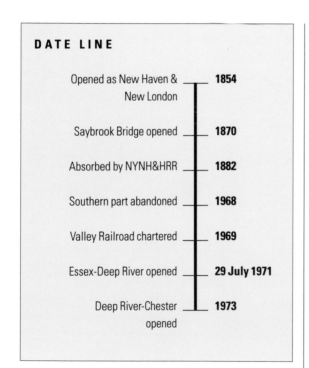

DATE LINE

Opened as New Haven & New London	**1854**
Saybrook Bridge opened	**1870**
Absorbed by NYNH&HRR	**1882**
Southern part abandoned	**1968**
Valley Railroad chartered	**1969**
Essex-Deep River opened	**29 July 1971**
Deep River-Chester opened	**1973**

operating it as an excursion line for tourists. Excursion trains began to run between Essex and the next station, Deep River, a distance of 2½ miles, on 29 July 1971. Two years later, a further 3½ miles to Chester were opened. The Railroad now owns a total of 21 miles of standard-gauge line.

The trains consist of well-restored coaches and a parlor car, hauled by steam locomotives in the manner of a 1920s branch railroad. The line has five steam locomotives, including one built in 1989 by the Tang-Shan locomotive works in China, one diesel locomotive, eight heavyweight passenger cars from Lackawanna Central of New Jersey and New Haven, and 20 freight cars.

The trains connect with boat cruises at Deep River. The complete train ride takes 55 minutes while the train-boat combination takes just over 2 hours. There are a number of attractions nearby, including the Shore Line Trolley Museum, Connecticut River Steamboat Dock, Submarine Museum, etc. A number of special events are held each year including the Murder Mystery Train in May, Halloween Ghost Train in October, a Jazz Festival, and of course Christmas trains.

ABOVE *A popular excursion is a combined train-boat trip. Here the train is seen at Chester where the river boat is waiting to take the passengers back to Essex.*

Illinois Railway Museum

I L L I N O I S

USEFUL DATA

Headquarters Illinois
Railway Museum Union,
Illinois 60180.

Phone 1 815 923 4391
(schedules).
Chicagoland: 1 800-BIG RAIL.
Information: (708) 834 6133.

Stations East Union depot.
Four streetcar stops.

Public access
by car from Interstate 90 and
US 20, Chicago 50 miles,
Rockford 40 miles.

Facilities
Bookshop, gift shop,
refreshments, picnic sites.
Free car parking,
comprehensive railroad
museum with artifacts.

The concept of the Illinois Railway Museum had its origins as long ago as 1941 when one of the largest Midwestern interurban railways was abandoned. This was the Indiana Railroad which owned some of the most technically advanced electric cars in the United States. One particular car, No 65, a lightweight high-speed unit built by Pullman in 1931, was much sought-after by railroad historians. The only way it could be secured financially in 1941 was to persuade another electric line in Iowa to purchase and run it. This became Cedar Rapids & Iowa City's primary service unit in World War II.

When CR&IC was abandoned in 1953, a group of ten enthusiasts acquired No 65 and moved it to North Chicago. To accomplish this task a non-profit educational corporation was established—the Illinois Electric Railway Museum.

Today the museum uses the vacant right-of-way of the former Elgin & Belvidere Electric railway, built in 1900 and abandoned as early as 1930 when the tracks were taken up and sold for scrap. The E&BER was owned by Bion J Arnold, an engineer of renown who also did some work on the London Underground. By 1966 some tracks had been relaid at Union, IL and the nucleus of the museum was established.

Such was the interest that additional cars were acquired from Chicago and Milwaukee, and the once great network of interurban lines of the Samuel Insull empire, and it was decided that examples of the more important types should be saved. The benefactor who had provided the initial track storage space had himself acquired a streetcar and several Chicago elevated cars, and agreed to the acquisition of a further two or three units.

As the collection grew so did the need to provide covered storage, and the IERM sought

RIGHT A 1918-built 2-10-0, formerly St Louis, San Francisco, (Frisco) No 1630 built by Baldwin is one of the many interesting exhibits at the Illinois Railway Museum.

ABOVE *All forms of traction feature in the museum as depicted here by diesel interurban and street cars of various types.*

a large plot of land (10 acres or more) to be its permanent home. After examining several sites it was finally decided to purchase the un-developed right-of-way of the former Elgin & Belvidere Electric just outside Union in McHenry county. At the same time it was decided to expand the scope of the Museum to include steam locomotives and main line rail-roads. The title was accordingly shortened to Illinois Railway Museum.

In March 1964 the Board of Directors authorized the purchase of 26 acres adjacent to the right-of-way with an option on another 20 acres and the relocation process began. On 23 August 1964 the process of moving some 42 cars and much material had been com-pleted by Museum members and their many friends. Money was borrowed to improve the site and to turn farmland into a railroad yard with vehicle access. By 1992 there were 1.5 miles of track under cover.

The mission of the Illinois Railway Museum is to demonstrate the vital role played by rail-roads in the growth of the Chicago area as well as the United States as a whole, through the preservation and operation of railroad and mass transit rolling stock and by the display of related artifacts in a realistic setting. Amenities are constantly being added and others improved.

There are two distinct divisions to the Museum's operating demonstration: the 5-

mile long mainline and the 1-mile long street-car loop. Steam, diesel and heavy electric trains run on the main line; interurban and elevated trains may run on either division, while streetcars are confined to the 1-mile loop. The main line is equipped with trolley wire charged at 600 volts dc.

Trains on the main line operate to regular schedules and depart from the Museum's East Union depot. The round trip to Kishwaukee Grove takes forty minutes passing a farmstead, a bit of Illinois prairie and over a grade cross-ing before dropping into the Kishwaukee Valley. Interurban and elevated trains depart from the 50th Avenue rapid transit station, then take the same route as the main line steam and diesel trains. Some interurbans make a circuit of the streetcar line before heading to the mainline.

Weekday operations are from Memorial Day to Labor Day and are usually operated only by electric cars. Weekend operation is more intense and includes both steam and diesel trains on the main line and extends from May into September and October. The Museum's main line runs parallel with a line of the Chicago & North Western from Rock-

ABOVE Chicago North Shore Brill Interurban car No 757 used on the "loop" and on the main line at times.

ford to West Chicago and there is an oppor-tunity to see their trains from the Museum.

The Museum contains probably the largest and one of the most varied collections of historical rolling stock. There are 21 electric streetcars, 33 interurbans including one of the famous Chicago, North Shore & Milwaukee "Electroliner," 24 rapid transit cars, 9 electric locomotives including one of the famous Pennsylvania GG-1s No 4939, 25 steam loco-

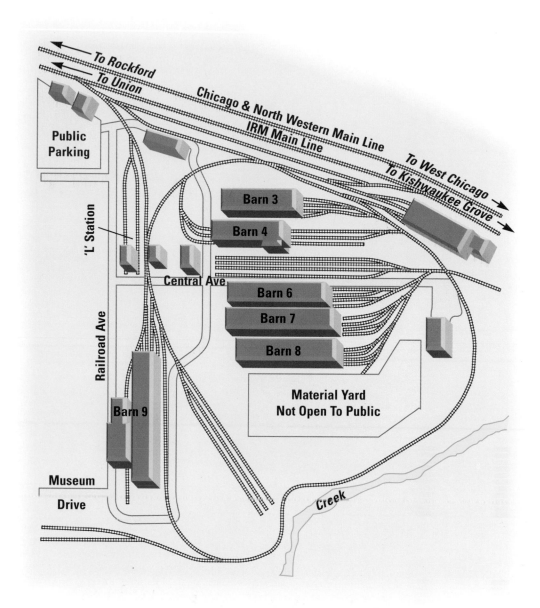

motives from switchers, a Shay to a Norfolk & Western 2-8-8-2 class Y3A. There are also 33 diesel locomotives including the original Delaware, Lakawanna & Western Box cab No 3001 of 1926, the remaining E5a of 1940, a Baldwin center cab and many others. There are 53 passenger and baggage cars and some 78 freight cars together with work vehicles of many different types.

The admission price includes unlimited rides on all equipment operating and all train departures are announced on the public address system. Streetcars may be used to view the various museum exhibits and can be boarded at the stops around the circuit.

Each building (there are seven open to the public) takes some 20–30 minutes to view and the diversity of equipment on display is truly remarkable. The museum is largely staffed by volunteers so that, except in the busier part of the season, on weekdays the ride is limited to

an electric powered streetcar on the main line from East Union depot. In the busy season an additional car runs on the streetcar loop.

On weekdays and holidays mainline steam or diesel-hauled trains operate on the main line and trips leave regularly from East Union depot as well as cars on the streetcar loop. If

ABOVE *Chicago & North Western 1518 – EMD 1948.*

ABOVE *This is one of the early Alco Box Cab switchers, although it is unusual to see it in Lackawanna ownership.*

one has plenty of time a self-guided tour of the display barns is well worthwhile. Barn 9 in particular includes the Zephyr "Silver Pilot" E-5 power car and the larger steam locomotives. The train operations, restoration and management of the museum is performed by volunteers and the Museum receives no operating funding from any government agency. Some 60% of the equipment has been donated by railroads and private individuals.

In addition to the normal scheduled attractions there are special days both in and outside the normal operating season and these are listed in the publicity leaflets obtainable from the Museum.

The Museum is a non-profit, volunteer organisation and is open daily from Memorial Day to Labor Day (29 May—first Monday in September). The sites includes a bookstore, giftshop and refreshment facilities and there is ample free car parking. Group rates are available by writing to the Group Sales Director.

The Illinois Railway Museum is situated about 50 miles northwest of Chicago at Union and may be reached from Interstate 90 by route 20, Marengo exit. From the west, Union is about 40 miles by Interstate 90 and route 20, Cherry-Belvidere exit. Drive east through Marengo on route 20 to Union.

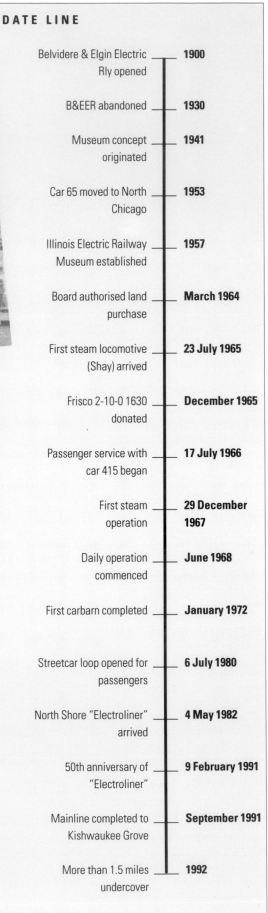

DATE LINE

Belvidere & Elgin Electric Rly opened	**1900**
B&EER abandoned	**1930**
Museum concept originated	**1941**
Car 65 moved to North Chicago	**1953**
Illinois Electric Railway Museum established	**1957**
Board authorised land purchase	**March 1964**
First steam locomotive (Shay) arrived	**23 July 1965**
Frisco 2-10-0 1630 donated	**December 1965**
Passenger service with car 415 began	**17 July 1966**
First steam operation	**29 December 1967**
Daily operation commenced	**June 1968**
First carbarn completed	**January 1972**
Streetcar loop opened for passengers	**6 July 1980**
North Shore "Electroliner" arrived	**4 May 1982**
50th anniversary of "Electroliner"	**9 February 1991**
Mainline completed to Kishwaukee Grove	**September 1991**
More than 1.5 miles undercover	**1992**

Whitewater Valley Railroad

INDIANA

DIRECT *A comparatively rare locomotive to find in preservation is this GE Bo-Bo on the Whitewater railway running beside the restored Whitewater Canal near Metamora, In.*

USEFUL DATA

Headquarters Whitewater Valley Railroad, PO Box 406, Connersville, IN 47331.

Phone (317) 825 2054; Year round: 825 4550.

Public Station Connersville.

Timetables by phone or mail.

Tickets from Station.

Reservations by phone or mail; reservations required for Christmas specials and school trips.

Public access by car on route 121 (Grand Avenue); US 52 from Indianapolis or Cincinnati. IS 70 and US 40 from Dayton. Car park.

Facilities Box lunches, if ordered before 11.30 am. Restaurants & lodgings in Connersville. Gift shop in Station. Canal House Museum. Rolling stock display.

The Whitewater Valley Railroad is a standard-gauge 16-mile tourist line running from Connersville to Metamora, Indiana. It crosses hilly country with 2% (1 in 50) grades, and runs over part of the original Whitewater Valley route, with views of the Whitewater Valley Canal.

The Railroad was incorporated in 1865. Its aim was to build a line from Harrison, Ohio, to Hagerstown, Indiana, along the towpath of the Whitewater Valley Canal. Once the railroad was built, it took the traffic from the canal, which was later allowed to become derelict. The WVR remained independent for some years, its chief business being the haulage of lumber and coal. It was absorbed with other small lines by the Big Four—Cleveland, Cincinnati, Chicago & St Louis—passing into the New York Central System and eventually the Penn Central.

In 1972, a group set up and operated tourist trains over part of the line. With the rapid failing of the Penn Central, which was shedding smaller lines, the group was able to purchase the Whitewater Valley Railroad in 1984, and began their operation on the 16-mile section from Connersville to Metamora, IN.

Trains are operated by steam or diesel locomotives. A special attraction is a Baldwin 2-6-2 of 1919, formerly owned by Florola Sawmill Co., which has a "balloon" stack. The 16-mile trip is full of scenic interest. At Metamora there is a two-hour layover which gives time

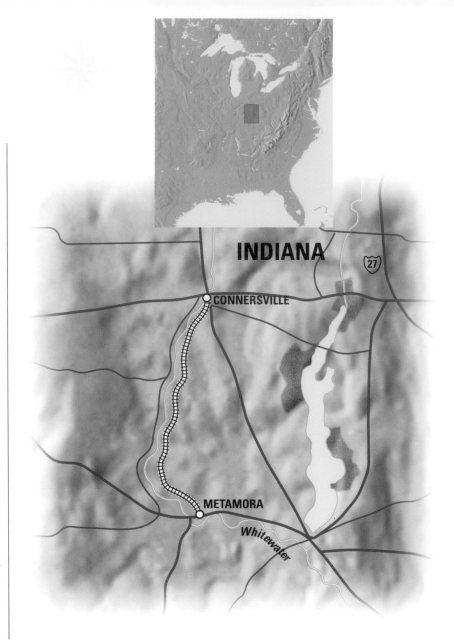

for sightseeing and shopping before returning to Connersville. Box lunches may be obtained by ordering before 11.30 am for delivery to the train before departure. There is a gift shop in the station at Connersville, and various pieces of rolling stock are on display nearby.

Steam and diesel-hauled trains are operated on weekends and holidays between early May and the end of October. Special trips are run for schools on Wednesdays, Thursdays, and Fridays in May; these need to be reserved in advance. There are Christmas runs during the last week of November and the first two of December on Fridays, Saturdays, and Sundays, which also must be reserved in advance. Except for the special trips, trains usually leave Connersville at noon and return from Metamora at about 5.30 pm.

There is no museum directly associated with the railroad, but nearby at Connersville is the Canal House Museum. Connersville station is on route 121 (Grand Avenue), about 1 mile south of the center of Connersville. Connersville is about 60 miles east of Indianapolis: US 52 to Rushville, which is 15 miles from Connersville. Cincinnati and Daemon, OH are also about 60 miles.

ABOVE *Another rare locomotive on the Whitewater is this Baldwin 2-6-2 of 1919.*

At the time of writing the boiler is under repair but the locomotive should be back in service by 1997.

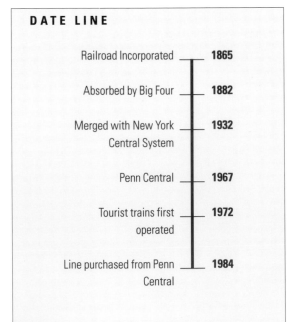

DATE LINE

Railroad Incorporated	**1865**
Absorbed by Big Four	**1882**
Merged with New York Central System	**1932**
Penn Central	**1967**
Tourist trains first operated	**1972**
Line purchased from Penn Central	**1984**

Boone & Scenic Valley Railroad

I O W A

USEFUL DATA

Headquarters PO Box 603, Boone, IA 50036.

Phone (800) 626 0319, (515) 432 4249

Main Station Boone.
Other Station: Fraser.
Flag Stops: West 15th Street, Boone, outward only; Riviera—YMCA Camp.

Timetables & Tickets from Headquarters in Boone.

Reservations required for bus tour groups & charters.

Public access
by bus from Ames. By car from Highway 30. From Des Moines Airport 50 miles. Car park. Facilities for disabled visitors.

Facilities
Museum with around 20 locomotives & cars, & souvenir shop. Trolley rides most weekends. Boone has ample food & lodging.

RIGHT *The Boone and Scenic is another line which has acquired a locomotive from China. This time it is a class J8 2-8-2 and was the last to be built by the Datong locomotive works in 1988.*

The Boone & Scenic Valley Railroad operates a standard-gauge line over 12 miles of the former Chicago & North Western line, between Boone and Wolf Crossing in central Iowa. The line is notable for a magnificent "trestle," a 156-foot-high bridge, 784 feet long, over Bass Point Creek, known as the "High Bridge."

The line's original owner was the Boone Valley Coal & Railway Company, which was chartered on 23 February 1893 to haul coal from Fraser coal mines over a 3½ mile line, to a connection with the former Minneapolis & St Louis Railroad at Fraser Junction near Wolf. It was opened later the same year. In 1899 a survey was made to the west, towards Boxholm & Gowrie, for a line to connect with the Chicago Rock Island & Pacific. Before this could be completed, the coal company was purchased by the Marshalltown & Dakota Railroad. The track reached Gowrie in 1900, a distance of 18 miles.

In 1902 construction commenced from Gowrie towards Rockwell City, with grading also from Gowrie towards Boone. In 1903 the line was completed, running over the Des Moines Bridge and the wooden trestle High Bridge to Boone and westward to Rockwell City. The Fort Dodge, Des Moines & Southern, an interurban railroad, was incorporated in 1906, with plans to connect Boone, Des Moines and Fort Dodge, crossing the High Bridge near Boone. Electric interurban cars began operation on 4 November 1907, and steam freight trains continued to operate over the line between Newton and Rockwell City, under the company title of Newton & North Western Railroad.

In 1912, following severe damage by floods on Bass Point Creek, the wooden trestle was replaced by a steel structure. It was the highest bridge on any electric interurban in North America. Later, in 1914, the wooden bridge over the Des Moines River was also replaced

ABOVE *Hand signals used during shunting movements.*

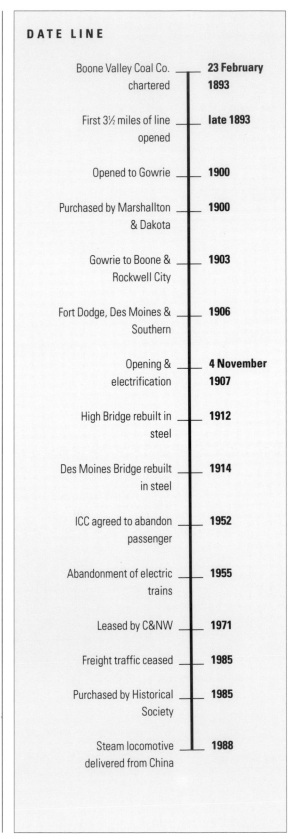

DATE LINE

Boone Valley Coal Co. chartered	**23 February 1893**
First 3½ miles of line opened	**late 1893**
Opened to Gowrie	**1900**
Purchased by Marshallton & Dakota	**1900**
Gowrie to Boone & Rockwell City	**1903**
Fort Dodge, Des Moines & Southern	**1906**
Opening & electrification	**4 November 1907**
High Bridge rebuilt in steel	**1912**
Des Moines Bridge rebuilt in steel	**1914**
ICC agreed to abandon passenger	**1952**
Abandonment of electric trains	**1955**
Leased by C&NW	**1971**
Freight traffic ceased	**1985**
Purchased by Historical Society	**1985**
Steam locomotive delivered from China	**1988**

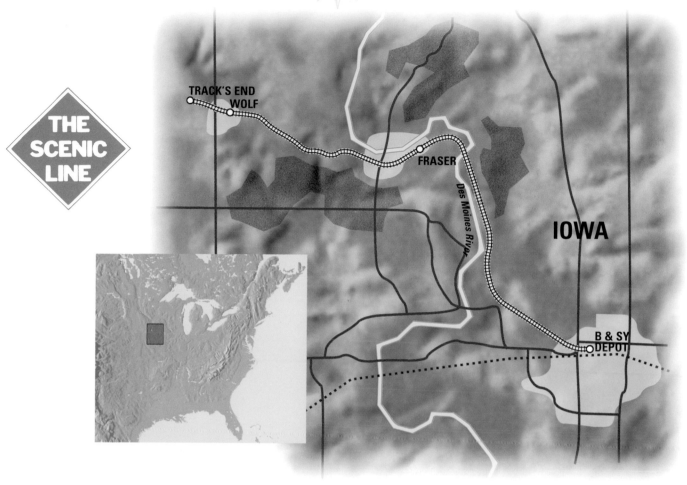

THE
SCENIC
LINE

by a steel structure. Although it was 694 feet long, the height it was constructed above the river bed was only 35 feet.

Overhead wires were erected over the Newton & Northwestern between Midvale and Hope, but in 1908 the N&NW went bankrupt. It was purchased in 1909 by the Fort Dodge, Des Moines and Southern Railroad, but a year later this also failed, and in 1913 the road was sold at foreclosure to another company of the same name.

The line was always primarily a freight carrier, and by 1930, main-line passenger service was down to four trains a day in each direction, reducing to two in 1935. In 1940 things went better, and a service of four trains was re-introduced, but following World War II business decreased again. In 1952 the ICC permitted abandonment of passenger services, but they continued to operate until 1955, by which time electric interurban operation had also ceased.

Most of the Fort Dodge Line's branches were abandoned in the 1960s, and the remainder were leased by the Chicago & North Western in 1971. In 1983 most of the main line was abandoned. Freight traffic ceased, and in 1985 the Boone Valley Historical Society purchased 11 miles from Boone to Wolf Crossing, including the famous High Bridge, for operation as the Boone Valley Scenic Railway. The line offers steam operation and throughout there are excellent views over the Des Moines river valley.

The present length of the run is just under 10 miles, and a possible extension of about a mile is contemplated to the Fairground in Boone. The Main Station is at 11th and Division Streets in Boone, and there is another station in Fraser. The round trip takes about 2 hours. The maximum gradient is 1% (1 in 100), climbing out of the Des Moines valley toward Boone.

The principal attractions are the High Bridges and the working steam locomotive, a 2-8-2 tender locomotive No. JS 8419, "The Iowan," which was built new in 1988 in China—the last to be built by the Datong works. There are also three working EMD diesel-electric locomotives and three electric locomotives from Chicago, South Shore & South Bend and Charles City Western. A

ABOVE *One of the main features of the Boone & Scenic Valley Railroad is the spectacular high trestle over Bass Point Creek, 156ft high and 784ft long. Originally built of wood it was reconstructed in steel in 1912.*

trolley service is operated Saturdays, Sundays, and holidays from downtown Boone to Harrison Street Depot.

Passenger rolling stock consists of four former electric cars, one Rock Island Line and five Lackawanna locomotive hauled cars. There is no freight traffic. Boone was once the junction between the C&NW and the Milwaukee Road, but there is now no main line depot. At Wolf there was a junction with the Minneapolis & St Louis Railroad. There are a number of other attractions in or near Boone, including a Railroad Museum in nearby Moingona. Boone was the birthplace of Mamie Eisenhower.

Trains run on a daily schedule of one train each way from the Saturday of Memorial Day

weekend to the last day of October. On Saturdays, Sundays and holidays there are two extra trains each way, while "Puffer Billy Day Specials" operate as required for four days on the weekend following Labor Day. These trains run beyond Fraser to climb the 2.447% (1 in 41) grade to Wolf. Steam is normally scheduled for Saturdays, Sundays and holidays. There is usually no need for reservations except for groups and bus tours, which should call the depot in advance. Special charter trips can also be arranged.

Boone is 42 miles from Des Moines and 17 miles west of Ames, from which there is a bus service. By car, access is best from highway 30 at the south edge of Boone. Des Moines airport is 50 miles.

Western Maryland Scenic Railroad

MARYLAND

USEFUL DATA

Headquarters Western Maryland Scenic Railway, 13 Canal Street, Cumberland, MD 21502.

Phone (301) 759 4400.

Fax (301) 759 1329.

Public Stations

W. Maryland Station Center, Cumberland; C&P Depot, Frostburg.

Timetables & Tickets from Headquarters.

Reservations call (800) TRAIN 50 or (301) 759 4400.

Public access

WM Station Center from Interstate 68.

Facilities

Museums at Cumberland & Frostburg. Gift shop at Cumberland. Restaurants at Frostburg & Cumberland.

The Western Maryland Scenic Railroad operates a 17-mile stretch of line between Cumberland and Frostburg over tracks that were once part of the Western Maryland & Pennsylvania Railroad, using steam and diesel motive power.

The Western Maryland Railroad originated in 1852, when a charter was granted on 27 May to the Baltimore, Carroll & Frederick Rail Road to build a line from Baltimore through Westminster to Hagerstown, MD. The name was soon changed to the Western Maryland Rail Road, and the line was opened as far as Union Bridge in November 1862. It figured in the Battle of Gettysburg in 1863. The line reached Cumberland in 1906, meeting the Cumberland and Piedmont Rail-

way. In 1908 the WMRR went bankrupt, and in 1910 it was taken over by the Western Maryland Railroad, which immediately began construction of the 86-mile extension northwest to a connection with the Pittsburgh & Lake Erie at Connellsville. This was opened on 1 August 1912, and contains the part now operated by the Western Maryland Scenic Railroad.

In 1967, B&O and C&O applied to take control of the Western Maryland Railroad, and this was granted by the ICC. In 1973, the Chessie System (later CSX) was incorporated to control B&O and C&O and Western Maryland, and the WM applied to abandon the line between Hancock, Cumberland and Connellsville. While some parts were aban-

RIGHT *Baldwin 2-8-0 No 734 of 1916 prepares to leave Cumberland with a well-patronised special train for Frostburg.*

ABOVE *Baldwin 2-8-0 No 734 is turned on the turntable watched by a group of interested spectators.*

doned, the line from Cumberland through Frostburg to Mount Savage remained until 24 August 1986. The last train was a revenue freight from the brickworks at Mount Savage, MD. Since the route is particularly scenic, a group set about reopening at least part of the line as a tourist railroad, and the Western Maryland Scenic Railroad came into being. It is a non-profit organization supported by the cities of Cumberland and Frostburg, by Allegheny County and by the State of Maryland, which purchased the right of way from Cumberland to Frostburg.

The WMSR maintains the track, at a cost averaging $100,000 annually. Half the revenue from the State's purchase goes to operating costs; the remainder was used to match grants from the Department of Economic and Employment Development and the Appalachian Regional Commission for the purchase and upgrading of equipment. This brought the total funding to $2,350,000. In addition, the National Railroad Historical Society, Maryland State Historical Society and the C&O Canal National Historical Preservation Society all have an interest.

Only three years after its closure, the line was reopened in 1989. Steam passenger excursions were resumed in 1993. In addition to the Cumberland–Frostburg run, a partnership developed with the Baltimore Orioles baseball franchise, CSX and MARC, which has resulted in four successful seasons of baseball trains to Orioles Park at Camden Yards. The WMSR also runs other trips over various routes, in conjunction with CSX, for Mainline Fall Foliage excursions. Routes covered have been Terra Alta, Grafton and Harper's Ferry, and Connellsville, PA, the latter over the rival ex-B&O route.

The line runs from Cumberland through a breach in the Allegheny Mountains known as the Narrows, over an iron truss bridge, round Helmstetter's Horseshoe Curve and through the 1,000-foot-long Brush Tunnel. Grades are steep with 2.8% (1 in 36), which, combined with Helmstetter's curve, gave severe operating headaches in steam days, when pusher locomotives were used to assist the heavy freights. Motive power today comes from the Baldwin Consolidation, a 2-8-0 No. 734 dating from 1916, which was steamed again in 1993. It has

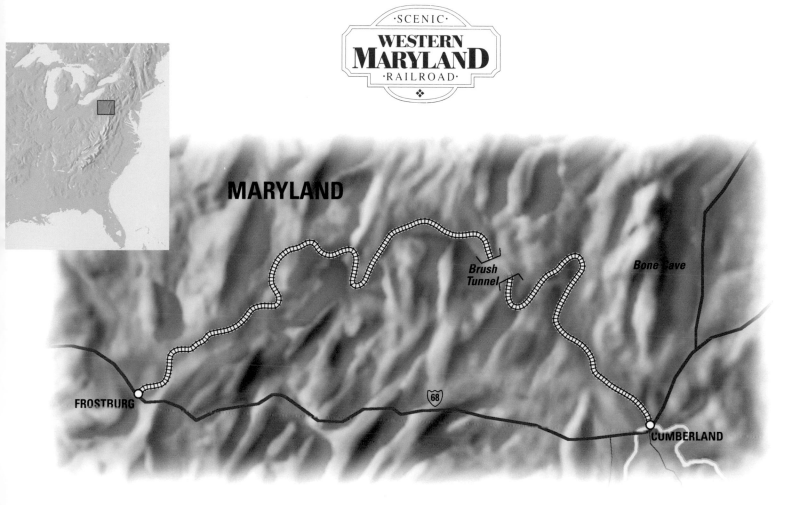

·SCENIC·
WESTERN
MARYLAND
·RAILROAD·

MARYLAND

FROSTBURG

Brush
Tunnel

Bone Cave

68

CUMBERLAND

been lovingly restored and is now called Mountain Thunder. Also there are two EMD GP30s, which came respectively from Conrail and Reading. The 17-passenger cars are interesting too, having come from a variety of different railroads; four are rented. There are no plants to extend the line but the Railroad hopes for more rolling stock, major improvements to the workshops at Ridgeley, and a turntable.

The program for 1996 begins in April, with one diesel-hauled train on weekends. From May to the end of September, a steam-hauled train runs Tuesday–Sunday. October has two trains per day Tuesday–Sunday (one train only from 27 October). November one train weekends only and to mid-December one train only. A round trip takes 3 hours, including 1½ hours at the Old Depot Center at Frostburg. There are special events throughout the operating season, including evening dinner trains, fall foliage excursions, and "Santa's Express." Reservations are not required but are strongly recommended.

DATE LINE

WMRR chartered	**27 May 1852**
Opened to Union Bridge	**November 1862**
Reached Cumberland	**1906**
Opened to Connellsville	**1 August 1912**
B&O, C&O control	**1967**
Chessie System	**1973**
Mount Savage & Frostburg closed	**24 August 1986**
Western Maryland Scenic RR open	**1989**
Steam locomotive introduced	**1993**

Huckleberry Railroad

M I C H I G A N

USEFUL DATA

Headquarters Genesee County Parks & Recreation Commission, 5045 Stanley Road, Flint, MI 48506.

Phone (810) 736 7610 or (800) 648 PARK.

Public Station Crossroads Village Depot.

Timetables & Tickets by phone or mail from Headquarters.

Public access
by car from I-69 or I-75, then I-475. Fully accessible for wheelchair & handicapped visitors.

Facilities
Café, snack bar, museums, rides, etc.

In the state of Michigan, a few miles north of Flint, the Genesee Country Parks and Recreation Commission operates Crossroads Village, a replica of a Victorian-era country town, complete with the Huckleberry Railroad, a 3-foot-gauge steam railroad built in 1976 to fit in with the theme of the village. It operates over a portion of the former Flint & Pere Marquette Railroad.

The F&PMRR was chartered in 1871 and was completed to Fostoria, OH, about 30 miles south of Toledo, in 1880. It also ran northwest to Pere Marquette (now Ludington) on the eastern shore of Lake Michigan. Part of the F&PMRR was the former Port Huron & Northwestern, a 3-foot-gauge line built between 1879 and 1992, running from Port Huron to Saginaw. These and others were consolidated to form the Pere Marquette Railway in 1901. All of the railroads in this part of Michigan were built to serve the lumber industry. By the end of the 19th century they were feeling the results of the decline in the lumber trade as the forests became depleted; consolidation was intended to make one larger and more powerful road. By the mid-1920s the PMR was also carrying coal from the Chesapeake & Ohio, with an interchange with the Hocking Valley (also controlled by the C&O) at Toledo. In 1928 the PMR was incorporated into C&O control.

The PMR merged fully with C&O on 6 June 1947, but carried on an almost independent existence at first as the Pere Marquette District, later part of C&O's Northern Region. The PMR gradually lost its separate identity, until Amtrak revived the name in 1984 for a new Chicago-Grand Rapids train. The line through Flint was closed to all traffic in 1975. It was reopened as a tourist attraction in 1976, but with 3-foot gauge replacing the original standard gauge. The line runs for 8 miles through the Genesee Recreation area; there are no plans for an extension.

RIGHT Former Denver & Rio Grande 2-8-2 No 464 stands at the water tower preparing to depart on its run through the Genesee Country Park and Crossroads village.

MICHIGAN

HUCKLEBERRY RAILROAD AND CROSSROADS VILLAGE

Mott Lake

Flint

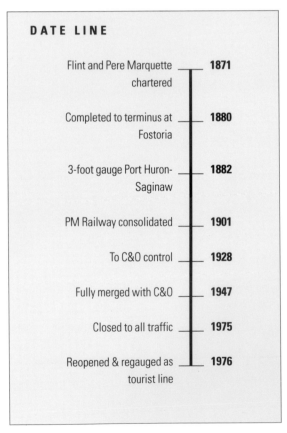

DATE LINE

Flint and Pere Marquette chartered	**1871**
Completed to terminus at Fostoria	**1880**
3-foot gauge Port Huron-Saginaw	**1882**
PM Railway consolidated	**1901**
To C&O control	**1928**
Fully merged with C&O	**1947**
Closed to all traffic	**1975**
Reopened & regauged as tourist line	**1976**

Crossroads Village is a "living history" village operated in conjunction with the railroad. There are 30 historic structures, all timber-built, including timber mills, a cider mill, blacksmith, printer, the doctor's and lawyer's offices, etc. The automotive pioneers were at work in this area—Flint is only about 65 miles from Detroit—and the carriage-building trade was well established in the area before the automobile came along.

The Huckleberry Railroad operates throughout the day. Trains depart hourly from the Crossroads Depot, usually hauled by a Baldwin 4-6-0 from Alaska or a 2-8-2 from the Denver & Rio Grande. A little out of character are the two diesel locomotives, but these are used as backup or for shunting (switching). The round trip takes approximately 35 minutes.

The Village is staffed throughout the year, but it is normally open to the public daily from June to August and on weekends in September. There are special Halloween Ghost Trains in October. During December there is a major holiday lighting display for "Christmas at Crossroads"; the railway runs Thursday–Sunday until about 10 December, and then Thursday–Saturday until the Saturday before Christmas and for the last five days to December 30. Reservations are not normally necessary, but are strongly recommended for Halloween and Christmas.

Crossroads Village may be reached from I-75 or I-69 by following I-475 to Saginaw Street, then north to Stanley Road, east to Bray Road and south to the village. Nearby are the Flint Cultural Center, Pennywhistle Place, and Frankenmuth.

St Louis Iron Mountain & Southern Railroad

M I S S O U R I

ABOVE *St Louis Iron Mountain & Southern began life as a 5ft gauge line. In due course it was converted to standard gauge and now employs a 1946-built H K Porter 2-4-2 tender locomotive seen here on a tourist train.*

The name of the St Louis Iron Mountain & Southern Railroad was revived from a long-time predecessor of the Missouri Pacific, for a tourist railroad that operates over the tracks of a short line, the Jackson & Southern Railroad, which was established to operate a Missouri Pacific branch from Delta to Jackson.

The original St Louis & Iron Mountain Railroad was chartered in 1851 to build southwest from St Louis to Ironton, to carry iron ore mined in Iron Mountain. It opened to Pilot Knob in 1858, with a track gauge of 5ft 6in. In 1869 it completed a line from Bismark to the Mississippi River and a connection by ferry to the Mobile & Ohio; this was so important that the road converted to 5-foot gauge, which was then the standard in the south. Other extensions took the road to Poplar Bluff and then to Little Rock, Arkansas. In 1874 the Iron Mountain consolidated with the Cairo & Fulton to become the St Louis, Iron Mountain & Southern. Conversion to standard 4ft 8½in gauge was carried out around 1886, and in the early 1990s the road was absorbed by the Missouri Pacific.

A proposal was made for abandonment in 1984, but the Jackson Industrial Development Corporation needed to maintain a link to Jackson. They purchased the 18½ miles of track to Delta, and a "short line," the Jackson & Southern Company, was formed with one diesel locomotive and a handful of wagons. Today there is no freight traffic on the line.

In 1984 a group of local steam enthusiasts had the idea of running a steam train so that others could enjoy and relive part of the country's heritage. The group raised money to purchase equipment and arranged for trackage rights from the Jackson Industrial Development Corporation. On 18 April 1986 the inaugural train ran. In 1990, stockholders purchased the track and right-of-way. Now, two or three permanent staff, plus an army of volunteers belonging to the "Friends of Steam Railroad-

BELOW *65-ton Whitcombe industrial switcher No 911 used in the winter months, here coupled to Southern Pacific SD40 No 8319.*

USEFUL DATA

Headquarters PO Box 244, Jackson, MO 63755-0244.

Phone (314) 243 1688 or (800) 455 RAIL.
Manager: Joyce Baker.

Main Station Jackson.

Timetables & Tickets
Depot, Jackson.

Reservations call Depot.

Public access

12 minutes NE of Cape Girardeau Intersection of 25, 34, 61 and 72 in Jackson, county seat of Girardeau County. 110 miles south-east of St Louis and 180 miles north of Memphis TS, on I-55. Car park. Facilities for disabled visitors.

Facilities

Dinner trains, reservations essential; light refreshments on trains.

ing" (a non-profit support group), run tourist trains part or all of the way between Jackson and Delta. Trains operate from Jackson to Gordonville (5 miles), Jackson to Dutchtown (8 miles) and Jackson to Delta (18 miles), round trips taking 1 hour 20 minutes, 2 hours and 5 hours respectively.

There are two coal-fired steam locomotives. One, a 2-4-2 tank switcher built in 1946 by H. K. Porter of Pittsburgh, Pennsylvania, was formerly with the Central Illinois Public

Service Company in Meredosia. From 1974 to 1981 it was with the Crab Orchard & Egyptian Railroad, another tourist line, who purchased a tender to work with it, giving increased water and fuel capacity. The StLIM&S purchased it with its tender in 1984. There is also a Baldwin-Lima-Hamilton Whitcombe diesel, which is used during the winter months and as backup to the steam locomotive. Passenger cars have been rebuilt from Central Illinois Public Service electric multiple unit vehicles

ABOVE *H K Porter 2-4-2 No 5, formerly of Crab Orchard & Egyptian RR crosses the trestle over a tributary of the Mississippi.*

BELOW *The new 'James Gang' of 1996 – the Bollinger County Posse is a search and rescue group affiliated to the County Sheriff.*

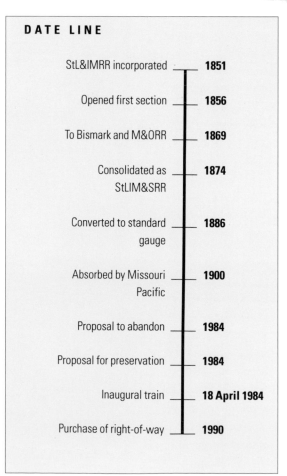

of 1926. There are also two cabooses, both of which can be rented for parties by arrangement with the station.

Public services are operated throughout the year, but the main season is from the beginning of April to the end of October, with four round trips to Gordonville each weekend. A Saturday night dinner train runs to Dutch-town—a two-hour round trip—but on one Saturday night each month this is replaced by a "Murder Mystery" train to Delta and back, providing dinner at a family restaurant and entertainment on board—a five-hour round trip. Light refreshments are served on other trains. Throughout the season there is a pro-gram of special events, and themes are provided on all weekends, including staged "Train Robberies." Missouri's first known train robbery, on 31 January 1874, was by the Great Jesse James!

Jackson Station is at the intersection of highways 25, 72, and US 61. Jackson is about 110 miles southeast of St Louis on Interstate 55, and about 6 miles northwest of Cape Girardeau, where there is a Heritage Museum.

DATE LINE	
StL&IMRR incorporated	**1851**
Opened first section	**1856**
To Bismark and M&ORR	**1869**
Consolidated as StLIM&SRR	**1874**
Converted to standard gauge	**1886**
Absorbed by Missouri Pacific	**1900**
Proposal to abandon	**1984**
Proposal for preservation	**1984**
Inaugural train	**18 April 1984**
Purchase of right-of-way	**1990**

Conway Scenic Railroad
N E W   H A M P S H I R E

USEFUL DATA

Headquarters Conway Scenic Railroad, PO Box 1947, Norcross Circle, North Conway, NH 03860.

Phone (603) 356 5251.

Public Stations North Conway, Conway, Bartlett, Crawford Notch, Fabyan (1 September 1996)

Timetables & Tickets from Headquarters; dining train.

Reservations (603) 356 5251, ext 19.

Public access by car on US 302 from Portland, Maine, or from US 3 east from Twin Mountain. Assistance available for special needs passengers.

Facilities Museum & gift shop at North Conway. Refreshments, display of restored cars, operating turntable, roundhouse & model railway.

RIGHT *The scenic nature of the Conway Scenic Railroad is well demonstrated by this view of F9A No 6516 crossing Willey Brook Bridge within view of Mount Washington, New Hampshire.*

CONWAY SCENIC RAILROAD

The Conway Scenic Railroad operates standard-gauge trains from a beautifully restored station in North Conway, New Hampshire, along the Saco River Valley to Conway, Bartlett and Crawford Hatch, over part of the old Boston & Maine line between Rochester, NH and Whitefield.

In 1872 the Portsmouth, Great Falls & Conway Railroad opened a branch to Conway. The village developed into a summer resort and in 1874 the Railroad erected a large wooden station (depot) at North Conway. This building has been meticulously restored, and now contains a museum and numerous railroad artifacts of a vanished era.

In 1878 the PGF&C became part of the Eastern Railroad, which was in turn absorbed in 1890 by the Boston & Maine. The Conway branch did well. When North Conway developed into a winter sports area in the 1930s, passenger traffic increased—only to be eroded by the relentless advance of the automobile. By the late 1950s, rail traffic had dwindled away. The last passenger train left North Conway on 2 December 1961. Freight traffic continued for a little over ten years, but was finally withdrawn on 30 October 1972.

Three men formed the Conway Scenic Railroad, a private corporation, in 1974. After long negotiations with the Boston & Maine Railroad, they bought the depot and the Conway Branch with 7½ miles of track from Conway to Intervale, north of the junction with the former B&M line from Portsmouth. Train operation began on 3 August 1974 over the 5½ miles between Conway and North Conway. Operations today are run jointly with the Boston & Maine RR Historical Society and the 470 Railway Club.

Conway Scenic Railroad also leases the 52.4 miles of former Boston & Maine RR from Center Conway to Whitefield, NH, now owned by the State of New Hampshire. This allows trains to operate to Bartlett, a further

10½ miles, and from 1 September 1995 to Crawford Notch, 24 miles from North Conway. It is planned to extend operations a further 4.3 miles to Fabyan on 1 September 1996.

The line runs across lush fields and woodlands and through the Mt Washington Valley, with views of Mt Washington (6,288 feet, notable for the Mt Washington Cog Railway) and the White Mountains. The line crosses the East Branch, Ellis and Saco Rivers over Frankenstein Trestle and Willey Brook Bridge, and past sheer bluffs, steep ravines, cascading brooks and streams. In the fall, the colors of the trees in these parts are legendary.

At Conway the original freight house still remains, while at Glen there is the original station house (now privately owned), although trains do not sop there. Bartlett has a freight house, and a roundhouse remains but is not in use. The station at Crawford Notch is a

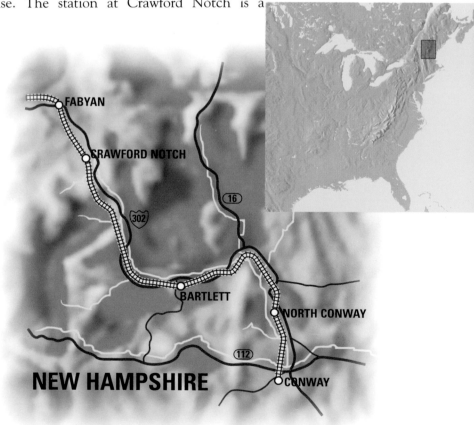

scheduled stop, but the buildings are privately owned. With the extension to Fabyan, travelers will find the station in use as a privately-owned restaurant.

But the major attraction, apart from the trains, must be the station house at North Conway. All the structures there are on the National Register of Historic Places. This is the main operations center and includes the roundhouse, yards, and the freight house, which contains a model-railroad room.

Currently the Railroad has three steam locomotives dating from 1910 to 1921, and six diesel locomotives including two F-7s and two FP-9s. There are 10 passenger cars in service, and another six under (or awaiting) restoration. Other vehicles are either on display or used for work trains and storage. Trains may be operated by steam or diesel locomotives between North Conway and Conway, but diesel locomotives are used on the longer runs to Bartlett and Crawford Notch.

To quote the official brochure, "Trains run rain or shine . . . mid-April to mid-December," weekends at each end of the season, working up to daily depending on the time of year. Passengers may make reservations for all or part of the journey from North Conway to Crawford Notch. In addition to the normal trains, on which refreshments are available,

ABOVE *Ex-Reader RR oil burner 2-6-2 No 108 stands in the magnificently-restored North Conway depot.*

DATE LINE

First railroad to Conway	**1872**
Absorbed into Eastern RR	**1878**
Absorbed by Boston & Maine	**1890**
Last passenger train	**2 December 1961**
Last freight train	**30 October 1972**
Reopened by Conway Scenic RR	**3 August 1974**
Extended to Crawford Notch	**1 September 1995**
Extension to Fabyan's expected	**1 September 1996**

the Chocoruna Dining Car specials are run for both lunch and dinner from mid-June to mid-October, for which it is best to make advance reservations (phone 603-356-5251, ext 19). There is a program of nine or 10 special events throughout the operating season, from Easter through to Christmas. North Conway is about 140 miles north of Boston, MA, and 60 miles west of Portland, ME, on Route 302.

Cumbres & Toltec Scenic Railroad

N E W   M E X I C O

USEFUL DATA

Headquarters 1. Antonito
Depot, PO Box 688, Antonito,
CO 81120.
2. Chama Depot, PO Box 789,
Chama, NM 87520.

Phone Antonito: (719) 376
5483. Chama: (505) 756 2151.

Timetables & Tickets
Reservations recommended
by phone or mail from either
depot.

Reservations (603) 356
5251, ext 19.

Public access
no public transport available.
By car: Antonito is on US
285, 30 miles south of
Alamosa. Chama is on US 84
and ST 17, 80 miles west of
Alamosa.

Facilities
Snacks & souvenirs on all
trains. Hot meals at Osier.
Restroom facilities (simple)
on all trains and at Osier
stop.

The Cumbres & Toltec Scenic Railroad is the longest and highest narrow-gauge steam railroad in the United States. It runs on a part of the 3-foot-gauge line built in the late 1870s by the Denver & Rio Grande Railway to reach the southwestern part of Colorado. The original line ran from Pueblo south through Walsenburg, then west to Alamosa and Antonito, and on to Chama in New Mexico. It was continued to Gunnison and Durango, Colorado, in 1881. The Scenic Railroad uses the line between Antonito and Chama, which is 7,863 feet above sea level. It negotiates the Cumbres Pass. The summit of the line is at 10,015 feet; it then drops down to Osier and Antonito (7,888 feet). The nature of the terrain means that there are many curves, and the gradient averages 1.4%

(1 in 71) on the New Mexico side of the Pass. There are two tunnels. The line passes through the Toltec Gorge, and crosses the Colorado/New Mexico border no less than eleven times!

Conversion to standard gauge was carried out on the main D&RGW routes in the early part of the century, and by 1921 only two major routes remained, of which the line from Alamosa to Durango and Silverton was one. There was also a branch south from Alamosa to Sante Fe, New Mexico. By 1955 only the Alamosa-Durango line, with branches to Silverton and Farmington, remained.

During the winter of 1965 the line over the Cumbres Pass was closed for five months—there was not enough traffic to make it worthwhile to keep it clear. In 1967 all traffic over

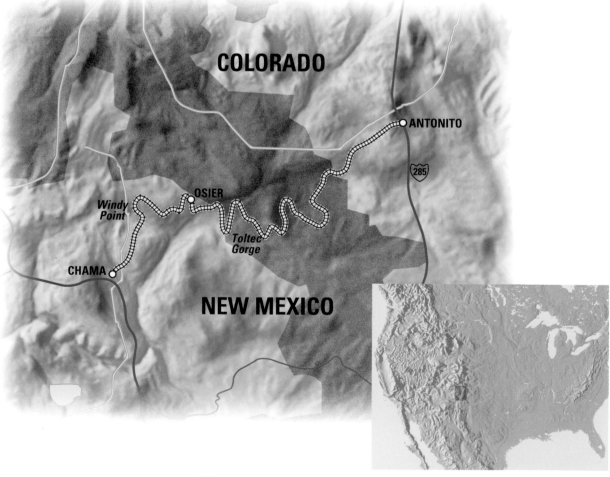

the line ceased, leaving only the Durango & Silverton line open for ore and occasional passenger traffic. In 1968, the 64-mile line from Chama to Antonito was purchased, together with the cars and locomotives

DATE LINE

Construction began	**March 1880**
Completed to Chama	**31 December 1880**
First train	**January 1881**
Closed to passengers	**31 January 1951**
Last charter train	**1966**
Closed to all traffic	**8 December 1968**
New Mexico & Colorado purchased	**July 1970**
First tourist train ran	**June 1971**

necessary to operate it, by the states of New Mexico and Colorado. The line is now operated for the two states by Kyle Railways

Trains are operated in the summer season between the two terminals. Normally a train departs from each at about the same time; the trains meet at Osier, CO, where lunch can be eaten and the two locomotives are exchanged. The locomotive having come from Chama takes the train back to Antonito and vice versa. Passengers can either make the whole journey, returning by van, or only half, returning by the other train from Osier to the terminal of origin.

The line has nine steam locomotives, of which only four are active (all ex-D & RGW Baldwin 2-8-2s), and one diesel switcher. There are 39 coaches and 65 wagons.

This is an extremely scenic line passing through some very rugged country. Apart from the two tunnels there are some high steel trestle bridges where the line passes back and forth over water-courses. It can be cold in the Rockies, even in mid-summer, and warm clothing is highly recommended!

ABOVE LEFT A *Cumbres & Toltec train crosses over one of the spectacular high trestles en route between Chama and Osier.*

ABOVE *To represent an authentic trip of the 1950/60s No 489 was repainted in Rio Grande livery. It is pictured near Coxo on the climb to Cumbres summit. In the background is Windy Point.*

LEFT Former Denver & Rio Grande 2-8-2 No 488 prepares to leave for a journey over the highest preserved narrow gauge line in the United States.

ABOVE A group of youthful travellers about to sample a train ride to the altitude of 10,015 feet over the Rockies.

East Broad Top Railroad

P E N N S Y L V A N I A

USEFUL DATA

Headquarters East Broad Top Railroad, Rockhill Furnace, PA 17249.

Phone (814) 447 3011.

Public Station Orbisonia.

Rockhill Trolley Museum
Railways to Yesterday Inc., PO Box 203, Rockhill Furnace, PA 17249.

Phone (814) 447 9576, (215) 965 9028 & (717) 367 6754.

Public access
US 522, 15 miles north of Exit 13 on Pennsylvania Turnpike. From east use Exit 14. About 50 miles south of Altoona.

Facilities
Roundhouse & souvenir shop.

Nearby attractions
Rockhill Trolley Museum, Raystown Lakes and Lincoln Caverns.

The East Broad Top Railroad was the last 3-foot-gauge common carrier in the United States east of the Mississippi River, lasting until 1956. Its principal business was as a coal carrier. Today it operates as a tourist railroad over 5 miles of track from Orbisonia, Pennsylvania, north to Colgate Grove.

The Railroad was chartered in 1856 as the East Broad Top Railroad and Coal Company, to mine and transport coal from Broad Top Mountain, a plateau in Pennsylvania south of the Juniata River (midway between Philadelphia and Pittsburg). A track gauge of 3 feet was chosen by the company's directors, and construction began in 1872. The line was opened from Mount Union on the Pennsylvania main line, south to Orbisonia, in 1873. There was a further extension south and west to Shade Gap and Robertsdale in 1874.

Although the EBT's main business was carrying coal, limestone, timber and bark, it operated a few passenger trains as well. It was plagued with mining strikes as well as flooding

rivers and creeks; it saw hard times in the 1890s, but was rehabilitated in the early 1900s. It adopted automatic couplers as late as 1908 and air brakes in 1913.

In 1919 the railroad was bought by a coal mining company, Madeira, Hill & Co., who installed a coal-cleaning plant at Mount Union and facilities for changing trucks on standard-gauge cars, so that cars from the Pennsylvania RR could be run over the EBT lines. Bankruptcy followed in 1937, and the EBT was bought in 1938 by the bond holders, who reorganised as the Rockhill Coal Company. The Shade Gap branch was used to carry materials for the building of the Pennsylvania Turnpike in 1939.

After World War II, despite a series of crippling strikes, the road remained in business and even contemplated changing to diesel; but with the decline in coal use caused by oil and gas, the Rockhill Coal Company closed its mines and offered the EBT for scrap to the Pennsylvania RR, who declined the offer. The

RIGHT *One of the original East Broad Top Baldwin 2-8-2s, No 12, built in 1911 with a train of vintage clerestory passenger cars about to leave Orbisonia.*

PENNSYLVANIA

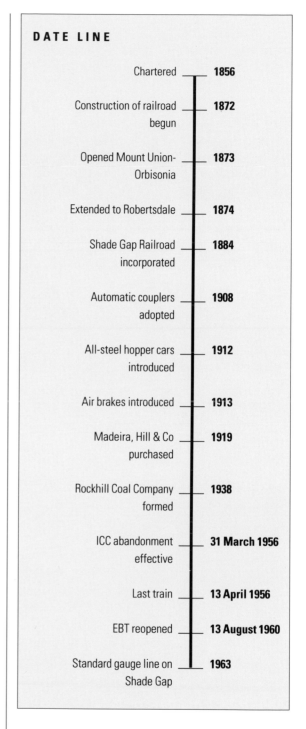

DATE LINE

Chartered	1856
Construction of railroad begun	1872
Opened Mount Union-Orbisonia	1873
Extended to Robertsdale	1874
Shade Gap Railroad incorporated	1884
Automatic couplers adopted	1908
All-steel hopper cars introduced	1912
Air brakes introduced	1913
Madeira, Hill & Co purchased	1919
Rockhill Coal Company formed	1938
ICC abandonment effective	31 March 1956
Last train	13 April 1956
EBT reopened	13 August 1960
Standard gauge line on Shade Gap	1963

ICC approved abandonment from 31 March 1956, and on 13 April 1956 the last train ran. The locomotives and cars were stored on the property until they were bought by a scrap dealer, Nick Kovalchick, who petitioned against dismantling the mines and resumed mining activity in 1957.

The year 1960 was the bicentennial of Orbisonia, and Kovalchick was asked if the railroad could be resuscitated for the celebration. The East Broad Top reopened on 13 August 1960, since when it has been operated as a tourist railroad during the summer. Another part, the portion of the Shade Gap branch just south from Orbisonia, was relaid with standard-gauge track by Railways to Yesterday, which operates a 1¼ mile trolley museum line from a station close to EBT's Orbisonia station. Their stock includes an Electroliner from the old Chicago, North Shore & Milwaukee Railroad.

EBT still operates three of the same Baldwin 2-8-2 steam locomotives and some of its passenger cars. A 50-minute round trip covers the 5 miles of scenic track to the north of Orbisonia. There are six steam, one electric and two diesel locomotives, one electric motor coach, eight passenger cars and 175 wagons.

Operation is from June to October at weekends, and some special events are held, including a Fall Spectacular (phone for details).

Knox, Kane & Kinzua Railroad

P E N N S Y L V A N I A

USEFUL DATA

Headquarters Knox &
Kane Railroad, PO Box 422,
Marienville, PA 16239.

Phone (814) 927 6621, (717)
334 2411.

Public Stations
Marienville, Kane.

Timetables by mail from
Headquarters.

Tickets reservations
recommended to ensure a
seat! 10% deposit required
with reservation. Deposit
refunded if canceled more
than 48 hours before
intended journey.

Public access
only by road

Facilities
Museum of railroad items &
artifacts at Marienville Area
Railroad & Historical
Museum across street from
station. Lunch boxes by
application in advance. No
refund if canceled less than
48 hours in advance. Cost
about $4.00.

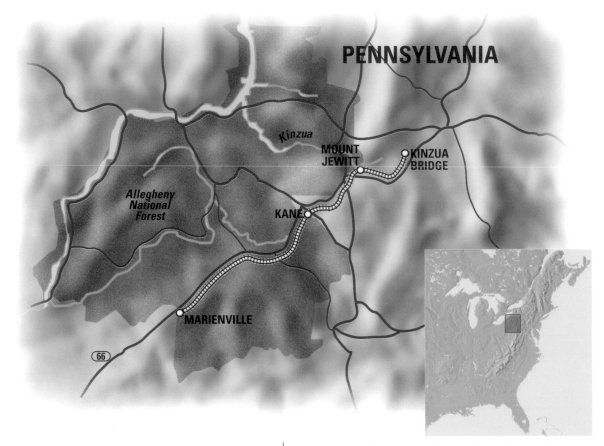

The Knox, Kane & Kinzua operates 48 miles of standard-gauge line between Marienville and Kane, Pennsylvania, which includes the famous 2,052-foot-long Kinzua bridge, at the time of its construction in 1882 the highest in the world at 301 feet. Even today it is the second highest in the USA.

In 1881 a narrow-gauge line was completed by the Pittsburgh, Bradford & Buffalo Railroad from Knox, PA, to Marienville, extended to Kane in 1882. The next extension, to Mt Jewett, included the Kinzua Bridge and opened in 1883, at which point the line was taken over by the Pittsburgh & Western Railroad. The Bridge was a relatively light structure and could not support heavier locomotives and rolling stock; in 1900 it was rebuilt. In the next year, the P&WRR was taken over by the Baltimore & Ohio Railroad, who in 1911 converted the line to standard gauge. B&O continued to run both passenger and freight

trains until January 1933, after which they substituted mixed trains. By then, the line carried a relatively light load. The mixed trains ended in 1937.

Train excursions to the Kinzua Bridge were popular in earlier times and continued until 21 June 1959. The structure is of such historical importance that on 16 August 1963, Governor William W. Scranton signed a bill establishing Kinzua State Park, thus preserving this National Landmark. In 1977 it was placed on the National Register of Historic Places, and in 1982 it was designated a National Historic Civil Engineering Landmark.

B&O continued to run freight trains until 1982, when the Knox & Kane Railroad purchased the tracks. In 1986 the company purchased the right-of-way of the abandoned Erie branch from Kane to Mt Jewett, which included the Bridge, and relaid the tracks on it so that trains could run across and back. It is a

DATE LINE

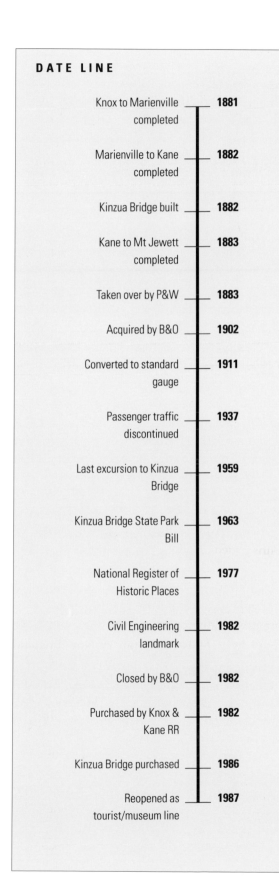

Knox to Marienville completed	**1881**
Marienville to Kane completed	**1882**
Kinzua Bridge built	**1882**
Kane to Mt Jewett completed	**1883**
Taken over by P&W	**1883**
Acquired by B&O	**1902**
Converted to standard gauge	**1911**
Passenger traffic discontinued	**1937**
Last excursion to Kinzua Bridge	**1959**
Kinzua Bridge State Park Bill	**1963**
National Register of Historic Places	**1977**
Civil Engineering landmark	**1982**
Closed by B&O	**1982**
Purchased by Knox & Kane RR	**1982**
Kinzua Bridge purchased	**1986**
Reopened as tourist/museum line	**1987**

96-mile round trip from Marienville to the Bridge, and a 32-mile round trip from Kane. Currently there are two steam locomotives, a Baldwin 2-8-0 of 1927 and a 2-8-2 built by the Tang-Shan Works in China in 1989. The two diesel locomotives are both of 1957 vintage—an EMD GP9 and an Alco S-6. There is also an interesting collection of passenger cars, mostly ex-Lackawanna.

The Kinzua Bridge attracts intense interest, and reservations are necessary to travel there from either Marienville or Kane. In addition, as the round trip from Marienville takes about eight hours, a lunch box is recommended, which may be ordered and paid for in advance. The line operates Friday, Saturday, and Sunday in June and September, Tuesday– Sunday in July and August, Tuesday–Sunday the first two weeks in October, and Saturday and Sunday the last two weekends in October. There is one train per day leaving Marienville at 8.30 am and Kane at 10.45 am, returning to Kane at 2.30 pm and Marienville at 4.40 pm.

Marienville is 110 miles north east of Pittsburgh and 75 miles south east of Erie, PA, and may be reached from Route 66. Kane is also reached by Route 66 and Route 6, and is 105 miles south west of Buffalo, NY, and 47 miles from Salamanca, NY. Both are close to the 500,000-acre Allegheny National Forest.

TOP *The famous Kinzua Bridge in Pennsylvania built in 1882 was then the highest in the world at 301 feet. It is 2,053 feet long and was rebuilt in 1900. It is today preserved as a National landmark.*

ABOVE *Today two steam locomotives may be used; one, shown here is a Baldwin 2-8-0 of 1927 formerly owned by the Huntingdon & Broad Top Mountain; the other was imported from China.*

Steamtown National Historic Site

P E N N S Y L V A N I A

USEFUL DATA

Headquarters Steamtown National Historic Site, Superintendent, 150, South Washington Avenue, Scranton, PA 18503-2018.
Phone (717) 340 5200.
Timetables excursion train schedules from museum by mail or phone.
Entrance fee for site and excursion trains, payable on entry to Visitor Center.
Public access
by car from Interstate 81, exit 52. Ample car parks. Facilities for disabled visitors.
Facilities
full museum of railroad rolling stock & equipment. Light refreshments & rest rooms. Restaurants & lodgings in Scranton.

ABOVE *Canadian Pacific 4-6-2 No 2317, built by Montreal Locomotive Works in 1926, leaves Steamtown with a main line* *excursion over the former Lackawanna line to Moscow, Pa.*

Steamtown, at Scranton, Pennsylvania, was established on 30 October 1986 to further public understanding and appreciation of the role steam railroading played in the development of the United States. Steamtown is the only place in the National Parks System where the story of steam railroading, and the people who made it, is told.

The former Delaware, Lackawanna & Western Railroad had a large yard at Scranton, where it had lines to Northumberland, PA, and Binghampton, Syracuse and Buffalo, NY. Scranton was established by George and Seldon Scranton in 1853. They formed the DL&W by merging three joining railroads: the Cayuga & Susquehanna, the Lackawanna & Western and the Delaware & Cobb's Gap. It was through them and anthracite that Scranton became an important industrial center. Four other roads ran through Scranton: the Central of New Jersey, the Delaware & Hudson, the Erie, and the New York, Ontario & Western. In addition there was an electric short line, the Lackawanna & Wyoming Valley railroad, which began operating in 1903. At its height, the DL&W operated about a thousand miles of main line and branches between Hoboken, NJ, and Buffalo, NY. Parts are still operated by Conrail and New Jersey Transit.

The idea of a "Steamtown" was first proposed by F. Nelson Blount, A New England seafood processor, who began to assemble a collection of standard-gauge steam locomotives in the 1950s and 60s. By 1966 his collection was established in Bellows Falls, VT, and

Labels within the illustration: Bridge 60 · Lackawanna Avenue · State Office Building · Excursion Loading Platform · Oil House (Bookstore) · The Mall at Steamtown · PARKING · Theater · 1 · 2 · 4 · 3 · 6 · 5 · Mall Ramp · RIVER · Locomotive Repair Shops · Green Sand Storage Bin

excursion trains were operated over a portion of the defunct Rutland Railway. Blount was killed in a plane crash in 1967, but his Steamtown continued to operate.

In 1984 the Steamtown Foundation for the Preservation of Steam and Railroad America, Inc. brought the collection to Scranton, which seemed a more appropriate center. The large yards had been closed by Conrail in 1980 following acquisition of Erie Lackawanna in 1976. When Steamtown National Historic Site was created, the yard became part of the National Park Service, so in effect the present owner is the Department of the Interior, United States Government. Ever since the site was established in 1984 there has been continuous development, along with the usual controversy that troubles national government-financed institutions. New facilities have nonetheless been built, including a roundhouse. There was a Grand Reopening and Dedication over the weekend of 1–4 July 1995.

The Steamtown collection consists of locomotives, freight cars, passenger cars, and permanent-way maintenance equipment from several historic railroads. Locomotives range from a tiny industrial switcher built in 1937 by H. K. Porter, to a huge Union Pacific Big Boy built in 1941 by the American Locomotive Company (Alco). The oldest locomotive is a freight locomotive built by Alco in 1903. At present, Steamtown has 29 steam locomotives from the USA and Canada, three diesel-electric locomotives and one electric passenger car, together with 47 other passenger cars and a representative number of freight cars (the latter are for exhibition only). There is also one passenger car from the former Great Western Railway of Great Britain.

The site covers 52 acres. A Visitor Center provides a guide to the attractions and collection. The History Museum gives an overview of the railroad industry from the early times to the present day, together with a time-line of the history of the DL&W from the early 19th century to the mid-20th. The restored roundhouse is based on the 1902–37 building and is used to store, maintain and display locomotives from the collection. A raised walkway gives views of work in progress on the exhibits. As

ABOVE *A Bird's eye view of Steamtown shows how the former roundhouse fits into the present complex, together with the Mall, the theatre and the excursion loading platform.*

RIGHT *Part of an advertisement of the former Dickson Manufacturing Company of Scranton, Pa, advertising locomotives of "every style and size". Even then attention was given to complete interchangeability!*

DATE LINE

D&H Canal Co. test *Stourbridge Lion*	1829
Scranton Brothers form DL&WRR	1853
Scranton locomotive shops closed	1949
Erie Lackawanna RR formed	1960
Steamtown at Bellows Falls	1966
F. Nelson Blount killed	1967
Conrail formed	1976
Scranton Yards closed	1980
Steamtown moved to Scranton	1984
Congress establishes Steamtown NHS	1986
Restored and recreated roundhouse opened	1995

in all roundhouses, the centerpiece is the turntable, measuring 90 feet. One section of three bays survives from the original building of 1902. There is a Technology Museum, which looks at the technological changes and advances in railroads over the years, and includes exhibits covering locomotives, track, architecture, engineering, signaling and safety. There is also an operating model of the DL&W Scranton yard.

Conducted tours and excursions of the yards, roundhouse and locomotive repair shops are run daily. On certain days there are steam rail excursions, including a ride over 13 miles of the former Lackawanna main line from Scranton to Moscow, PA. Other privately-sponsored main line excursions may run from time to time; for example, Fall Foliage trips were run from Scranton to Pocono Summit in October 1995.

A typical excursion schedule includes two trains to Moscow and back on Friday, Saturday and Sunday of Memorial Day weekend; Thursday, Friday, Saturday, Sunday and holidays from the beginning of June to Labor Day weekend; Friday, Saturday, Sunday, and holidays in October. One trip only is run each weekend in November to the first in December.

Scranton is in the northeast corner of Pennsylvania and is best reached from I-81 and Pennsylvania Turnpike extension (Philadelphia Binghampton), exit 52. The Museums and historic site are open every day except Thanksgiving, Christmas and New Years Day.

Strasburg Rail Road

P E N N S Y L V A N I A

USEFUL DATA

Headquarters Strasburg Rail Road, PO Box 96, Strasburg, PA 17579–0096.

Phone (717) 687 7522.

Public Station Strasburg.

Timetables & Tickets from Headquarters and East Strasburg Passenger Station. Timetable details by phone.

Public access
Amtrak train to Mount Joy or Lancaster, then by taxi. By car from route 741. Car park.

Facilities
Picnic area at Groff's Grove (Cherry Hill), Toy Train Museum. Red Caboose Lodge Motel. Railroad Museum of Pennsylvania in Paradise Lane over route 741.

RIGHT *In its earlier times it is likely the Strasburg Railroad employed mainly small locomotives for its 4½ mile route. Today it has a 1925-built Baldwin from the former Great Western of Illinois – No 90 – seen here en route for Paradise.*

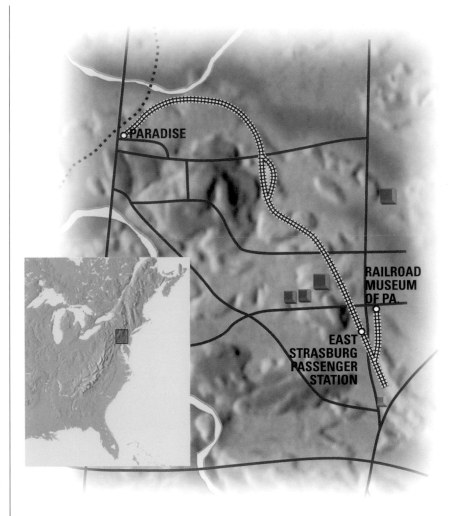

The Strasburg Rail Road is the oldest railroad in the USA still operating under its original charter. It was also one of the first railroads in the USA to go after the tourist business, and is the nation's oldest "short line" railroad. The Railroad was incorporated on 9 June 1832 in the first term of President Andrew Jackson. Trains first operated between Strasburg, in Lancaster County, Pennsylvania, and Paradise (railroad name Leaman Place), a distance of 4½ miles. Paradise was a junction with the now electrified Philadelphia-Harrisburg main line of Amtrak, formerly the Pennsylvania Railroad.

The Strasburg was chartered in 1851. Like many other American railroads, it alternately prospered and fell on hard times. Its first major economic setback came at the turn of the century, when a streetcar line was built between Lancaster and Strasburg; it took most of the Strasburg's passenger traffic, and passenger trains were discontinued, although a mixed train continued to run for some time.

Carload freight to and from the Pennsylvania Railroad provided the major part of the Strasburg's income and kept the line solvent, until highway improvements following World War II diverted most of its traffic to trucks. By the mid-1950s, the road was feeling the pinch badly. In 1957 severe hurricane storms caused so much damage from washouts and fallen trees that an embargo was placed on all incoming carload freight. The owner was reluctant to spend any money on rehabilitation, and petitions for abandonment followed.

While the petitions were being considered, a local industrialist and rail enthusiast, the late Henry J. Long, tried to organize a group to purchase the property at scrap value, to restore and preserve the railroad and to operate it as a hobby. After a long and sometimes frustrating battle, Long managed to get a group together. Acting as its trustee, he purchased the fifty outstanding shares at $450 each. On 1 November 1958 he tendered a cheque of $18,000 to the Homsher Estate, the former owner, and the railroad was saved from the scrap merchant.

The new owners, a group of 24 individuals, had many obstacles to overcome. Apart from the bad state of the permanent way, the track at the Strasburg end had been obliterated at the railroad crossing by the resurfacing of highway 741. With the railroad, the new owners had acquired a four-wheel Plymouth gasoline-mechanical locomotive built in 1926. This was refurbished by the Reading Railway, and after repairs to the track, it was available to earn some money if a passenger car could be obtained. The first of these to arrive was ex-Reading Railway No. 90849. On 4 January 1959 the Plymouth and coach made two trips the length of the line. Later there was even an occasional freight run, but compared to passengers these did not produce much revenue.

Since that time more stock has gradually been acquired. In 1960 the first steam locomotive, ex-Canadian National 0-6-0, built by Baldwin in 1908, arrived and was numbered 31. Various coaches were located, acquired and moved to the railroad. Not long after No. 31 was put to work hauling trains, problems arose with the permanent way and it had to be relaid.

Over the years, a good selection of locomotives and rolling stock has been built up. The Strasburg now has five steam locomotives,

one of which is the property of the Railroad Museum of Pennsylvania (also situated in Strasburg). There are now 18 coaches, including five built by Pullman between 1896 and 1906. The place of honor is taken by the restored Parlor car Marian, which was researched, designed and re-built in the Strasburg's car shops in 1988, under the direction of Vice President and Chief Mechanical Officer Linn W. Moedinger, from an old open-platform passenger car.

The Railroad Museum of Pennsylvania, operated by the Pennsylvania Historical and Museum Commission, is just across the street from Strasburg station on Paradise Lane. It has one of the largest collections of locomotives and cars in North America, chiefly from the former Pennsylvania Railroad. Some are

BELOW *From time to time locomotives are leased from other lines or societies. Here is a classic eight-wheeler – 4-4-0 No 1223 – built in 1903 and leased from the Pennsylvania Museum.*

under cover and many more outside (the outdoor exhibits may only be seen weekends from May to October). Among others there is a replica of the Camden & Amboy's John Bull, which is operated on special occasions.

Trains run on weekends from the third weekend in March through April, and daily from May to November, except Thanksgiving Day. Santa Specials are run on the first two weekends in December. The frequency of service changes with the season, with an hourly service in summer, except Sundays when there are afternoon trains only. Extra trains may be run as needed.

The Railroad Museum at Strasburg is open weekends in April and November, the first two weekends of December, and during Christmas week; also Good Friday, Easter Monday and Thanksgiving Friday. It opens daily from May to October. In addition to full-size exhibits, there is a model railway.

A combined visit to the Strasburg Rail Road and the Railroad Museum is highly recommended. Strasburg lies between Lancaster and Harrisburg, PA and may be reached by route 741 or from routes 30 and 896 from IH 83. The nearest Amtrak stations on the suburban system are Mount Joy and Lancaster.

DATE LINE

Incorporated	**9 June 1832**
Chartered	**1851**
First scheduled passenger train	**December 1851**
Last passenger train	**about 1902**
Abandoned	**1957**
Purchased by preservation group	**November 1958**
First passenger train	**4 January 1959**
First steam locomotive arrived	**1960**
Last 2-10-0 in USA purchased	**1968**
150th anniversary	**9 June 1982**
Parlour Car Marian completed	**1988**

Texas State Railroad Historical Park

T E X A S

USEFUL DATA

Headquarters Texas State Railroad, PO Box 39 Rusk, TX 75785.

Phone (903) 683 2561. Texas residents: (800) 442 8951.

Public Stations Rusk Depot and Palestine Depot.

Timetables & Tickets

reservations recommended. Office open 8.00 am to 5.00 pm seven days a week. Payment required when reservations made. Special train may be rented.

Public access

Rusk station is on US 84, 2½ miles west of Rusk. Palestine station is 3½ miles east of Palestine on US 84. 120 miles southeast of Dallas. 150 miles north of Houston. Car parks in Rusk & Palestine.

Facilities

small theater at Rusk. Refreshments on all trains. Restaurants and lodging in Rusk & Palestine.

ABOVE *Now operated by the Texas State Railroad Historical Park No 500, formerly Santa Fe "Pacific" No 1316, built by Baldwin in 1911 has two admirers.*

The Texas State Railroad Historical Park, about 120 miles from Dallas and 150 miles from Houston, was created in 1972. The bulk of the former Texas State Railroad was conveyed to the Texas Park and Wildlife Department to preserve the operation of steam locomotives and recreate railroading's golden age. The railroad offers rides over 25 miles of track through pine woods and rolling hills to Palestine Park.

Construction of the Texas State Railroad was begun in 1896 by the State Prison System as a plant facility of the penitentiary then at North Rusk. The first five miles were built, using convict labor, to serve an iron-smelting plant at the Prison and other industries in Rusk. This was financed partly from penitentiary funds, partly from the sale of bonds to the State Permanent School Fund, and partly by legislative appropriations.

It was ten years before the line reached Maydelle, and the final 22 miles from Maydelle to Palestine were completed in 1909. Except for the locomotive driver (engineer), prisoners made up the train crew; but when passenger service was extended to Palestine, a full-time staff of nine was employed.

In 1913 the iron plant closed, and in 1917 the penitentiary was converted into a state mental hospital. From then on, the line ran only intermittent service. The railroad was leased to the Texas & New Orleans—later Southern Pacific—in 1921 for freight traffic. The lease was with the Texas Southeastern Railroad from the early 1960s until they

ABOVE *Texas State No 400, in this rural scene, was formerly owned by the Tremont & Gulf – later part of the Illinois Central – and as No 30 was a 2-8-2 built by Baldwin in 1917.*

ceased freight operations on 31 December 1969, when they moved their rolling stock to Diboll. Union Pacific still leases just over 3½ miles at the Palestine end to serve a meat-packing plant.

The line has been authentically restored to represent the late 1890s—which has led to its use in movies and TV—and a ride on it is pure nostalgia. Rusk Depot is three miles west of Rusk City, Cherokee Country, and has been built to resemble a turn-of-the-century depot. State prisoners were again used to rebuild the line, from Ellis and Eastham prison farms, spending about 10 hours each day on renovation work. There is only one community on the route, at Maydelle, which was established in 1910 principally because of the Texas State Railroad. It is now the seat of the TSRR maintenance operation, and has the railroad's only turntable. Maydelle has been used many times

as a backdrop for movies.

The line crosses a number of bridges: the one at Talles Creek is 724 feet long, and that at Neches River is 1,100 feet long. There is a passing loop at Mewshaw siding, in the I.D. Fairchild State Forest, and a wye at Jarvis Crossing allows train engines to be turned at the Palestine end of the line. Palestine Depot, also built to resemble a turn-of-the-century depot, is located 3 miles east of Palestine City. Here the line joins the Union Pacific, whose Red River Operation employs around 450 people. The line has five steam locomotives built between 1901 and 1927, and three diesels built between 1944 and 1953.

Trains run weekends from the third weekend in March to the last weekend of May, with two Fridays in March and one in April, and from 3 August to the last weekend in October, plus the first three Saturdays of November.

ABOVE *No 500 again; in this view about to leave Rusk depot.*

From the end of May to the end of July, trains run from Thursday to Sunday. There are two rostered trains each day, one starting from Rusk and one from Palestine, and numerous other special runs and displays.

The Park covers about 110 acres and there are 30 miles of track. In addition to the railroad, Rusk Park has 94 campsites and a stocked 15-acre lake with paddle boats; Palestine Park has 14 campsites and a ½-acre lake. As the Railroad Park is visited by around 230,000 tourists each year, reservations are strongly recommended. The train starting from Rusk has 505 seats and that from Palestine has 485 seats.

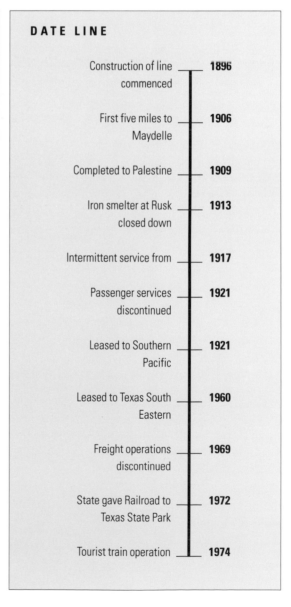

DATE LINE

Construction of line commenced	**1896**
First five miles to Maydelle	**1906**
Completed to Palestine	**1909**
Iron smelter at Rusk closed down	**1913**
Intermittent service from	**1917**
Passenger services discontinued	**1921**
Leased to Southern Pacific	**1921**
Leased to Texas South Eastern	**1960**
Freight operations discontinued	**1969**
State gave Railroad to Texas State Park	**1972**
Tourist train operation	**1974**

Mount Rainier Scenic Railroad
W A S H I N G T O N   S T A T E

USEFUL DATA

Headquarters Mount
Rainier Scenic Railroad, PO
Box 921, Elbe, WA 98330.

Phone (294) 926 3044.

Public Station Elbe, WA.

Timetables by phone or
mail.

Tickets from Elbe station.

Public access

by car from Tacoma on Route
7, from south from I-5, take
route 12 to Morton, then
route 7 north to Elbe. Car
park.

Facilities

Snacks at Elbe & Mineral.
Restaurant next to station at
Elbe.

The Mount Rainier Scenic Railroad operates on a 7-mile stretch of a branch formerly belonging to the Milwaukee Road (originally the Tacoma Eastern) from Elbe, Washington State, to a logging display and picnic area at Mineral. Mount Rainier Scenic also has trackage rights to run passenger excursions over the Chehalis Western Railroad.

Lines in the northwest of the USA were absorbed by the Northern Pacific, the Great Northern, or the Milwaukee Road: Chicago, Milwaukee, St Paul & Pacific. The area is dominated by the Rocky Mountains, and sparsely populated except for the coastal areas. It is rich in timber, and a number of small branch lines were built to carry lumber to the main rivers or the coastal ports. The Tacoma Eastern was one of these, and was eventually taken over by the Milwaukee Road.

The Chehalis Western is a recent creation. It is a Class II road with about 165 miles of line, and has its headquarters at Tenino, on

RIGHT Mount Rainier consists of two operations – the principal one being a former logging line. Here three truck Heisler No 91 of 1930, formerly owned by the Kinzua Pine Mills takes a train through former logging country.

the line from Seattle to Portland, Oregon. This line was formerly the Great Northern Railway line from Vancouver, British Columbia, to Portland.

The Mount Rainier Scenic line runs south from Elbe on the Alder Lake at about 1,300 feet above sea level, crosses an 800-foot-long trestle bridge over the Nisqually River, and climbs with stretches of 3% (1 in 33) gradients to Mineral, in full view of Mount Rainier (14,410 feet) to the northeast. Mount St Helens (8,364 feet), of 1980 eruption fame, is about 35 miles due south.

There are three steam locomotives, a Porter 2-8-2 and two "Logging" railroad locomotives, one a three-truck Climax and one a three-truck Heisler. There are three diesels, two Alco and one EMD, and also some coaches and an open car with bench seating.

Trains are scheduled for weekends from Memorial Day weekend to the end of September. Trains run daily from mid-June to Labor Day and there are normally three return trips each day. In spring and fall there are "railfan" special excursions; these usually run over Chehalis Western tracks. Adverse weather may lead to cancellation.

Elbe is about 40 miles south-southeast of Tacoma on route 7. If coming from the south, take US 12 east from I-5 to Morton, then route 7 north to Elbe. Snacks are available at both Elbe and Mineral, and there is a railroad-theme restaurant next to Elbe station. Nearest lodging accommodation is at Ashford, 7 miles away.

ABOVE *Scenic excursions are also run from Elbe on the Alder Lake to Mineral with magnificent views on Mount Rainier.*

Mid-Continent Railway Museum

W I S C O N S I N

USEFUL DATA

Headquarters Mid-Continent Railway Historical Society Inc., North Freedom, WI 53591-0358.

Phone (800) 930 1385, (608) 522 4261.

Public Station North Freedom.

Timetables by mail or phone.

Tickets reservations by mail or phone (608) 522 4261. Answering service on (800) 930 1385.

Public access

from Interstate south from Wisconsin Dells to Baraboo, then right on 136 to North Freedom and left on County PF to MCRM depot.

Facilities

Museum of motive power & rolling stock. Gift shop & refreshments in depot.

RIGHT *A fascinating night-time scene as former Chicago & North Western 10-wheeler 1385 gets hold of its train over snow-covered tracks leaving North Freedom.*

The Mid-Continent Railway Museum was founded in Milwaukee by the Mid-Continent Railway Historical Society in 1959 for the educational and historical benefit of the public in an effort to reconstruct a small portion of history known as the golden age of railroading. Its first season was in Hillsboro, Wisconsin, in 1962; one year later it moved to the La Rue branch built from North Freedom by the Chicago & North Western.

The La Rue branch was built in 1903 to serve iron mines. The possible presence of iron had been recognized as early as 1882, and by 1885 a small deposit of surface iron was being worked by a farmer, who produced a mineral (barn) paint for local sale. By 1887, red metallic ore had been discovered by other farmers when digging water wells. The euphoria created by these finds had resulted in mining companies being set up, the most successful of which was the Douglas Iron Mining Co., so named for its discovery of good deposits on the Douglas farm property. This site, near the present day La Rue, became the location of the Illinois mine, later known as the Baraboo Iron Range.

Early iron was brought into North Freedom—for a time renamed Bessemer—by horse, and shipped out by the Chicago & North Western Railroad. Mining fortunes fluctuated between 1887 and the turn of the century. In 1890 the town of North Freedom regained its former name, and it was in that year that the first marketable ore was discovered some 3½ miles away by W. G. La Rue. Another good deposit was discovered by a company soon to become famous as the International Harvester Co. This was the Illinois mine, about ¼ mile west of the present location of La Rue.

All this caused the C&NW to survey a number of routes between North Freedom and the Illinois mine. Construction of a spur was authorized in August 1903 and started one

ABOVE *Two vintage steamers, former Western Coal & Coke by Montreal Locomotive Works, 4-6-0 No 1 and Saginaw Timber by Baldwin a 2-8-2 No 2 work a vintage freight train.*

month later. The 3½-mile spur was completed in early December 1903 for an actual cost of $40,533.72. Some 25,000 tons of ore was already awaiting shipment. The first ore was shipped by rail on 10 March 1904 in a train of 14 cars, each carrying 45 tons, to the International Harvester smelters in Chicago. By 1908 the workings were being flooded; the expense of pumping rendered the mine unprofitable and operations were suspended.

By 1906, United Steel had purchased another mine, the Iroquois, and requested C&NW to run a spur to it. The terrain required a roundabout route: a little over one mile of track was laid to cover a straight-line distance of about 600 feet! The mine was working by 1909 and the spur opened in 1910; mine-working was abandoned in 1914.

In August 1918, the C&NW removed the track to the Illinois mine and the spur to the Iroquois. With the end of mining, the town of La Rue died. As early as 1911, however, deposits of quartzite had been discovered, and in 1917 a Pittsburgh company opened a quarry

south of La Rue and asked C&NW to extend their track to the new site. By October 1917, approximately 4,000 feet of track had been completed. Quarrying continued until, in 1960, changes in steelmaking and rising labor costs led to a decline in the quartzite-quarrying operation, which shut down in 1962. Shipping from the stockpile continued for a short while. C&NW added the branch to its list of abandonments.

In May 1963, the Mid-Continent Railway Museum purchased the branch from C&NW and began to develop it into a historical railroad specializing in equipment and operation of the 1885–1915 era. The line runs for about 4 miles through the pleasant woods and farmland scenery of the Baraboo River valley, from North Freedom to Quartzite Lake. The C&NW depot at North Freedom has been restored to the 1894 style, with a gift shop and fascinating displays. The museum grounds and buildings house many examples of steam locomotives, vintage passenger cars, freight cars and cabooses, all beautifully restored.

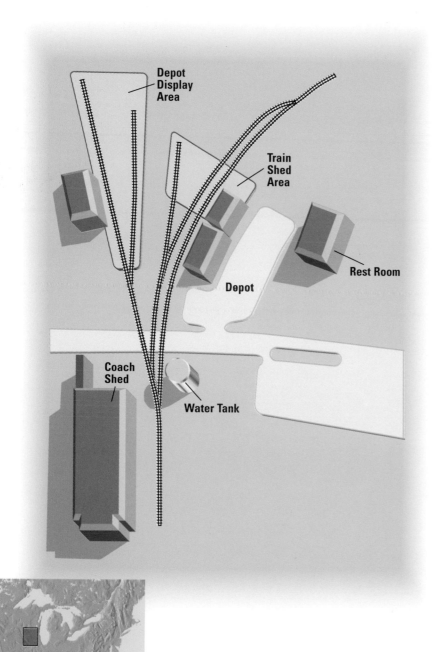

Depot
Display
Area

Train
Shed
Area

Rest Room

Depot

Coach
Shed

Water Tank

Currently the museum owns 10 steam locomotives and holds four owned by members. Two are normally used: a C&NW Alco 4-6-0 of 1907, and a Baldwin 2-8-2 formerly owned by the Saginaw Timber Co. In addition, there are 5 diesel locomotives (one privately owned), one gas mechanical and one gas-electric. Steam is the normal motive power, backed up by diesel when necessary.

Some special trains are run with meals and first class service, but the normal train service is four trains each day from mid-May to late August, weekends from end April to end October, and public holidays. Four special events are Independence Day weekend, Autumn Color trains two weekends in October, Santa Express in late November, and Snow Trains in mid-February. School trips are run in May and September.

North Freedom is about 45 miles northwest of Madison, Wisconsin, west on 136 from the intersection of highways 12, 33, and 136 in West Baraboo. Follow County Highway PF to North Freedom; MCRM is ½ a mile west from the 4-way intersection.

DATE LINE

C&NW spur to mines authorized	**August 1903**
Construction started	**September 1903**
Spur completed	**December 1903**
First train of iron ore	**10 March 1904**
Track to quartzite quarry opened	**October 1917**
Track to Illinois mine removed	**August 1918**
Quartzite quarry closed	**1962**
Branch on C&NW abandonment list	**1963**
Purchased by MCRM	**May 1963**

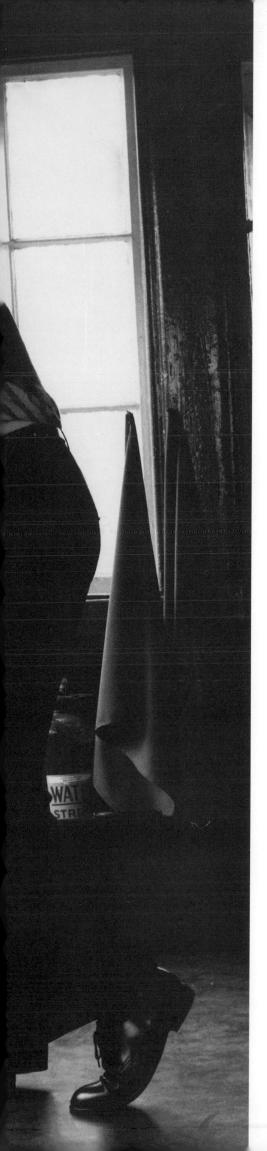

BRITISH ISLES

Bluebell Railway, East Sussex, England

Severn Valley Railway, Hereford & Worcester, England

Great Central Railway, Leicestershire, England

National Railway Museum, North Yorkshire, England

North Yorkshire Moors Railway, North Yorkshire, England

West Somerset Railway, Somerset, England

Keighley & Worth Valley, West Yorkshire, England

Clonmacnoise & Offaly Railway, County Offaly, Ireland

Isle of Man Steam Railway, Isle of Man

Manx Electric Railway, Isle of Man

Strathspey Railway, Inverness-shire, Scotland

Festiniog Railway, Gwynedd, Wales

Talyllyn Railway, Gwynedd, Wales

Bluebell Railway

EAST SUSSEX, ENGLAND

USEFUL DATA

Headquarters Sheffield Park Station, Uckfield, East Sussex TN22 3QL.

Phone (01825) 723777.

Public Stations Sheffield Park, Horsted Keynes, Kingscote.

Timetables & Tickets by phone or mail from Headquarters. Tickets on sale at stations and on special bus.

Public access

Bus from Haywards Heath main line station (summer) or Horsted Keynes village. Car to Sheffield Park. Special bus from East Grinstead station to Kingscote—no public road access to Kingscote.

Facilities

Food, shop, museum and locomotive depot at Sheffield Park.

The rescue of the Bluebell Railway in south-east England was the pioneering effort of British standard-gauge railway preservation. The Railway operates a part of the former Lewes & East Grinstead Railway in the county of East Sussex.

East Grinstead is a country town close to the Surrey–East Sussex border. From 9 July 1855, it was served by a branch from Three Bridges on the London–Brighton main line, but there was no direct connection to London until 10 March 1884. The Lewes & East Grinstead, a little over 20 miles long, was one of a number of rival proposals for railroads between London and the growing coastal town of Brighton, whose population tripled between 1841 and 1876. After many difficulties the line was completed with the help of the London, Brighton & South Coast Railway. After it opened, on 1 August 1882, it was taken over by them.

As a secondary route to London, the line was engineered for double track, although this was only laid on the northern 6.4 miles from Horsted Keynes and the branch from the London–Brighton main line at Haywards

PREVIOUS PAGE The key to safe and efficient working is the "Tower" or Signal Box. This is the interior of a box at Bewdley on the British Severn Valley Railway with the signalman setting up the road for the next departure on 9 May 1981.

RIGHT *A beautifully turned-out Maunsell "S15" class 4-6-0 of 1936 No 847 hauls the prestige replica "Golden Arrow" between*

Sheffield Park and Horsted Keynes on the pioneer of British standard gauge preserved railways.

Heath. The 10.8 miles from Horsted Keynes to the junction with the Lewes and Tunbridge Wells line remained single, as it never generated the traffic expected. It was always a rural secondary line, although in 1899 it was used by six direct trains between Brighton and London. There were still three direct trains in 1955.

In 1954, trying to reduce its deficit, the British Transport Commission closed many unprofitable secondary lines. The Lewes and East Grinstead line was costing £68,000 a year with a revenue of only £9,000. In the spring of 1955, notice was given of the withdrawal of trains between East Grinstead and Lewes on 13 June 1955. Due to a strike of footplatemen, the last train actually ran on 28 May 1955.

A local resident, Miss R. E. M. Bessemer, pointed out that closure went against the Act of Parliament that authorized the railroad, which required that four trains run each day calling at certain stations. After much publicity in the national press, the line was reopened to passenger traffic on 7 August 1956. Four trains were restored between East Grinstead and Lewes for a further period of 19 months, but they ran at times that were not coordinated with other services, and for only a short period in the middle of each day.

Following a 3-day public hearing, the line was eventually closed after the last train on 16 March 1958. This attracted a sympathetic crowd of hundreds, and stirred unprecedented public awareness. A nine-coach train was run that day, the longest seen on the line for many years. The line remained unused for a time, and the section between Horsted Keynes and

East Grinstead was kept on a "care and maintenance" basis, being used by a few "Ramblers" special trains and for storage of wagons. The branch (electrified in 1935) between Horsted Keynes and Haywards Heath remained open for another five years.

Four railway-enthusiast students, Chris Campbell, David Dallimore, Martin Eastland and Alan Sturt, vowed to keep the line alive if at all possible. On 15 March 1959, a year after the last train ran, they organized a meeting in Haywards Heath, which was well attended. The Lewes to East Grinstead Railway Preservation Society was formed and a committee elected. Money was not available to purchase the whole line, so the Society decided to concentrate their efforts on the section between Sheffield Park and Horsted Keynes, known as the Bluebell Line for its profusion of spring flowers. Instead of an outright purchase, British Railways agreed to a seven-year leasing arrangement for £34,000.

After much negotiation and restoration work had been done, mainly by volunteer labor, the Ministry of Transport inspected the line and passed it fit for use, granting a Light Railway Order on 27 July 1960 for the Society to run trains, at a maximum speed of 25 mph, between Sheffield Park and a temporary platform just short of Horsted Keynes. The first train ran on 7 August 1960. The connecting line to Haywards Heath remained open and, when Horsted Keynes Station opened, acted as a feeder for a time.

The Bluebell Railway Preservation Society

BELOW *The front page of the LB&SCR timetable (price 2 pence) calls attention to it being the cheapest route to many of the popular Continental destinations.*

purchased the five-mile stretch of line and its two main stations outright. Electric trains from Haywards Heath were withdrawn on 27 October 1963; this effectively isolated the Bluebell from the main-line system. Nevertheless the line has flourished and has been extended in three stages to Kingscote, one station short of East Grinstead.

The original aim was a "living museum" line. Starting with just two small 0-6-0 tank locomotives and two coaches, a large collection of historic rolling stock representing the age of steam was built up over the next thirty years. Now there are some three dozen steam locomotives and the same number of coaches, mostly coming from the former railroads of Southern England.

Since 1970 the ultimate goal has been to reach East Grinstead and to meet up again with the main-line system. Following the

RIGHT *The beautiful liveries of late Victorian locomotives are depicted by this former South Eastern & Chatham railway "C" class 0-6-0 No 592 of 1902 about to leave Horsted Keynes for Sheffield Park.*

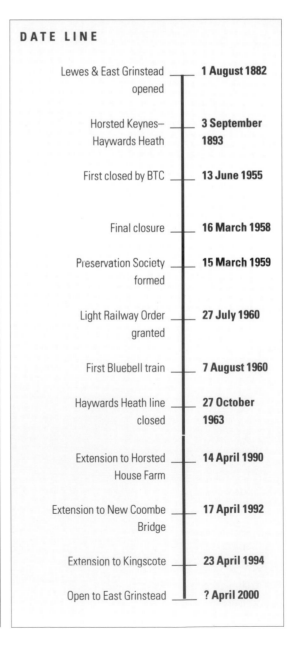

ABOVE *A busy day on the Bluebell Railway at Horsted Keynes with a rebuilt "Merchant Navy" class 4-6-2 leaving for the north.*

RIGHT *A magnificent sight – "Merchant Navy" No 35027 "Port Line" leaving Sheffield Park with a train for the then northern terminus of the line – West Hoathly on 8 March 1990.*

special inquiry, government approval was granted in 1985. On 17 April 1992, trains were extended 2.3 miles to the site of the former West Hoathly station. The work included the renovation of a 730-yard tunnel. On 23 April 1994, a further 1.9-mile extension was opened to the beautifully renovated Kingscote station; this involved the building of an entirely new bridge. Work is now in hand on the final 2.2 miles to East Grinstead, which includes the 308-yard-long Hill Place or Imberhorne Viaduct. It is expected that this will be completed by the year 2000.

The line has been fully signaled from the start. Sheffield Park has locomotive workshops, and there are covered-carriage and wagon workshops at Horsted Keynes. The Railway employs a basic staff of 20 specialists, but the greater part of the work is undertaken by volunteers drawn from a membership of nearly 8,000. Some 300,000 visitors a year travel the line.

The Bluebell line has featured in a number of movies where scenes from earlier times have involved travel by steam train, making good use of the carefully restored period locomotives and rolling stock. Some locomotives are wholly owned, some are owned privately by other groups who have joined with the Bluebell. Refreshments are provided on certain trains at various times of the year. The Bluebell celebrated its 35th anniversary on 7 August 1995.

DATE LINE

Lewes & East Grinstead opened	**1 August 1882**
Horsted Keynes– Haywards Heath	**3 September 1893**
First closed by BTC	**13 June 1955**
Final closure	**16 March 1958**
Preservation Society formed	**15 March 1959**
Light Railway Order granted	**27 July 1960**
First Bluebell train	**7 August 1960**
Haywards Heath line closed	**27 October 1963**
Extension to Horsted House Farm	**14 April 1990**
Extension to New Coombe Bridge	**17 April 1992**
Extension to Kingscote	**23 April 1994**
Open to East Grinstead	**? April 2000**

Severn Valley Railway

HEREFORD & WORCESTER, ENGLAND

The Severn Valley Railway runs between Kidderminster Town and the ancient town of Bridgnorth to the west of Birmingham. The line now open was part of a route built between 1858 and 1862 from Droitwich to Shrewsbury, to provide a more direct line between the two cities than the Great Western route through Birmingham. It was absorbed into the Great Western 1870.

Kidderminster was not on the original route, and was connected by a spur from Bewdley in 1878 to allow trains access from Birmingham to Bridgnorth, Tenbury Wells and Woofferton on the direct Hereford-Shrewsbury line. This was a joint line with the London & North Western Railway, opened in 1852–3.

The new line through Bridgnorth gave the GWR an independent line between Hereford and Shrewsbury, albeit a somewhat longer route, with connections to Birmingham once the Kidderminster link had been established. It was also a secondary route from London via Oxford, but it never achieved the importance expected of it. Following the Beeching "rationalization" of railroads, passenger traffic was withdrawn in 1963 and freight in 1969.

The River Severn, Britain's longest river, flows from its principal source in the Cambrian Mountains in Plynlimon, east towards Shrewsbury, then south to the Bristol Channel. The 1862 rail route followed the valley of the Severn south to Bewdley, and then turned away southeast to join the 1852

ABOVE *The Severn Valley line runs representatives of both main and branch line trains. Here is a typical branch line train near Arley hauled by ex Great Western "Pannier" tank 0-6-0 No 5764 built in 1929.*

USEFUL DATA

Headquarters Severn Valley Railway Co. Ltd., Bewdley, Worcs DY12 1BG.

Phone (01299) 403816.

Public Stations Bridgnorth, Hampton Loade, Highley, Arley, Northwood Halt, Bewdley, Kidderminster Town.

Timetables by mail from Headquarters.

24-hour phone (01299) 401001. Trains run every weekend, daily mid-May to end September, all school holidays.

Tickets from main stations.

Public access

Midland Red bus X92 to Kidderminster and Bewdley or 890 to Bridgnorth. Main Line Rail to Kidderminster, immediate connection to SVR station. Through tickets available from all manned Main Line Stations. Car parks: at all stations. Disabled: Special vehicle to carry wheelchairs with advance notice.

Facilities

Food & drink: all stations & most trains.
Bars at Bridgnorth and Kidderminster.
Souvenir shops: Bridgnorth, Bewdley, Kidderminster Town.
Model railroads: Bewdley, Kidderminster, Hampton Loade.
Museum: at Kidderminster.

RIGHT *One of the spectacular features of the Severn Valley Railway is the beautiful long-arch bridge taking the line over the river Severn.*

Evesham–Worcester–Birmingham line at Hartlebury.

By the time the line closed, there was a growing movement for the preservation of lines of special interest. The principal town, Bridgnorth, was a center of attraction: it is really twin towns, the High Town and Low Town connected by many flights of steps, with ruins of a 12th century castle and the steepest funicular railway in Britain. It was from here in 1965 that the newly-formed Several Railway Company, headed by Michael Draper, began the task of rebuilding the railway.

First, enough money had to be raised to purchase the line from British Railways. Fundraising began almost as soon as the final closure was completed, and as instalments were paid, the work on the first section from Bridgnorth to Hampton Loade progressed. On 25 June 1970, the final balance was paid. A Light Railway Order had already been obtained, and the inaugural train ran, hauled appropriately by a restored Great Western Railway 0-6-0, No. 3205, on 28 June 1970.

The next two sections of line were completed to Bewdley by 18 May 1974, and on that day one of the former GWR diesel railcars, No. 22, made the first direct passenger trip between Bridgnorth and Bewdley. The latter point became the permanent headquarters of the railway, and was the end of the line for the next six years. The extension to the ultimate goal, Kidderminster, was a more difficult task, as it included a splendid curved viaduct on the approach to the town. For a time a connecting service of lightweight diesel multiple units ran to and from Kidderminster, until the extension was opened fully in 1984.

A new terminal station was built in the former goods yard of the British Railways station at Kidderminster Town, and there is a connection with the main line to Birmingham, Worcester, and London. Special trains from distant destinations can be received and run over the SVR to Bridgnorth.

The route follows the right bank of the Severn and crosses to the left bank on a beautiful metal long-arch bridge built in 1861, the Victoria Bridge, between Arley and Northwood Halt. The stations have all been meticulously restored, and the new station at Kidderminster is in the same style of architecture. The distance from Bridgnorth to Kidderminster is 16¼ miles.

The Railway hosts more main-line locomotives than any other preserved line in the

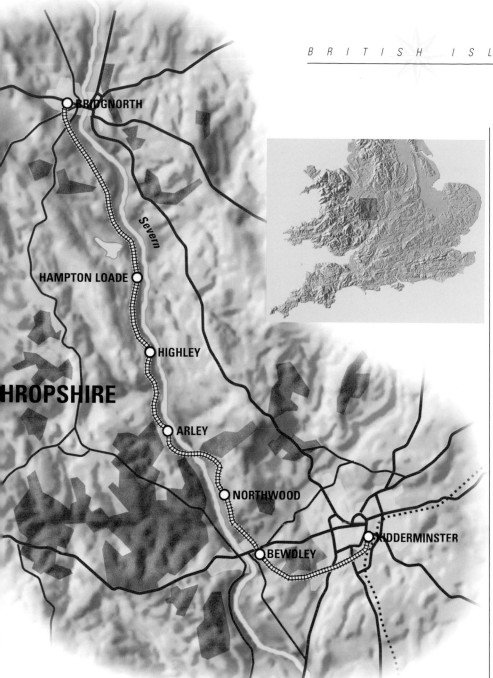

HROPSHIRE

BRIDGNORTH

Severn

HAMPTON LOADE

HIGHLEY

ARLEY

NORTHWOOD

KIDDERMINSTER

BEWDLEY

SEVERN VALLEY RAILWAY

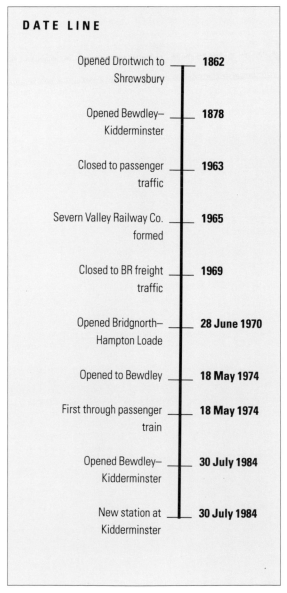

DATE LINE

Opened Droitwich to Shrewsbury	**1862**
Opened Bewdley– Kidderminster	**1878**
Closed to passenger traffic	**1963**
Severn Valley Railway Co. formed	**1965**
Closed to BR freight traffic	**1969**
Opened Bridgnorth– Hampton Loade	**28 June 1970**
Opened to Bewdley	**18 May 1974**
First through passenger train	**18 May 1974**
Opened Bewdley– Kidderminster	**30 July 1984**
New station at Kidderminster	**30 July 1984**

country. While the normal service is based on steam locomotives, supplementary trains with diesel locomotive haulage are run and listed in the timetables. The Railway is host to many locomotives owned by other associations or privately. Currently there are 27 steam locomotives, 11 diesel locomotives, 78 hauled coaches, and four diesel multiple unit coaches. There are also more than 100 goods vehicles.

Trains run weekends year-round, with a daily service from May to early October. The SVR is noted for its annual program of special events. There are Steam Enthusiasts' weekends in April and September; Santa Specials at the end of November and in December; Mince Pie Specials in December/early January; Friends of Thomas the Tank Engine weekends in June and September; and an annual Diesel Gala weekend.

Great Central Railway

L E I C E S T E R S H I R E ,   E N G L A N D

USEFUL DATA

Headquarters Great Central Railway (1976) plc, Loughborough Central Station, Great Central Road, Loughborough, Leics LE11 1RW.

Phone (01509) 230726.

Public Stations

Loughborough Central, Quorn & Woodhouse, Rothley, Leicester North.

Timetables & Tickets from main stations, inquiries to Headquarters.

Public access

from Loughborough Main Line station (15 mins walk). Trent, South Notts, and Midland Fox buses—some Midland Fox services pass bottom of Great Central Road. Car parks at Quorn & Rothley. Accommodation for disabled visitors.

Facilities

Refreshments on most trains. Sunday lunch on midday train; evening dining trains some Saturday nights; information & reservations from railway. Shop, museum, and depot at Loughborough.

RIGHT *"Flying Scotsman" is one of the best known of all British steam locomotives. Here it takes a train of VIPs on its first trip over the restored Great Central Railway out of Loughborough on 12 December 1992.*

ABOVE *Another famous former L&NER Streamliner, "A4" 4-6-2 No 60007 "Sir Nigel Gresley" speeds a train through Swithland on 3 January 1995.*

The Great Central Railway, as it now exists, was rescued by the Main Line Preservation Group, formed in 1969 to purchase the section of railway from Nottingham (Ruddington, about 4 miles south of Nottingham center) to Leicester (Abbey Lane), part of the former Great Central Railway. The aim was to run a main line so that steam locomotives could be operated at realistic speeds, recreating for future generations the magic of main-line steam locomotive operation. The Group gathered support and began raising funds for the purchase of the line, soon gaining charity status to become the Main Line Steam Trust in 1971.

The Great Central Railway, the successor to the Manchester, Sheffield & Lincolnshire Railway, was the last main line to reach London in 1899. It was the ambition of the Chairman, Sir Edward Watkin, to have a through train running from Manchester to Continental Europe through a Channel Tunnel—Watkin was the founder of the original Channel Tunnel Company. When setting out the London extension, therefore, he had it built to a loading gauge similar to that of the Northern Railway of France, of which Watkin was also a Director.

Construction of the "London Extension" commenced in 1894, and the permanent way was ready for coal trains in July 1898. Watkin's railroad was renamed the Great Central Rail-

ABOVE *In keeping with its "Main Line" status large locomotives are the order of the day and here former LMS "Duchess" No 46229 "Duchess of Hamilton" arrives at Leicester North with the 10.15 from Loughborough on 9 August 1994.*

way. It ran south from Sheffield through Nottingham, Leicester, and Rugby to a new terminus at Marylebone in West London. The first direct passenger train ran in March 1899.

By the mid-1950s, competition from trucks and private automobiles was having a serious effect on rail traffic. The main line south of Rugby served only rural communities before reaching the counties north of London. There was a choice of routes from Sheffield, Nottingham, and Leicester to London, and in the Beeching "rationalization" of main routes, the majority of the Great Central south of Sheffield was closed. The first sections to go were those from Sheffield to Nottingham and from Rugby to Aylesbury on 5 September 1966. The section between Nottingham, Leicester, and Rugby was reduced to single track and remained for a time, but this too closed on 3 May 1969.

The Trust paid substantial monthly interest charges to British Railways, the owners of the

track, to ensure that the track would be retained. The original valuation had been £96,000, so the Trust began raising money as quickly as it could; but, with the price of scrap rising rapidly, BR revalued the line in 1975 at £279,000, and gave the Trust three months to purchase or the track and ballast would be removed. It seemed impossible to raise that amount of money in such a short time, so the Trust's Directors formed the "Great Central Railway Company (1976)" in order to raise money through a share issue. Funds were still short of the required sum by the deadline, so the Company eventually purchased the section south from Loughborough to Rothley (5½ miles). Fortunately, Charnwood Borough Council bought the land from Loughborough to Birstall (north of Leicester) and granted the Company a 99-year lease from 21 April 1978 at a reasonable rent, which is reviewed every seven years.

The Company is developing the site at

BELOW *Things are not always what they seem! For the Christmas Gala of 1994 former LMS "Jubilee" class 4-6-0 No 5593 "Kolhapur" masqueraded as No 5552 "Silver Jubilee"!*

Leicester North, constructing a prestigious new station with buildings featuring the "house style" of the old Great Central Railway. In addition, work is in progress to restore the section between Rothley and Loughborough to double track.

At the time, the Company was disappointed not to get the northern part of the line. It has not been forgotten, however, and the most ambitious plan yet is a proposed northern extension of 10 miles from Loughborough to Ruddington. Work is proceeding from the northern end, and while this is not expected to be completed for another five years—it will require substantial funding—acquisition of land and some work has already

ABOVE *Travelling Post Offices were a familiar scene and here one is being enacted on the Great Central.*

begun, with two miles of track rebuilt by March 1995. A single track still exists over much of the line's length, with a connection to the main line at Loughborough, but this is in poor condition. There are also some bridges to be replaced, one of which will have to be 85 feet long.

Nevertheless, trains have already been run over a small part of the route that is connected to the Nottingham Heritage Centre, built on the site of a former Ministry of Defence depot, where there is a small locomotive depot. The next stage is an extension to the next station, Rushcliffe Halt. This is expected to be in operation by Easter 1997.

The present southern section from Loughborough operates on Saturdays, Sundays and public holidays throughout the year, every day over Easter, and daily from the beginning of May to the end of September. There is an impressive collection of main line locomotives and visiting locomotives during the operating season. Currently the Company has 18 steam and seven diesel locomotives.

Passenger trains are normally operated, with steam haulage predominating. From time to time, demonstration "period" goods and mail trains, and some named, limited-stop trains, are run. Most trains have refreshment facilities. More than a dozen special or Gala events are arranged at weekends throughout the year.

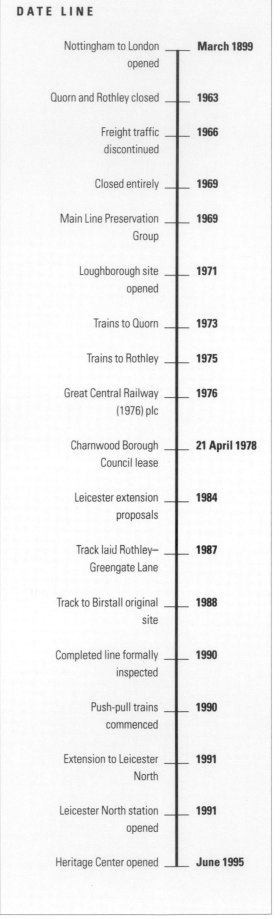

DATE LINE

Nottingham to London opened	**March 1899**
Quorn and Rothley closed	**1963**
Freight traffic discontinued	**1966**
Closed entirely	**1969**
Main Line Preservation Group	**1969**
Loughborough site opened	**1971**
Trains to Quorn	**1973**
Trains to Rothley	**1975**
Great Central Railway (1976) plc	**1976**
Charnwood Borough Council lease	**21 April 1978**
Leicester extension proposals	**1984**
Track laid Rothley– Greengate Lane	**1987**
Track to Birstall original site	**1988**
Completed line formally inspected	**1990**
Push-pull trains commenced	**1990**
Extension to Leicester North	**1991**
Leicester North station opened	**1991**
Heritage Center opened	**June 1995**

National Railway Museum

N O R T H   Y O R K S H I R E ,   E N G L A N D

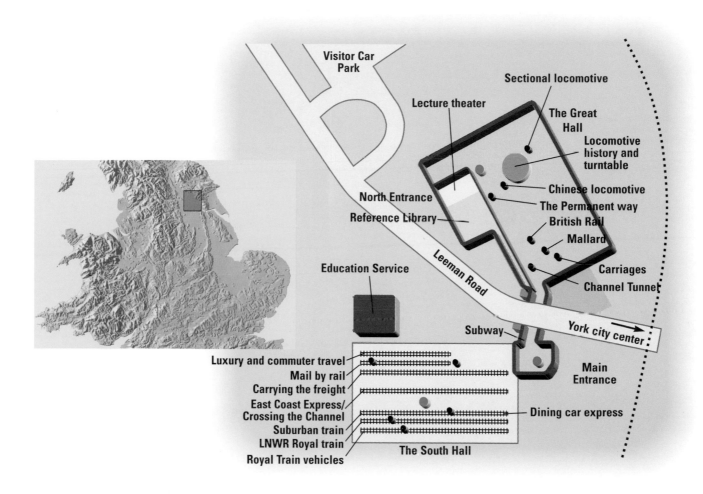

USEFUL DATA

Headquarters The
National Railway Museum,
Leeman Road, York YO2 4XJ.
Phone (01904) 621261.
Fax (01904) 611112.
Admission fee charged;
special rates for groups.
Public access
Ten minutes on foot from
York Main Line station. Car
park.
Facilities
Lecture theater,
refreshments, shop.

The National Railway Museum was opened in York in 1975. It is probably the largest national museum entirely devoted to railroads.

The idea of a British railway museum was first proposed in the Victorian era. The mechanically-operated railway was first developed in Britain; towards the end of the 19th century, as people began to look back and assess the extraordinary changes that had occurred, some felt they ought to be commemorated. Several countries had already established railway museums. The first to open were in Hamar, Norway, in 1897, and at Nurnberg, Germany, in 1899. There was talk of doing something similar in Britain in the 1890s and again in 1908, but nothing came of it at that time.

The idea never went away; it was first realized through the energy and enthusiasm of J. B. Harper and a small group of men on the North Eastern Railway, in whose territory railroads had been born. When it became certain that the North Eastern Railway would lose its identity under the Railways Act of 1921, these men began collecting relics, and stored them in the Company's offices in York.

It was the centennial celebrations of the opening of the Stockton and Darlington Railway in 1925 that began to generate a strong interest in the history of railroads in Britain. The London & North Eastern Railway (of which the North Eastern was now a part) decided to open a public railroad museum into which relics could be moved. An ideal building was the old locomotive erecting shop of the former York & North

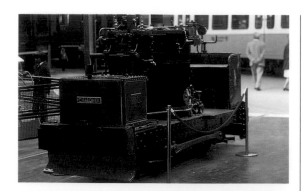

RIGHT *Among the varied selection of exhibits is this narrow-gauge vertical boiler 0-4-0 tank locomotive by de Winton of Caernarvon.*

ABOVE *The famous "Mallard", still the holder of the world's speed record for steam – 126 mph on 3 July 1938 – on the right of this picture. Next to "Mallard" is the last steam locomotive built for British Railways, class 9 2-10-0 No 92220 "Evening Star".*

Midland Railway in Queen Street, York. There the first railway museum in Britain was opened in 1927. It soon grew crowded, and by 1956 it was full to overflowing with locomotives, carriages, wagons and a wide variety of historical exhibits. While none of the other three companies at first showed much interest, eventually locomotives from their constituents arrived: Columbine, City of Truro and Gladstone.

One other place, the Science Museum in London, had already assembled an important collection of railway relics, a collection superior to that of any other national museum in Europe. There were other smaller collections in Edinburgh, Newcastle, Liverpool and Hull.

With the nationalization of the railroads in 1947, a new chance arose. The British Transport Commission, set up to manage the nationalized undertaking, assumed responsi-

bility for the materials and the history of the former private companies, and a Department of Historical Relics was set up.

The museum at York was full, and the site was too small for any further extension. Then London Transport offered the disused tram depot in Clapham, South London. While not an ideal site, it was something. A new Museum of British Transport was opened there in 1961, with John Scholes as Curator until 1963. At the same time, an agreement was made with Corporation of Swindon for a museum devoted entirely to the former Great Western Railway. In Scotland, a Museum of Transport was set up in Glasgow, including a significant railway section.

This was a time of rapid technological change, with steam being phased out; older pieces of equipment, large and small, were in danger of being destroyed. Finally, in the Transport Act of 1968, the Government relieved British Railways of the responsibility and set up a new museum. It was a branch of the Science Museum, but based in York.

York was a good choice because it had its own place in railway history. It was George Hudson's town, the base from which he built up his railway empire in the 1840s, and the meeting-point of seven lines from London, Sheffield, Leeds, Harrogate, Newcastle, Scarborough, and Hull. York had been the administrative center of the former North Eastern Railway since 1854; it had large railroad works for the building and repair of locomotives and rolling stock, and it was the headquarters of one of the five regions of British Railways.

In 1973 the former motive-power depot was overhauled by British Railways and skilfully adapted to its new purpose. Exhibits were moved from Clapham and from the old York museum. The opening was fixed for 27 September 1975, the 150th anniversary of the opening of the Stockton and Darlington Railway. The date was met, and the new museum was opened by the Duke of Edinburgh. That York was the right choice was demonstrated by the two million visitors in the first year, compared to the half million estimated.

ABOVE *This is a general view of a selection of many of the varied exhibits to suit all ages and tastes. There is no doubt the collection requires much time to view and absorb the wealth of railway history.*

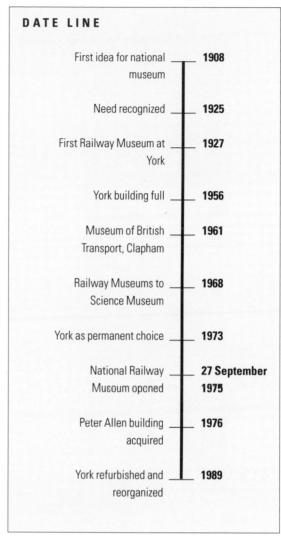

DATE LINE

First idea for national museum	**1908**
Need recognized	**1925**
First Railway Museum at York	**1927**
York building full	**1956**
Museum of British Transport, Clapham	**1961**
Railway Museums to Science Museum	**1968**
York as permanent choice	**1973**
National Railway Museum opened	**27 September 1975**
Peter Allen building acquired	**1976**
York refurbished and reorganized	**1989**

The Museum holds many more locomotives and other rolling stock than can be exhibited at one time. Some is operational, and various items are in the care of preserved railways, being operated and maintained on an agency basis. Steam, diesel and electric locomotives are included in the exhibits. Right by the entrance to the main hall is Agenoria, built by Foster, Rastrick & Co. at Stourbridge in 1829, a close relative of the Stourbridge Lion, the first steam locomotive to run on the Delaware & Hudson in the United States. There is a cutaway "Merchant Navy" class, No. 35029 Ellerman Lines, which has an electric motor to turn the wheels, and the locomotive Mallard, which still holds the world speed record for steam, 126 mph—and many more.

Since the museum was opened, two further buildings have been added. One, adjacent to the main exhibition hall, was the former diesel traction maintenance shop, complete with wheel-drop and overhead cranes. This is now used for most of the engineering tasks that arise, including the complete overhaul of the largest steam locomotives.

The other new building, named after Peter Allen, the first chairman of the Museum's committee, is on the other side of Leeman Road and was the former LNER goods depot. At first used for storage and then for carriage and wagon restoration, it now has a section built to resemble part of a terminal station. This has been used for filming movies.

The museum has recently been renovated. Displays are arranged to tell the story of train travel, using models, exhibits and well-made figures. The museum includes two model railroads, and it has its own 7¼-inch-gauge miniature railroad. There is a lecture theater, refreshment rooms, a shop and various display areas.

The National Railway Museum is in Leeman Road, York, 10 minutes' walk from York main-line station and ¾ mile from the city center. The entrance is on a level with the road, but above the main hall, which is down a small flight of steps. An elevator is available for disabled people. The refreshment rooms and shop are by the entrance. There are small display areas outside. A charge is made for admission. There is ample car parking.

North Yorkshire Moors Railway

N O R T H   Y O R K S H I R E ,   E N G L A N D

USEFUL DATA

Headquarters Pickering Station, Pickering, North Yorkshire YO18 7AJ.

Phone (01751) 472508/473535.

Public Stations Pickering, Grosmont, Goathland, Newtondale Halt, Levisham, others.

Timetables from Headquarters & Grosmont.

Public access
Train from Whitby & Middlesborough. Bus service Malton-Pickering, York or Scarborough-Pickering, also Whitby-Goathland & Pickering. Car parks: Grosmont, Goathland, Levisham & Pickering. Disabled visitors welcome; special attention given with advance notice.

Facilities
Depot: Grosmont. Shops: Pickering, Goathland. Refreshments: most trains, & at Grosmont, Goathland & Pickering. Museum: at locomotive depot in Grosmont.

RIGHT *A busy scene at the North Yorkshire Moors Railway's main locomotive depot. In this view locomotives of the former North Eastern and London & North Eastern Railway are represented.*

Picture a beautiful National Park of wild, rolling country, 400–600 feet above sea level; imagine a railway running from north to south with trains of vintage rolling stock hauled by beautifully maintained steam (and sometimes diesel) locomotives; and you have the North Yorkshire Moors Railway.

In the 1830s, the "Railway King" George Hudson had become friendly with George Stephenson. They both saw the city of York as the pivot of a north-south line from London via Birmingham or Rugby to Newcastle. Stephenson's goal was actually a railroad between London and Edinburgh, via Leeds and Newcastle, and he was deeply involved with the North Midlands Railway, already authorized from Birmingham to Leeds. The York & North Midlands Railway was to form an integral part of his route to Edinburgh.

Hudson had, as early as 1834, cherished a scheme to make Whitby into a coastal resort and connect it to York by railroad. In 1827 he inherited £30,000 from a relative in Whitby. He and Stephenson had taken an immediate liking to each other, and Hudson persuaded Stephenson to engineer a line through Malton to Scarborough, with a branch from Malton along the dales of the North York Moors to Whitby, as an adjunct to his York & North Midlands Railway.

The Whitby-Pickering Railway was incorporated in 1833 and opened in 1835; the York & North Midlands Railway was incorporated in 1834 and opened in 1839, and the Whitby and Pickering became part of it around 1840. It was absorbed by North Eastern Railway in 1854 and amalgamated into the London & North Eastern Railway in 1923.

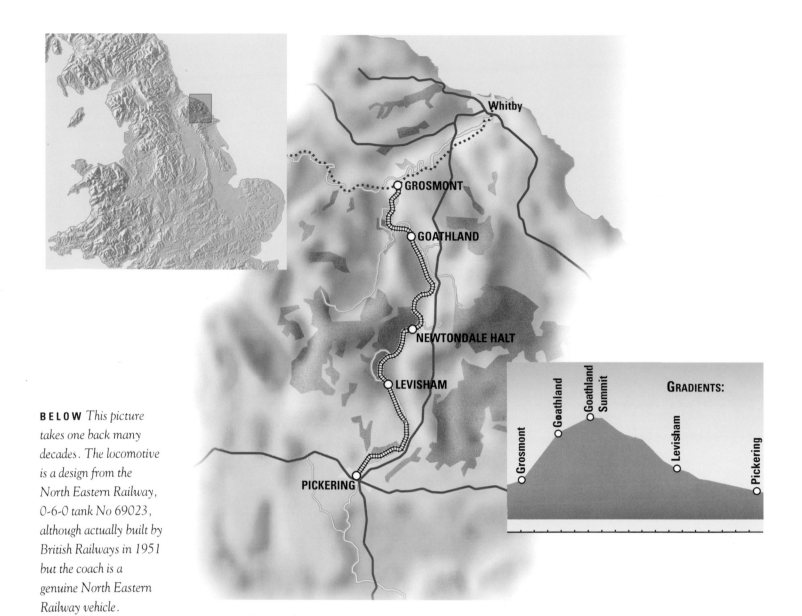

Whitby

GROSMONT

GOATHLAND

NEWTONDALE HALT

LEVISHAM

PICKERING

GRADIENTS:

Grosmont

Goathland

Goathland
Summit

Levisham

Pickering

BELOW *This picture takes one back many decades. The locomotive is a design from the North Eastern Railway, 0-6-0 tank No 69023, although actually built by British Railways in 1951 but the coach is a genuine North Eastern Railway vehicle.*

At one time Pickering was the junction of four lines, with two routes to York, one via Rillington and Malton, one to the east coast main line via Tollerton, and a line to Scarborough. With the Beeching "rationalization," all passenger services except the Middlesborough line were withdrawn from Whitby Town on 3 May 1965. The line from Malton to Whitby via Pickering was finally closed in 1968. Negotiations began immediately to save this historic line before British Railways could remove the track. The North York Moors Historical Railway Trust was set up and, working closely with the North York Moors National Park, took quick and vigorous action to get the line running again between Pickering and Grosmont. The inaugural train

ABOVE *The locomotive is "K1" No 2005, one of a class of 70 locomotives which, although built just after Nationalisation, bears all the hall marks of the LNER including the lovely apple-green livery.*

under the new management ran on 22 April 1973. The Railway is now one of the main attractions for railway enthusiasts and tourists.

Pickering is the headquarters of the Railway, which runs 18½ miles through delightful scenery across the moors and dales to Grosmont, where there is a connection with the Middlesborough–Whitby line.

The Trust hopes to run direct trains from the NYMR to Whitby in the future. Operation is mainly by steam locomotives, but in dry weather, diesel locomotives may be substituted. The North Yorkshireman Dining Train and Moorlander Lunch Train run regularly, and one of the former Great Western Railway Special Saloons can be rented for weddings, conferences, etc.

A Museum associated with the Railway is located at the Locomotive Depot in Grosmont. There is an extensive collection of main-line locomotives as well as industrial steam and diesel locomotives. The Railway is also host to locomotives owned by other individuals or groups, some of which may move their locomotives to other lines from time to time. Of course, the same applies in reverse! There are 16 steam and diesel locomotives on the line at present, together with

40 passenger coaches and some 20 goods vehicles. The line is open daily from the last week in March to the end of October, and again in December for Santa Specials and other Christmas services.

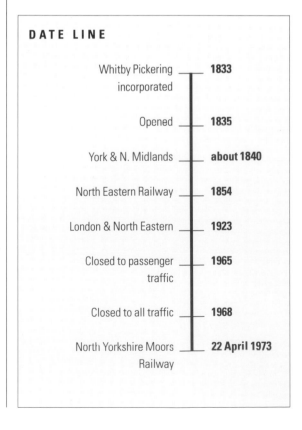

DATE LINE

Whitby Pickering incorporated	**1833**
Opened	**1835**
York & N. Midlands	**about 1840**
North Eastern Railway	**1854**
London & North Eastern	**1923**
Closed to passenger traffic	**1965**
Closed to all traffic	**1968**
North Yorkshire Moors Railway	**22 April 1973**

West Somerset Railway

S O M E R S E T ,   E N G L A N D

USEFUL DATA

Headquarters The Railway Station, Minehead, Somerset TA24 5BG.

Phone (01643) 704996.

Public Stations
Minehead, Dunster, Blue Anchor Bay, Washford, Watchet, Doniford Beach, Williton, Stogumber, Crowcombe Heathfield, Bishops Lydeard.

Timetables by mail from Headquarters; 24-hour "talking timetable": (01643) 707650.

Tickets for special trains details by mail, otherwise from stations, on train or special link bus from Taunton.

Public access
Main Line Rail to Taunton, then by special bus (WSR tickets valid); also Southern National bus 28A. Information: (01823) 272033.
Car parks: Bishops Lydeard, Williton (free). Minehead: pay car park only. Small car parks at all other stations. Most steam trains have a special coach for wheelchair passengers.

Facilities
Refreshments and bar facilities on most steam-hauled trains. Refreshments at Minehead & Bishops Lydeard. Limited shops: Minehead —"Buffer Stop Shop" has full range of railway books, etc. Bishops Lydeard has a well-stocked shop.

The West Somerset Railway is Britain's longest preserved railway. It runs from Bishops Lydeard near Taunton to Minehead, just short of 20 miles.

A standard-gauge mineral railway, the West Somerset Mineral Railway, was incorporated in 1855 to bring iron ore from the Brendon Hills to the small port of Watchet, on the Bristol Channel, for shipment to South Wales. The West Somerset Railway Company, was promoting a broad-gauge line from

ABOVE *It is perhaps a little strange to find a locomotive of the former Somerset & Dorset Railway working on a former Great Western* branch line but today the S&DJR has gone so it is good to see 2-8-0 No 88 still working near to its original territory.

Watchet Junction (now Norton Fitzwarren) on the Bristol & Exeter Railway to Watchet. They wished to make a connection with the Mineral Railway, lay a mixed-gauge track, and

have running powers over a short distance. The Mineral Railway opposed this, and when the WSR Act was passed by Parliament in 1857, the two lines were completely separate and even served the harbor by two different piers. The WSR was opened to Watchet on 31 March 1862, and was worked from the start by the Bristol & Exeter Company.

The Mineral Railway gave up an extension, so the WSR proposed an independent extension of broad gauge in 1863, using about 2 miles of the Mineral Railway between Watchet and Washford, which would be converted to mixed-gauge. Again the Mineral Railway objected, so plans were finally deposited in November 1864 for an independent line. Agreement was later reached to lay the broad-gauge track on Mineral Railway land alongside the standard-gauge track. The WSR's application was agreed and the Minehead Railway Act received Royal Assent on 5 July 1865. The Company was unable to raise the capital and the application was set aside, but it was revived again in 1871. The Minehead extension was brought into use on 16 July 1874 and, as with the Watchet line, was worked by the Bristol & Exeter Railway Company. The Bristol & Exeter was fully amalgamated with the Great

Western Railway in 1875, but the Minehead branch was not fully absorbed until 1890. As with the other lines of the GWR, it was converted to standard gauge in 1892.

Minehead had been an important port from the Middle Ages to the late 18th century, when the harbor silted up. It began to attract tourists in the early part of the 19th century, and developed rapidly once the railroad arrived in 1874. The Minehead branch of the GWR was a popular line, and between the World Wars it carried fairly heavy traffic for a country branch line. The branch suffered from the rapid increase in automobile transport following World War Two. It managed to survive until 1971, when it was closed to both passenger and freight traffic. It was quickly taken in hand by the West Somerset Railway Preservation Association, and reopened in stages between 1976 and 1979. The section from Bishops Lydeard to Williton was opened on 22 October 1977, when ex-GWR Pannier No. 6412 worked the first train.

The glorious scenery of the north Somerset coast has helped the WSR to recapture the atmosphere of a Great Western Railway country branch line. There are 10 restored stations, including Bishops Lydeard and Minehead. The existing 2-mile link between

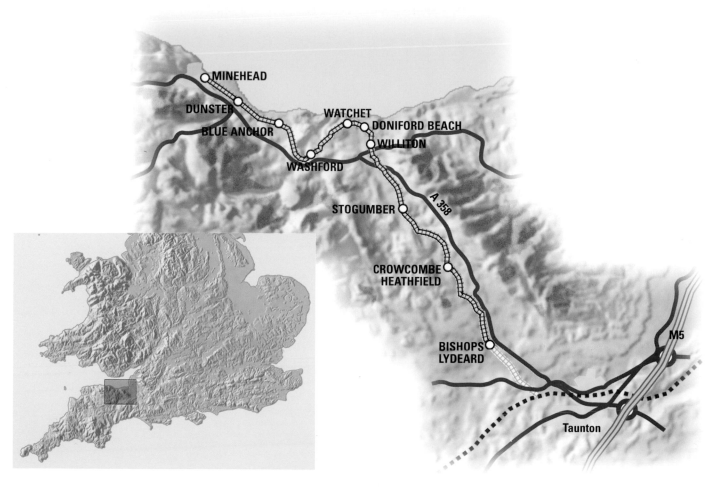

Bishops Lydeard and Norton Fitzwarren is used for Gala events and for the transfer of charter trains from the Main Line. There are depots at Bishops Lydeard, Williton, Washford, and Minehead.

The WSR has always operated a mix of steam and diesel motive power—this is largely due to the activities of the Diesel & Electric Preservation Group. Other groups involved with the operation of the Railway are the West Somerset Steam Railway Trust, the Somerset & Dorset Railway Trust and of course the West Somerset Railway Preservation Association. The timetables indicate which trains are diesel operated. Currently based on the West Somerset Railway are nine steam and nine diesel locomotives, two diesel multiple units, 20 passenger coaches, and over 50 goods vehicles.

The WSR runs a weekend-only service in the early part of March, then daily until the end of October (except certain Fridays in April, every Friday in October and four Sundays in November), and also daily from 26 to 30 December. There are Gala Days one weekend each month between April and October, and Santa Specials on certain Saturdays and Sundays in December.

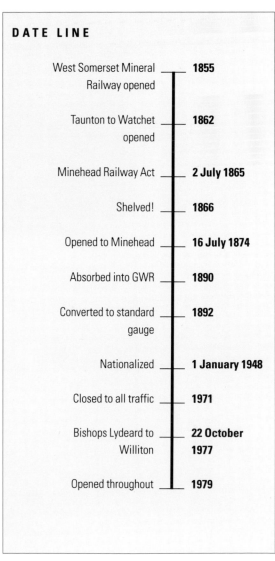

DATE LINE	
West Somerset Mineral Railway opened	**1855**
Taunton to Watchet opened	**1862**
Minehead Railway Act	**2 July 1865**
Shelved!	**1866**
Opened to Minehead	**16 July 1874**
Absorbed into GWR	**1890**
Converted to standard gauge	**1892**
Nationalized	**1 January 1948**
Closed to all traffic	**1971**
Bishops Lydeard to Williton	**22 October 1977**
Opened throughout	**1979**

Keighley & Worth Valley

WEST YORKSHIRE, ENGLAND

USEFUL DATA

Headquarters Haworth Station, Keighley, West Yorkshire, BD22 8NJ.

Phone (01535) 645214.

Fax (01535) 647317.

24-hour information (01535) 647777.

Timetables (01535) 647777 (24-hour service).

Tickets at all stations.

Reservations Haworth Office.

Public access

Train to Keighley. Many public buses to Keighley. Car parks at Keighley, Ingrow, Haworth and Oxenhope. Disabled visitors accommodated with advance notice.

Facilities

Museums at Oxenhope, Ingrow Railway Center. Depots: Carriage & Wagon, Oxenhope. Locomotives: Haworth. Refreshments: Oxenhope & Keighley. Refreshments car on some trains. Shops: Haworth, Oxenhope, Keighley, Ingrow Carriage Museum.

The Keighley & Worth Valley is the only complete branch line in the British Isles under independent control. The line runs from a junction some 17 miles from Leeds, on the line to Carlisle (Settle and Carlisle line), 4 miles south to Oxenhope, serving six stations.

The Keighley & Worth Valley Railway Company, in conjunction with the Midland Railway, built a line from Keighley principally to keep the woollen mills supplied with coal and to carry away their products. The fact that there are six stations in a distance of only 4 miles gives some indication of the importance of the railroad to the local community in the mid-Victorian era.

ABOVE *The Keighley & Worth Valley Railway was host for a period to former Metropolitan Railway 0-4-4 tank No 1 and two compartment coaches, making an attractive shot here in the distinctive brown livery.*

RIGHT *A British Railways standard class 2 2-6-0, No 78022, makes a good display of smoke and steam on a demonstration freight train.*

WORTH VALLEY

ABOVE *An ex-LMS "Black 5" No 5305 on a Wine and Dine train waiting to leave gas-lit Oxenhope station.*

The original line was opened on 13 April 1867 and operated at first by the Midland Railway company, who handed over to the London Midland & Scottish Railway in the amalgamation of 1923. It passed into the ownership of British Railways, London Midland Region, in 1948. In the 1950s the wool trade declined and many mills closed, while passengers turned to road travel. On 30 December 1961, passenger traffic was withdrawn, but the line continued to carry some freight. That too was withdrawn on 23 June 1962.

The Worth Valley line passes through some delightful scenery and its next-to-last station is Haworth, the former home of the famous Brontë family. Haworth has long been an English literary shrine, and this no doubt helped motivate those enthusiasts who worked to preserve the line. On 1 March

1962, the Keighley & Worth Valley Railway Preservation Society was formally constituted.

The usual problems arose in finding enough money to purchase the right-of-way, but this was accomplished and the complete line came into the ownership of the Society. The first locomotive arrived on 7 January 1965. By 29 June 1968 the necessary work had been accomplished for the inauguration of service, and on that day the first public train ran.

The aim now is to provide the atmosphere of the days of the steam railroad, although from time to time diesel locomotives are also operated. Stations are immaculate, as are the staff uniforms, and the atmosphere is friendly. Of the six stations (Keighley, Ingrow, Damems, Oakworth, Haworth and Oxenhope), Haworth is the most important. The railroad has its headquarters there, with locomotive work-

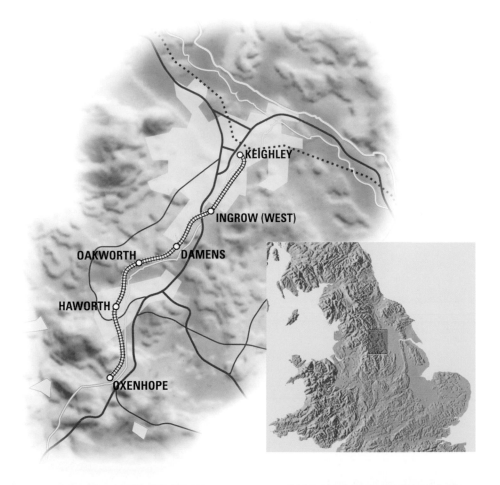

shops and depot, while carriages and wagons are based at Oxenhope.

At present, the railroad is host to some 30 steam and eight diesel locomotives, of both main-line and industrial types. The Society incorporates the Vintage Carriage Trust (museum at Ingrow), the Bahamas Locomotive Society, and the Lancashire & Yorkshire Railway Preservation Society. There is a wide variety of coaches from the British Railways era back to the 19th century.

The principal business of the line is passenger transport, but demonstration freight trains are run from time to time. Trains run on weekends throughout the year, and every day in the summer season, from mid-June to the end of

ABOVE *A vintage scene near Oakworth with an ex-L&NWR 0-6-2 "Coal Tank" No 1054 hauling an assortment of restored passenger cars in their original liveries.*

August. There are Santa Specials on weekends in December, and five or six special events throughout the season. An attraction between October and March is to travel during the twilight hours, when Britain's third largest collection of gas lighting can be seen.

Access from the main-line railway system is at Keighley, with cross-platform interchange if arriving from Leeds or Bradford. Ample car parks are provided at all stations. Generally, reservations are only necessary for large groups; otherwise tickets are easily obtainable on the day of travel.

WORTH VALLEY

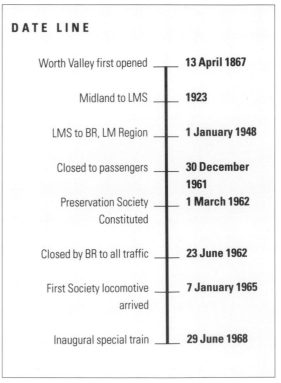

DATE LINE

Worth Valley first opened	**13 April 1867**
Midland to LMS	**1923**
LMS to BR, LM Region	**1 January 1948**
Closed to passengers	**30 December 1961**
Preservation Society Constituted	**1 March 1962**
Closed by BR to all traffic	**23 June 1962**
First Society locomotive arrived	**7 January 1965**
Inaugural special train	**29 June 1968**

Clonmacnoise & Offaly Railway

COUNTY OFFALY, IRELAND

The Irish Peat Board (Bord Na Mona) is a business that operates some 850 miles of 3-foot-gauge railways. It owns about 350 diesel locomotives and 5,400 wagons. Part of its operation is centered around Blackwater in County Offaly, and this unit has recently opened part of its operation to tourist passengers. It is not really a preserved railway, but it offers a unique opportunity to travel over a network of narrow-gauge lines.

For many years, railroads have been used to transport peat from the diggings in the Bog of Allen to the processing plants. While there are many well-defined routes, over which long trains of open bogie wagons are hauled by diesel locomotives, it is only since the 1960s that the Blackwater operation has included a power-station. This system has its own allocation of about 100 bogie wagons. Trains of peat going to the power-station cross the River Shannon by an impressive viaduct.

Groups of passengers have sometimes been transported over certain sections of the railroads by special arrangement, but in view of the growing interest in preserving Ireland's narrow-gauge railroads, it was decided in 1990 to carry passengers as a tourist attraction for a trial period of a month. This was so successful that a section has now been opened as a regular tourist experience. It is now known as the Clonmacnoise & West Offaly Railway. The railroad lies between two lines of Irish Rail. It runs as a separate business unit, and includes one regular circular route starting

USEFUL DATA

Headquarters
Clonmacnoise & West Offaly Rly Bord Na Mona, Shannon Bridge, County Offaly, Republic of Ireland.

Fax (353) 905 74210.

Public Station Blackwater Works.

Timetables & Tickets from Headquarters. Groups by special arrangement.

Public access
By Irish Rail to Athlone, Ballinasloe, Clara, or Tullamore, then bus or mini-bus by arrangement. By car to Shannon Bridge (L.27). Wheelchair access throughout.

Facilities
Outdoor machinery museum, craft shop, coffee. Car parks, picnic areas.

LEFT *A modern line designed for tourists and as an educational project near the center of Ireland, the Clonmacnoise & Offaly railway takes passengers around its peat bog workings in this attractive little diesel train.*

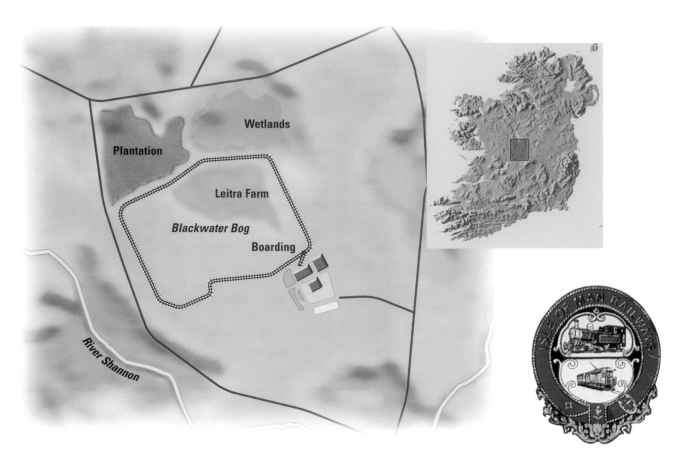

ABOVE *The attractive new station at Shannon Bridge is the starting point for the tour and this picture shows one of the newly-built cars for comfortable traveling.*

and finishing at the Blackwater works. There is one station area at present, but small platforms are being erected at sites of special interest or educational value, for example for bird watchers and naturalists.

Currently some 5½ miles of line are open for regular tours, but these may be varied or extended by special arrangement, and there are plans for longer and specialized trips. Three small diesel locomotives built by Hunslet or Ruston, of the same type as those used for hauling peat, are allocated to the line. There are two passenger cars, especially designed for comfortable traveling.

The line operates for tourists from early April to the end of October, but is available for coach reservations the year round. There is a large parking area that includes a craft shop and picnic areas, and there is an outdoor machinery museum. The site can be reached by Irish Rail to Athlone, Ballinasloe, Clara or Tullamore, and bus or mini-bus transfer can be arranged by prior notice. It is necessary to make arrangements in advance for groups, and for special or unusually long trips.

Isle of Man Steam Railway

ISLE OF MAN

USEFUL DATA

Headquarters Isle of Man Railways, Strathallan Crescent, Douglas, Isle of Man IM2 4NR.

Phone (01624) 663366.

Fax (01624) 663637.

Public Stations Douglas Port Soderick, Ballasalla, Castletown, Colby, Port St Mary, Port Erin, with halts (on request) at Santon, Ronaldsway, Ballabeg and Colby Level.

Timetables by mail from Headquarters. Reservations for parties of 20.

Tickets from booking offices at stations, or on trains.

Public access
to Douglas Airport, then bus or car to Douglas. By ferry from Heysham or Liverpool.

Facilities
Museum, shops, and refreshments.

RIGHT *This picture gives a foretaste of the beautiful country traversed by the IoM Steam Railway with a pair of 2-4-0 tank locomotives hauling a train toward Port Erin.*

The Isle of Man, lying in the middle of the Irish Sea equidistant from England, Ireland, Scotland and Wales, belongs to the English Crown but is not part of the United Kingdom. It forms what is called a crown dependency, and has its own parliament, the Tynwald. The Isle of Man Steam Railway offers a unique experience of traveling on part of a narrow-gauge railroad system that has a 125-year history. Steam has always provided the motive power, although two second-hand diesel rail-cars were introduced as an economy measure in 1961. Today steam locomotives dominate. They have all been carefully preserved and have the grace of a bygone age. It has been said that the Isle of Man Railway is the finest narrow-gauge steam railroad still operating.

Between 1860 and 1870, after a number of unsuccessful attempts, a meeting agreed in principle to form a railroad company to connect the four towns of Douglas (the capital), Peel, Ramsey, and Castletown, and later, when the breakwater had been completed, Port Erin. The latter would promote a shipping service to the Island from Holyhead.

Following a survey, the Isle of Man Railway was registered in December 1970 with a capital of £200,000. Mr Henry Vignoles was appointed Engineer to the Company, but by the time of the first General Meeting in December 1871, the capital sum had not been achieved. Overseas support was sought, and eventually the Duke of Sutherland, a supreme railroad enthusiast, became interested. The capital was

ABOVE *The attractive lines of 2-4-0 tank No 11 "Maitland" are clearly shown here as she heads a Douglas-Port Erin train.*

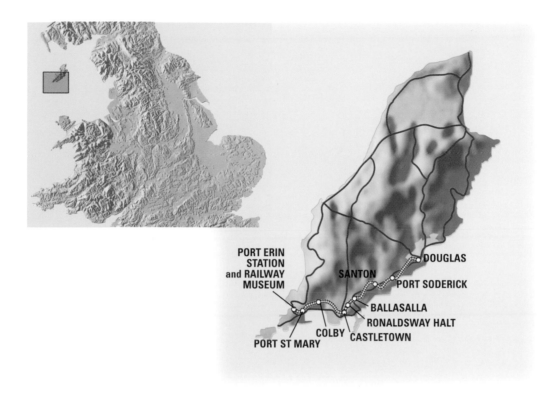

restored and the Duke of Sutherland was given the Chair, which he held for seven years.

After consulting a number of people, among them Robert Fairlie, Vignoles decided on Fairlie's advice to adopt the 3-foot gauge. This was extended also to the Douglas Horse Trams (1876) and the Manx Electric Railway (1893). The first line was from Douglas across the Island to Peel. It was started in 1872, and required considerable engineering work, including diverting two rivers to make way for the new station at Douglas.

Twelve miles were opened to Peel on 1 July 1873. Meanwhile work was progressing on the 15¼ miles of line to the southern tip of the Island at Port Erin. This proved to be a more difficult task, requiring impressive earthworks, and gradients were as steep as 1.67% (1 in 60). The line was opened to the public on 1 August 1874. It is this piece of line that operates today.

Ramsey was the next target, but the Isle of Man Railway Company (IMR) made it clear that they had no intention of adding to the Peel and Port Erin lines. The Ramsey line was built by a new company, the Manx Northern

Railway Company, which received powers to proceed with a line starting from St John's, some 3½ miles inland from Peel, covering 16 miles to Ramsey on the northeastern side of the Island. Work was completed in August 1879, and passenger services started in September.

At first the stations outside Douglas were simple, economical structures built from wood; but as the tourist industry grew, and

ABOVE *A train leaves Colby behind another beautifully-kept 2-4-0 tank locomotive.*

with it the fortunes of the railways, these buildings were gradually replaced by permanent structures of brick and stone, beginning with Douglas and Port Erin.

The Manx Northern had competition from the Isle of Man Tramways & Electric Power Company, who built a much more direct line from Douglas to Groudle and extended it to Ramsey (*see under* MANX ELECTRIC RAILWAY). There was some mineral traffic from lead mines, but it was of short duration. By 1904 they had approached the Isle of Man Railway (IMR) to buy them out. This, and the purchase of another small railway, the Foxfield, was accomplished in 1905.

By 1913, passenger numbers had topped one million. The outbreak of war in 1914 saw no immediate drop, as tourists continued to arrive at first, but during the following years they almost disappeared. Relief then came from the movement of troops and the large number of aliens detained on the island.

After the War, tourists returned, finances picked up and in 1925 the total number of passengers carried reached 1,344,620, a figure that was never again surpassed. Then buses began to take away traffic. The Railway pursued aggressive fare policies and shorter journey times, and eventually merged with the two rival bus companies. These strategies

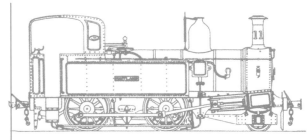

worked, even though there was still competition from private bus operators.

Then came World War II and its aftermath. By 1946, passenger carriage had almost reached its pre-war peak, but war had left the railroad in a run-down state, and costs rose astronomically. Heavy traffic lasted until 1956, after which receipts fell and expenses rose. Winter services were cut to the minimum or halted completely.

In May 1961, two diesel railcars were purchased from the County Donegal Railway in Ireland, which had closed the previous year. After a complete overhaul in Douglas shops, they were ready to run the winter services to Peel and back.

By 1965, losses had mounted so high that it was announced that winter services would be suspended for essential track repairs; but neither winter nor summer services recommenced in 1966.

ABOVE *Douglas station had acquired a new Booking Hall, raised platforms and Railway Company offices by 1901.*

LEFT *A line drawing of one of the standard Beyer Peacock 2-4-0 tanks – No 11 "Maitland".*

The railroad had many supporters, and the Tynwald Transport Commission recommended that the Peel line only should continue "as a tourist attraction". An Isle of Man Railway Supporters Association was formed to assist the railroad in whatever way it could. Fortunately the Marquis of Ailsa agreed to lease the whole railroad for 21 years, with the option of breaking the lease after five years. The losses continued, and by the end of 1968 both the Peel and Ramsey lines had seen their last trains. The Tourist Board offered to help keep the Port Erin line open for a further three years, and Lord Ailsa formed the Isle of Man Victorian Steam Railway Co. Ltd. Traffic showed a slight increase, track maintenance was undertaken, and many coaches were re-painted and upholstered. A new boiler was installed in No. 13 Kissack, which was back in service by 1971.

ABOVE *The Duke of Sutherland, railway enthusiast, financier, and Company Chairman when operations began in 1873.*

The Marquis of Ailsa exercised his option to pull out in 1971 after five years, and the Railway Company came back into the picture. Negotiations with the Tourist Board brought financial guarantees to cover the Port Erin line until November 1974. Overtime was reduced by operating Monday–Friday only. There was a Royal Visit in 1972, when the Queen traveled from Castletown to Douglas,

BELOW *The restored station buildings at Douglas.*

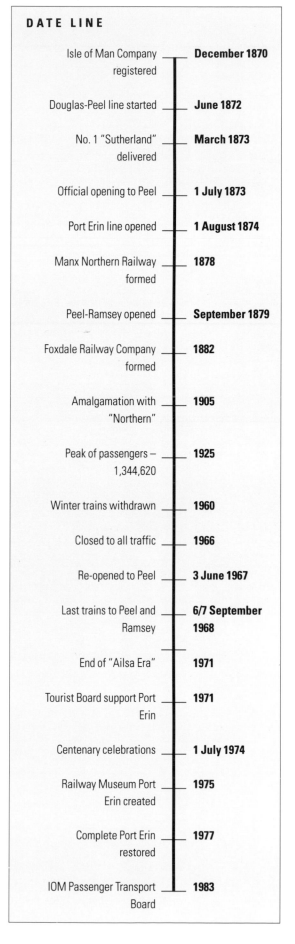

DATE LINE

Isle of Man Company registered	**December 1870**
Douglas-Peel line started	**June 1872**
No. 1 "Sutherland" delivered	**March 1873**
Official opening to Peel	**1 July 1873**
Port Erin line opened	**1 August 1874**
Manx Northern Railway formed	**1878**
Peel-Ramsey opened	**September 1879**
Foxdale Railway Company formed	**1882**
Amalgamation with "Northern"	**1905**
Peak of passengers – 1,344,620	**1925**
Winter trains withdrawn	**1960**
Closed to all traffic	**1966**
Re-opened to Peel	**3 June 1967**
Last trains to Peel and Ramsey	**6/7 September 1968**
End of "Ailsa Era"	**1971**
Tourist Board support Port Erin	**1971**
Centenary celebrations	**1 July 1974**
Railway Museum Port Erin created	**1975**
Complete Port Erin restored	**1977**
IOM Passenger Transport Board	**1983**

ABOVE *No 12 "Hutchinson" hauls a train through typical rural country near Port Erin.*

and that year saw passenger numbers at 71,879, the best for many years. The railway was back in business for its centennial, when special trains were run on Sunday, 1 July 1974.

In that same year Tynwald debated the fate of the remaining part of the system—the Peel, Ramsey, and Foxfield lines had all been dismantled and sold for scrap. The railroad was a tourist attraction, so support was continued to keep alive that part of the island's rich heritage. 1975 saw enough support for four trains to be run Sundays to Fridays on the Port Erin to Castletown section. This was extended to

Ballasalla in 1976, and by 1977 the line from Port Erin to Douglas was back in action.

Today the railroad is in good shape. Three of the later Beyer Peacock 2-4-0 steam tank locomotives, built between 1905 and 1908, survive, together with 0-6-0 tank Caledonia, built by Dübs & Co in 1885 for the Manx Northern Railway—this locomotive was returned to traffic in 1995. There are plans to restore another locomotive in the near future.

The 24 passenger coaches, nearly all bogie vehicles, were supplied to the railway between 1874 and 1926. All have been carefully restored. For shunting and standby duties there is one Schöma diesel-hydraulic locomotive.

The line passes through very scenic country, never far from the coast. Each of the five intermediate stations has something of special interest. All are now brick and stone-built structures. Port Erin station is in the heart of the town, which is a peaceful and beautiful resort with fine coast and hill scenery. The Steam Railway Museum, created in 1975, has an outstanding collection of locomotives, rolling stock and historical memorabilia, including the IMR's first locomotive, No. 1 Sutherland, and the last to be delivered, No. 16 Mannin of 1926. There is also a Royal Saloon, and the museum has a shop.

Trains run between Easter and the last weekend in October, with four trips daily between Easter and mid-July, the summer bank holiday to the end of September, and mid- to end October. From mid-July to end of August there are six trains Mondays to Thursdays, and four Friday to Sunday. Reservations are only required for groups of 20 or more.

The headquarters of the Railway are at Douglas, where there is a beautiful brick-built ticket hall adjacent to the former Railway Company offices. This contains a shop. The workshops and running shed are close by. Apart from the regular train service, evening excursion trains are run; these usually include a bar and refreshment car.

Douglas is the principal town, accessible by air from London (Heathrow) or from a number of regional airports. There are also ferries from Heysham and Liverpool.

Manx Electric Railway

I S L E   O F   M A N

Today the Manx Electric Railway and the Isle of Man Steam Railway, once competitors for traffic between Douglas and Ramsey, are under one administration. The Electric Railway runs from Derby Castle at the northern end of Douglas Bay to Laxey, where a separate line of different gauge runs to the top of Snaefell Mountain. From Laxey the Electric Railway continues to Ramsey. The Manx Electric Tramway, 17 miles long, is the longest electric tramway in the British Isles, and two of its cars are the oldest tramcars operating anywhere.

By 1880 the tourism boom was rapidly making the Isle of Man the "Playground of the North". Douglas had horse-drawn trams on a line running the 2-mile lengths of its promenade. The railroad (*see under* ISLE OF MAN STEAM RAILWAY) had reached both ends of the Island, but the picturesque northeast of the Island still had only limited access. One major attraction, the famous Laxey Wheel—still the largest working waterwheel in the world, with a diameter of 72½ feet—and mine workings (lead and zinc), could only be reached on foot or by horse-drawn carriage.

The first promotion was for a line of 2½ miles from the north end of Douglas Bay at Derby Castle. Work began early in 1893 on a 3-foot-gauge tramway to Groudle Glen, electrified at 500 V DC with overhead trolley current collection. This was completed in August 1893 and opened on 7 September,

USEFUL DATA

Headquarters Manx Electric Railway, Isle of Man Railways, Strathallan Crescent, Douglas, Isle of Man IM2 4NR.

Phone (01624) 663366.

Fax (01624) 663637.

Public Stations Douglas, Laxey, Ramsey.

Timetables from Headquarters or locally.

Tickets from stations.

Public access by air from London or regional UK airports. Ship from Heysham or Liverpool. Air from Dublin or Belfast.

Facilities Horse tram museum at Derby Castle.

LEFT *Contrasting styles (and gauges) of Manx Electric and Snaefell cars stand together at Laxey. The conventional trolley collector contrasts with the fixed bows of the Snaefell cars.*

ABOVE *Now more than a century old, one of the original motor cars hauls a cross-bench open trailer where the line runs alongside the main road in Laxey Bay.*

closing for the winter on 28 September 1893.

Three saloon cars of American design were built by G. F. Milnes of Birkenhead, England. These had an unusual rigid bow collector, which caused problems at first but was later modified with springs. Each car had four 25-hp electric motors made by Mather and Platt Ltd. of Manchester.

As soon as work had begun on this line, approval was sought for an extension to Laxey. This was obtained, and work commenced in February 1894. At the same time, a second track was laid to Groudle. Formal opening took place on Friday, 27 July 1894.

Having reached Laxey, the next challenge was the climb of 2,036-foot-high Snaefell, the island's highest point. This was a more difficult task, and would involve a gradient of 8.33% (1 in 12). At that time there was doubt that a gradient as steep as this could be climbed by rail adhesion alone, so the Fell Incline Railway System was employed. The Fell System, invented by John Barraclough Fell, involves a double-headed center rail, laid on its side, which is gripped by two horizontal driving wheels. It is used for traction when ascending a gradient, and for braking when descending. By the time construction started in 1895, it had been proved elsewhere that with electric traction it was possible to climb such gradients by adhesion alone, so the Fell Gear was discarded for traction but retained for braking.

Work commenced in January 1895, but due to the space required for the Fell Gear, the track gauge was increased to 3ft 6in, making it impossible to inter-run with the Douglas-Laxey cars. Construction work was assisted by using Caledonia (borrowed from the Manx Northern Railway) to work material trains between Douglas and Laxey. Construction was so quick that the 4½ miles of line, to an altitude of 1,992 feet, were opened to the public on 21 August 1895.

Six tramcars were built by G. F. Milnes, similar to another four cars built for the Douglas-Laxey line. They had 48 seats and were carried on two four-wheel tracks, each with two 25-hp traction motors. Sprung bow collectors were again provided. To supply the additional power, a power-station was built at Laxey with five 120-hp steam engines. The trams were so popular that an extension to Ramsey was approved by Tynwald (the Manx

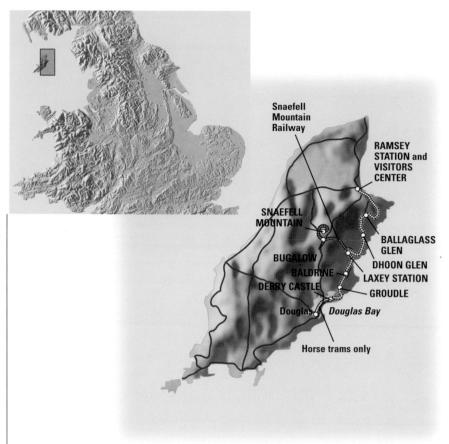

Parliament) in May 1897, and construction commenced in August, assisted by renting two locomotives, this time from Isle of Man Railway. The civil engineering work was difficult, but in spite of this, trams began running to Ballure on 2 August 1898. The official opening was performed by the Lieutenant Governor, Lord Henniker.

The line closed again on 24 October 1898, to allow further work to be carried out and to complete the extension to Ramsey. It reopened to Ballure on 17 June 1899, and to its new terminus at the Palace Concert Hall in Ramsey on 24 July 1899. The distance from Douglas, Derby Castle, was 17 miles.

From Laxey, the line was electrified on the now-familiar overhead trolley system, and at the same time the Douglas-Laxey section was brought into line. Nine open cross-bench cars were provided. Originally only five were motored and four used as trailers, but in 1903, all were converted to motor cars.

Financial problems hit the original Isle of Man Tramways & Electric Power Company in 1900, and by 1902 the company was re-organized as The Manx Electric Railway Company. By 1907 it had laid the foundations of a Company that was to endure for half a century as a private enterprise. Much of the original installation, an early example of electric traction, was experimental, and after a short time it became obsolete. The early DC generators had to be replaced, and an AC distribution system with converter equipment was substituted.

After two World Wars and declining traffic, proposals were made in 1953–4 and again in 1956 to close the lines. Tynwald decided that as the value (to the tourist industry) of such an historic railroad was incalculable, it should be run as a Government enterprise. In April 1957 a Bill was passed to that effect. The railroad would be purchased, and a 10-year program of renovations would be initiated

ABOVE *A car ascends to Snaefell where the gradient steepens to 8.33% (1 in 12). The Fell center rail, used for braking, is clearly visible.*

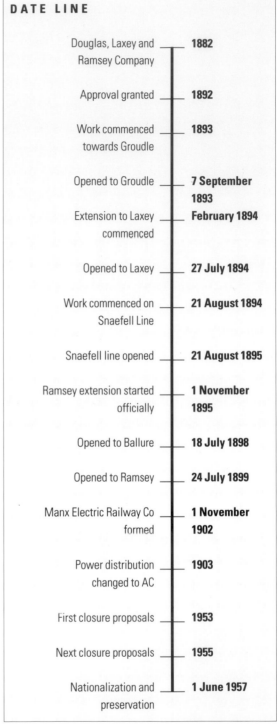

DATE LINE

Douglas, Laxey and Ramsey Company	**1882**
Approval granted	**1892**
Work commenced towards Groudle	**1893**
Opened to Groudle	**7 September 1893**
Extension to Laxey commenced	**February 1894**
Opened to Laxey	**27 July 1894**
Work commenced on Snaefell Line	**21 August 1894**
Snaefell line opened	**21 August 1895**
Ramsey extension started officially	**1 November 1895**
Opened to Ballure	**18 July 1898**
Opened to Ramsey	**24 July 1899**
Manx Electric Railway Co formed	**1 November 1902**
Power distribution changed to AC	**1903**
First closure proposals	**1953**
Next closure proposals	**1955**
Nationalization and preservation	**1 June 1957**

ABOVE *A visit to the Isle of Man would not be complete without a trip on the horse-drawn trams. Here a car leaves Derby Castle for the journey along Douglas Bay.*

under the newly-constituted Manx Electric Railway Board. Today the preservation and maintenance of the steam and electric railroads is the responsibility of the Chief Engineer. Maintenance and overhaul of the coastal cars takes place at the Derby Castle Depot, where some of the original buildings and equipment remain in use.

A trip on this early example of an electric tramway is a unique experience, while the ride on the Snaefell Line gives wonderful views over the Irish Sea.

The Derby Castle terminus is at the northern end of Douglas Promenade, and is served by the Horse Tramway and frequent bus services; the Steam Railway terminus is at the southern end. Bus service 30 connects the Steam Railway and the electric tramway. A regular daily service of trams is operated from the beginning of April to the last Sunday in October, but in summer special trips and extra cars run between the timetabled trips. The trip from Douglas to Ramsey takes 1¼ hours.

The Snaefell Mountain Railway operates daily between the end of April and the last Sunday in September, with regular departures from Laxey between 10.30 am and 3.30 pm (weather permitting).

At Groudle Glen there is a 2-foot-gauge steam railroad, operated by the Isle of man Steam Railway Supporters Association, which runs from the Tramway Station (12 minutes from Derby Castle). This railroad has been restored from the one that originally ran through the Glen to the cliff tops. Trains run during the summer every Sunday, on public holiday Mondays, and on Tuesday and Wednesday evenings in July and August. An evening tram shuttle operates Monday–Saturday, 15 July to 31 August.

The Horse Tram depot at Derby Castle has a fine collection of horse and tramway relics.

Strathspey Railway

I N V E R N E S S - S H I R E ,   S C O T L A N D

USEFUL DATA

Headquarters Strathspey Railway, Aviemore Speyside Station, Dalfaber Road, Aviemore, Inverness-shire PH22 1PM.

Phone (01479) 810725.

Fax (01479) 811022.

Public Stations Aviemore, Boat of Garten.

Timetables write with SAE to Headquarters.

Tickets from stations.

Bookings for Clansman (essential) phone: (01479) 831692. write to: David Dunnett, Clansman Bookings, Boat of Garten Station, Boat of Garten, Inverness-shire PH24 3BH.

Public access

Main Line train to Aviemore. Express bus to Aviemore. Local service to Boat of Garten. Car parks: Aviemore & Boat of Garten. Disabled: access at both stations—contact for directions or group access.

Facilities

Refreshments on most trains. Special Morning Coffee and Afternoon Tea trains. Picnic tables at Boat of Garten. Souvenir shops: Aviemore & Boat of Garten. Museum: small relics at Boat of Garten. Depot: Aviemore—no public.

ABOVE *0-6-0 saddle tank No 9 "Cairngorm" leaves Boat of Garten with a train for Aviemore.*

Between the Cairngorm and Monadhliath Mountains in the Scottish Highlands lies the resort town of Aviemore, on the railway from Perth to Inverness. From there, the Scottish Strathspey Steam Railway runs some 5 miles to the traditional highland village of Boat of Garten. The route follows the course of the River Spey—the Strath Spey.

Railroad building in Scotland developed rather more slowly than further south, as it was a larger task. While Glasgow and Edinburgh had trains as early as 1848, such towns as Inverness, Aberdeen and Perth had to wait longer. Inverness and Aberdeen had been linked with Edinburgh on a circuitous route by 1855–60, and Inverness with Aberdeen in 1858. The railroad to link Inverness with Perth had to negotiate the mountainous Highland Region. A line was completed between Forres and Perth from a junction with the Inverness-Aberdeen line in 1863. It was the line south of Forres that incorporated the Aviemore-Boat of Garten section, opened in 1865 as the Inverness and Perth Junction Railway. This was almost immediately amalgamated with other lines into the Highland Railway. In turn, the Highland Railway was amalgamated into the London Midland & Scottish Railway in 1923.

In 1866 a rival line opened from a junction with the Forres line just north of Boat of Garten to Craigellachie, known as the Strathspey Railway because it followed the River Spey for most of its route. This line became part of the Great North of Scotland Railway, and was amalgamated with the London & North Eastern Railway in 1923.

Going north from Aviemore, the Inverness & Perth Junction Railway followed the River Spey (Strath Spey) through Boat of Garten to Grantown-on-Spey (where the rival GN of S line also had a station), then turned north to the Moray Firth. For most of its route it followed the River Findhorn, joining the line from Aberdeen at Forres, which ran due east to Inverness. This remained the main line until 1898, when the direct line from Aviemore through Carr Bridge to Inverness was opened. This took the through traffic, reducing the Forres line to secondary importance.

These railroads, in remote, under-populated parts of the country, were non-competitive, but they were the lifelines of the communities they served—until the growth of automobile transport.

By the 1960s, many lines were carrying little traffic. Those that were not major life-lines were closed, among them the Forres-Boat of Garten-Aviemore line and the other line (formerly part of the rival London & North Eastern Railway) from Boat of Garten to Elgin and Keith (and Aberdeen). Boat of Garten station was closed on 2 November 1964, and passenger traffic ceased on 18 October 1965. The line was not ideal for heavy trains: to cross Dava Moor, it climbed from Grantown-on-Spey to a summit of 1,052 feet above sea level. The line closed altogether on 16 June 1966.

Almost immediately a group of enthusiasts, with support from the Scottish Tourist Board, took up the task of preserving some of this historic railway. The station at Boat of Garten —the name is from the ferry boat that was used to cross the River Spey before the bridge was built—was meticulously restored, along with the 5 miles of track to an independent station at Aviemore.

The line was reopened, and the first trains ran again on 22 July 1978. An extension towards Grantown-on-Spey is now under way, and the 4 miles to the next station at Broomhill should be completed by the time

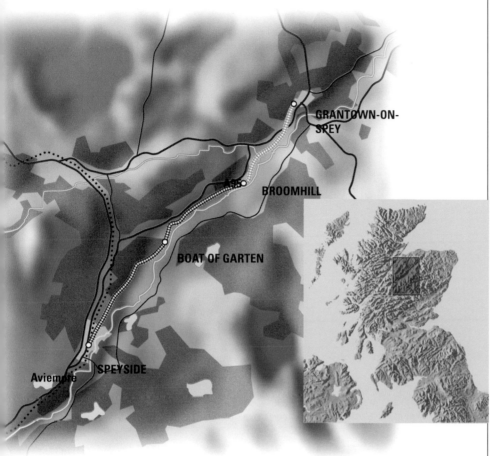

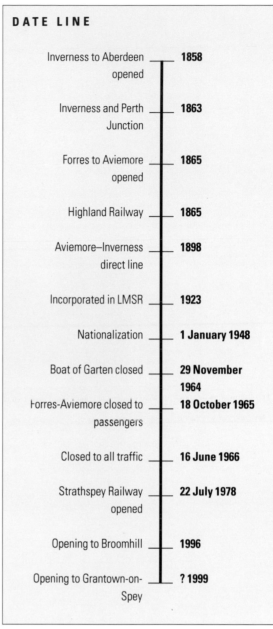

DATE LINE

Inverness to Aberdeen opened	**1858**
Inverness and Perth Junction	**1863**
Forres to Aviemore opened	**1865**
Highland Railway	**1865**
Aviemore–Inverness direct line	**1898**
Incorporated in LMSR	**1923**
Nationalization	**1 January 1948**
Boat of Garten closed	**29 November 1964**
Forres-Aviemore closed to passengers	**18 October 1965**
Closed to all traffic	**16 June 1966**
Strathspey Railway opened	**22 July 1978**
Opening to Broomhill	**1996**
Opening to Grantown-on-Spey	**? 1999**

this book appears in print. The goal is Grantown, the center for salmon-fishing on the Spey, which is a further 3 miles. This could be completed by the end of the century.

Near Boat of Garten, the Royal Society for the Protection of Birds has a reserve at Loch Garten, with an observation point from which visitors can watch the ospreys (rare in the United Kingdom) in their nesting area. A special treat is a trip on the "Strathspey Clansman", which runs on Wednesdays in midsummer. On a fine day, the view of some of the highest mountains in Scotland is magnificent. This, combined with a four-course *table d'hôte* lunch served with fine wines and liqueur, helps to recall the great days of train travel.

Under normal conditions all trains are steam hauled, but diesel power may sometimes be used. The Railway operates nine steam and six diesel locomotives, as well as a diesel multiple unit set on special occasions. There are some 30 coaches, including three vintage coaches from Scottish pre-amalgamation days. In conjunction with the Railway, Classique Coaches operates vintage bus trips, which include the Speyside Heather Center, Broomhill Station, Dulnain Bridge and the RSPB reserve at Loch Garten.

The Strathspey Railway has a very small permanent staff, relying on its army of volunteers both to keep the line running and for work on the extension. Trains are operated on certain days in April, May, and October, and on most days from the beginning of June to the end of September, with a few special days around Christmas and the New Year. Special demonstrations, "Thomas the Tank Engine" days and other events are organized in the running season.

Festiniog Railway

G W Y N E D D ,   W A L E S

RIGHT *In 1962 the Penrhyn Railway had two powerful 0-4-0 saddle tank locomotives which were bought by the Festiniog. "Linda", converted to a 2-4-0, stands at Porthmadog Harbour station.*

USEFUL DATA

Headquarters Harbour Station, Porthmadog, Gwynedd L49 9NF.

Phone (01766) 512340 or 831654.

Public Stations

Porthmadog Harbour, Minffordd, Penrhyn, Plas, Tan-y-Bwlch, Dduallt, Tanygrisiau, Blaenau Ffestiniog.

Timetables & Tickets

Porthmadog Harbour, Blaenau Ffestiniog and on trains.

Public access

Minffordd & Blaenau Ffestiniog Main Line trains. Local Buses: Porthmadog, Minffordd, Tanygrisiau and Blaenau Ffestiniog. Car Parks: Porthmadog, Tan-y-Bwlch, Tanygrisiau, Blaenau Ffestiniog.

Facilities

Refreshments on most trains. Restaurant, museum, shop in Porthmadog. Café, shop in Tan-y-Bwlch. Shop in Blaenau Ffestiniog.

On 2 August 1946, the General Manager of the Festiniog Railway Company sent identical letters to the few remaining staff. One, addressed to T. J. Roberts, can be seen in the museum at Portmadoc and reads:

> *Dear Sir*
> *There will be no further traffic conveyed over this Railway and the service of the Staff is dispensed with. I therefore regret having to inform you that your services will not be required after tomorrow the 3rd instant.*
> *Yours faithfully, Robert Evans.*

The last passenger train ran on 15 September 1939, and the last slate train arrived at Minffordd from Duffys on 1 August 1946. From then on everything stood still; deterioration and vandals did their best to close the railway for ever.

On 27 July 1951, the *Railway Gazette* published the following letter from 17-year-old Leonard A. Heath Humphrys:

Proposed Festiniog Railway Preservation Scheme

> *Sir*
> *The Festiniog Railway, one of the few existing un-nationalized railways which operated during the war, but unfortunately closed shortly after it, is, it is hoped, to have a new lease of life. An organized attempt is to be made to save it from being abandoned and its priceless historical relics lost to the scrap-iron dealer.*
> *The Festiniog Railway is possibly the world's first narrow-gauge public railway. Locomotives introduced by Charles Spooner still exist after 83 years of hard work. In 1873 Charles Spooner introduced the first*

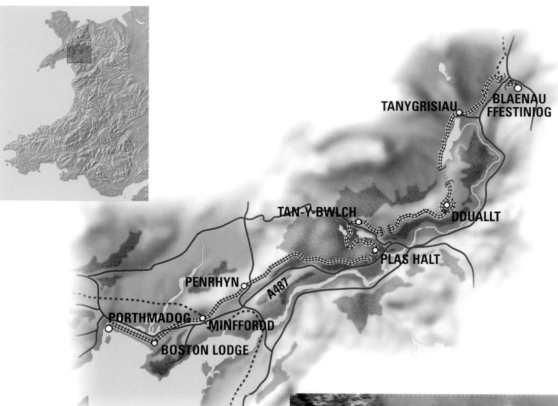

bogie carriage to Britain. This still exists at the railway's famous Boston Lodge Works and is now 78 years old.

The warrant of abandonment applied for by the railway company has been refused by the Ministry of Transport. A preliminary inspection of locomotives, and so on, is to take place, and it is hoped that a meeting will be arranged in the near future. I shall be pleased to hear from anybody interested in the scheme especially if they are in a position to help financially or professionally.

The Festiniog Railway in North Wales had been built originally to carry slate from quarries around Blaenau Festiniog. The route was surveyed by James Spooner, Thomas Pritchard and Spooner's two sons. It included

a tunnel of 730 yards. A gauge of about 2 feet was specified, actually 1ft 11½in. The first stone was laid by William G. Oakley, a local landowner, on 26 February 1833 at about the halfway point, and work began from both ends.

The civil engineering works are considerable. The track drops 700 feet in 12¼ miles. It winds around the contours of the land in sharp curves, crosses embankments as high as 60 feet built up on dry stone walls, and hugs the vertical rock-faces on ledges. The gradient

ABOVE *Restored double Fairlie No 10 "Merddin Emrys" was built in Boston Lodge shops in 1879 and is still going strong.*

ABOVE *"Merddin Emrys" traverses the new alignment after leaving the new Moelwyn Tunnel.*

averages 1.09% (1 in 92).

When the line was opened fully in 1842, trains of loaded wagons descended by gravity most of the way, with horse haulage over the embankment known as the Cob approaching Portmadoc Harbour. Speed was controlled by brakesmen and was in theory limited to 10 mph. Horses hauled the empty wagons back to Blaenau Festiniog in four stages, with stables at each stage. Horses were fed and carried back to the beginning of each stage in dandy-carts. A gravity-worked loaded train took 1 hour and 40 minutes, while an "up" train of empties took 5 hours and 50 minutes.

By the early 1850s, the company wanted to carry passengers. James Spooner died on 18 August 1856. His son Charles Spooner, who had helped his father build the line, transformed a horse-worked mineral railway into a miniature main line of world-wide influence.

Steam locomotives were now needed, but in the opinion of the experts, no locomotive engine could be planned to work on such a line. At a Board meeting in 1860, Charles Spooner was instructed to inquire about the practicability of using steam locomotives. The original track was realigned, the worst curves eased, cuttings widened and track relaid with new, heavier and better-supported rails. Thanks to an engineer, Charles Holland,

some 0-4-0 tank-tender locomotives were ordered from George England of New Cross in southeast London in 1862. The first two were delivered in July 1863, the third and fourth around February–March 1864.

On 23 October 1863, two special trains each carrying about 100 people, ran to Blaenau and back to Portmadoc. In June 1864, the Festiniog gave notice to the Board of Trade that they intended to operate a passenger service. An inspection carried out on 27 October by Captain H. W. Tyler revealed that some work was still needed. The Festiniog carried out his recommendations, and on 28 December 1864 they received the go-ahead. The official opening was on 5 January 1865, and passenger services began the next day. There were four stations: Portmadoc, Penrhyn, Hafod-y-Llyn and Dinas. The latter was closed when a new station was opened, serving Blaenau at Duffws. Later stations were Tan-y-Grisiau (opened 1866), Minffordd (1872), and Tan-y-Bwlch (1873; Hafod was then abandoned). A station existed at Dduallt sometime earlier.

Soon something more powerful than the 0-4-0s was needed. The answer was found in Robert Frances Fairlie's Patent 0-4-4-0, which was really two engines placed back-to-back on one frame. The first, called Little Wonder, was delivered in July 1869.

Slate traffic reached a peak in 1897 with 139,000 tons. Passenger traffic peaked in 1925, but road competition took its toll. Traffic had all but disappeared by the outbreak of World War II, with the last train before closure running in 1946.

The full story of the rehabilitation of the Festiniog is well covered in John Winton's book The Little Wonder. The first step was the acquisition of the Railway from its owners. Complicated negotiations by many enthusiastic people finally bore fruit. Alan Pegler, then a part-time member of the board of British Railways, Eastern Region, played a crucial role and, together with a number of colleagues, in November 1954 succeeded in acquiring the Festiniog Railway Company—a Company in its own right, as opposed to the Festiniog Rail-

DATE LINE

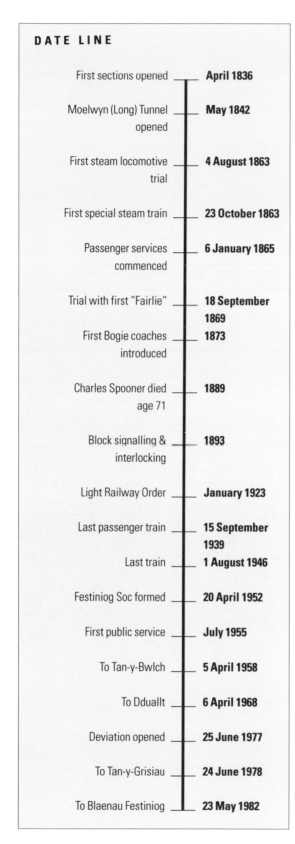

First sections opened	**April 1836**
Moelwyn (Long) Tunnel opened	**May 1842**
First steam locomotive trial	**4 August 1863**
First special steam train	**23 October 1863**
Passenger services commenced	**6 January 1865**
Trial with first "Fairlie"	**18 September 1869**
First Bogie coaches introduced	**1873**
Charles Spooner died age 71	**1889**
Block signalling & interlocking	**1893**
Light Railway Order	**January 1923**
Last passenger train	**15 September 1939**
Last train	**1 August 1946**
Festiniog Soc formed	**20 April 1952**
First public service	**July 1955**
To Tan-y-Bwlch	**5 April 1958**
To Dduallt	**6 April 1968**
Deviation opened	**25 June 1977**
To Tan-y-Grisiau	**24 June 1978**
To Blaenau Festiniog	**23 May 1982**

TOP "Linda" *and train arriving at Tan-y-Bwlch.*

way Society Limited. In their hands were now nearly 14 miles of well-engineered railroad, in a condition that varied from fair to terrible, much of it overgrown with trees and shrubs.

The locomotive stock was badly run down, but carriages, mostly under cover, were in reasonable condition. Boston Lodge Works were a wonderful example of 19th-century engineering shops, but the machinery had suffered years of idleness and the buildings were in a terrible state. So the Company and the Society, with a large army of volunteers, set about the work of restoration.

One major problem arose in the shape in the British Electricity Authority. They planned to flood the top part of the Festiniog Railway, including the Moelwyn Tunnel. A long, bitter—and successful—court case followed, during which the Railway built a "Deviation" including a spiral and a new, shorter, Moelwyn Tunnel. The Deviation opened to Tan-y-Grisiau (1978) and eventually to Blaenau Festiniog on 25 May 1982, running into a new station combined with the standard-gauge main line branch from Llandudno. The Railway's collection includes 16 steam locomotives, 13 diesel locomotives and 38 coaches (six are four-wheeled). The Railway celebrated its 150th Anniversary in April 1986. While there is still a large army of volunteers, the Company has a permanent staff of around 50.

Talyllyn Railway

G W Y N E D D ,   W A L E S

USEFUL DATA

Headquarters Wharf
Station, Tywyn, Gwynedd
LL36 9EY.

Phone (01654) 710472.

Public Stations Tywyn
Wharf, Tywyn Pendre,
Rhydyronen, Brynglas,
Dolgoch Falls,
Abergynolwyn, Nant
Gwernol.

Timetables & Tickets by
phone or mail from
Headquarters. Tickets at
Tywyn Wharf or on trains.
Groups by reservation.

Public access

Tywyn main line station; Bus
Gwynedd services to Tywyn.
Car parks Tywyn Wharf,
Dolgoch Falls &
Abergynolwyn. Special
limited facilities for disabled
visitors.

Facilities

Shops & food at Tywyn
Wharf & Abergynolwyn.
Museum: Tywyn Wharf.
Picnic areas: Dolgoch Falls &
Abergynolwyn. Workshops:
Tywyn Pendre.

*RIGHT The scenery has
not changed and, apart
from some of the vehicles
in the train this could be
a scene from the last
century as this Talyllyn
train approaches
Abergynolwyn.*

"We never closed" is the rightful boast of
this little railroad in West Wales. The
Talyllyn Railway opened on 1 December
1866, to carry slate from the Aberdovey Slate
Company's quarries to the sea. The original
intention was to build the line down the Afon
Fathew Valley to the sea, then to follow the
coast south to Aberdovey; but this was not
followed, as the Aberystwyth & Welsh Coast
Railway (later Cambrian Railway) was being
promoted. The Talyllyn's promoters settled for
a 6½-mile-long line to the coast at Towyn
(now Tywyn) with arrangements to transfer
goods for Aberdovey and Aberystwyth to the
main line company.

The Talyllyn was the first narrow-gauge
railway in the world designed from the start to
be operated by steam locomotives—those pre-
ceding it had first been worked by horse and
gravity. The decision to adopt steam locomotives was influenced by the FESTINIOG RAILWAY,
which had only two years earlier changed
from horses.

The Talyllyn Railway Act of 1865 insisted
on a gauge of not less than 2ft 3in, because
another line on the north side of the River
Dovey, the Corris Railway (opened in 1859),
had chosen that gauge, and there was the pos-
sibility that the two could join. The carriage
of passengers was included in the Act, as it
was expected that direct access to the Cambrian
Railway's passenger station at Towyn would
encourage passenger traffic.

At Towyn, slate-wagons were moved by
hand on to a track running parallel to the
former Cambrian Railway's sidings. Here the
slates were unloaded and loaded into the
standard-gauge wagons, also by hand. Passengers were carried, but clearances were so tight
that management restricted loading and un-
loading to one side only: doors were provided
on both sides of the coaches, but those on the
south side were permanently locked. As an
economy measure, lettering was also confined

ABOVE *The viaduct at Dolgoch Falls with No 3 "Sir Haydn" and train.*

to one side of each coach! The route was fairly easily graded, the maximum gradient being 1.67% (1 in 60). Speed was limited to 15 mph. Most trains were mixed, with up to 20 slate-wagons trailing behind the passenger coaches, the journey of 6½ miles taking about 40 minutes.

The two original locomotives survived for 80 years, but in 1945 the "Tal-y-llyn" had to be laid aside and the remaining one, "Dolgogh," was left to manage alone. By this time, the slate traffic had all but disappeared; but Sir Henry Haydn Jones, Member of Parliament, who had purchased the quarries and the line, decided that the little railroad should continue during his own lifetime at least, and the Talyllyn kept going. Sir Henry died in 1950. As a mark of respect, the management struggled on until October, when it finally had to admit defeat. Lady Haydn Jones and her daughter, the sole surviving shareholders, were advised to ask for an Abandonment Order and to sell the meager assets for scrap.

Tom Rolt was inspired by the idea of keeping the line open. On 11 October 1950, he and a group of enthusiasts sponsored a public meeting in Birmingham, and the Talyllyn Railway Preservation Society was formed. The Society's aim was to see the line continue working, not just to preserve it. Sir

Henry's executors were helpful, and Lady Haydn Jones transferred all her Talyllyn Railway shares, worth £1,350, to a new holding company.

The group of people who rescued the Talyllyn brought it out of decades of obscurity to become a living legend with the public and enthusiasts alike. In May 1976, after much hard work, an extension was brought into use, taking the Talyllyn beyond the original passenger terminus at Abergynolwyn along the mineral extension to Nant Gwernol.

The original line had been run on the "one engine in steam" principle: there were no signals or electric telegraph, and when a train was dispatched, it had to return before another could be sent out. When only two trains each way were required daily, that was no problem; but as tourists began to arrive in numbers, this had to change.

Formal inspection of the line was carried out by Col. McMullen before the preservation society was given permission to run passenger trains. He recommended that a single line staff should be carried by the driver. Later, with the provision of passing loops, three staffs were necessary. Greater flexibility is now needed, and electric train staff instruments have been installed to cover all of the passing-places. The Abergynolwyn-Nant Gwernol section is still operated by one train at a time, so the "staff and ticket" system is employed, although there is a loop and a siding at the end of the line. Originally there were two 0-4-0 locomotives and five four-wheeled carriages. Now there are six steam locomotives and three diesels, while passengers are conveyed in 13 four-wheel and 10 bogie coaches. There are also 45 wagons.

A journey over the 7¼ miles of line is a delightful experience. From Tywyn Wharf, the line runs north to Pendre, where the repair shops are situated, and then between stone walls and hedges through gently rising country to Rhydyronen, where the gradient becomes steeper as the line climbs the side of the Afon Fathew valley, through the woods to Dolgoch Falls. The country beyond is open and almost treeless as far as the original

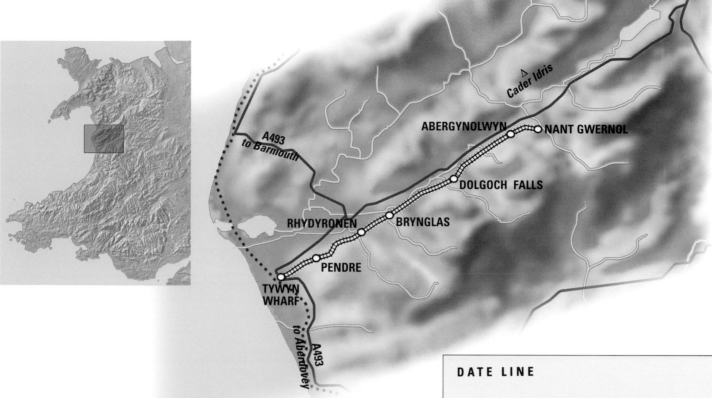

ABOVE *The "new" passenger terminus at Nant Gwernol with No 3 "Sir Haydn" running round the train to return to Twywn.*

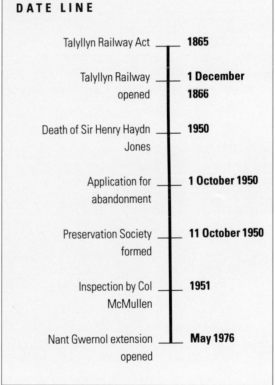

DATE LINE

Talyllyn Railway Act	**1865**
Talyllyn Railway opened	**1 December 1866**
Death of Sir Henry Haydn Jones	**1950**
Application for abandonment	**1 October 1950**
Preservation Society formed	**11 October 1950**
Inspection by Col McMullen	**1951**
Nant Gwernol extension opened	**May 1976**

terminus at Abergynolwyn, which is some 150 feet above the village of that name. The railway took its name from Talyllyn Lake, some 3½ miles further inland, which it never reached!

The section that runs on to Nant Gwernol has much of its length on a shelf cut into the valley flank. The shelf was widened and the rock wall was blasted in two places to ease the curves. A new station was built at Nant Gwernol on the site of the old sidings, below the three rope-worked inclines that took wagons to the quarries at Bryn Eglwys, some 330 feet above. From there an incline, also rope-worked, took wagons with supplies down to the village of Abergynolwyn, where rails were laid along the streets!

Today the railroad depends on tourists: as many as 11 trains are run in each direction at the height of the season. The two original locomotives can still be seen, and they have been joined by four more. One, rebuilt in 1964, carries the name Tom Rolt in memory of the first General Manager, the man whose vision made all this possible.

Ziller Valley Railroad

Zillertalbahn

A U S T R I A

USEFUL DATA

Zillertalbahn

Headquarters Zillerthaler Verkehrsbetriebe AG, A-6200 Jenbach, Austria.

Phone (43) 5244 2311 & 5353.

Fax (43) 5244 398339.

Timetables from main stations, travel agents and Headquarters.

Tickets from main stations. Group reservations from Headquarters and travel agents.

Achenseebahn

Headquarters

Bahnhofstrasse 3, A-6200 Jenbach, Austria.

Phone (43) 5244 2243.

Fax (43) 5244 22435.

Public access

by Austrian Federal Railways & bus from Innsbruck. By road along the Inn valley.

Facilities

Refreshments at main stations & on some trains. Museum at Innsbruck.

Austria adopted the unusual gauge of 760mm—a fraction under 2ft 6in—for the majority of its narrow-gauge railroads, unlike its European neighbors, who adopted the 1-metre (3ft 3in) gauge. The little line up the Ziller Valley to Mayrhofen in the Austrian Tyrol is not a tourist railroad in the strictest terms, since it was built to replace the stage-coaches used until 1902, and to perform a year-round service to its communities.

The Ziller Valley is the biggest and most famous of the many beautiful valleys of the Tyrol. The villagers were largely responsible for the worldwide fame of the Christmas hymn "Silent Night" ("Stille Nacht"). It was attributed to Franz Gruber and Joseph Mohr from the village of Obendorf, Salzburg. The manuscript was lost, and then found in 1818 by a Zillertaler, who took it home with him, producing it again in 1831 in Leipzig!

As early as 1868, there was discussion of a railroad to run from Jenbach in the Inn Valley, on the main line from Salzburg to Innsbruck, up the Ziller Valley to Zell-am-Ziller and possibly beyond. The river Ziller has its source close to the Italian border, and from the village of Mayrhofen, above Zell, to Jenbach, on the Inn, the fall is fairly gentle. The normal method of transport for visitors was stage-coach; travelers had to spend a night at Zell, 21km (13 miles) from Jenbach.

It took until 1899 for the government to concede that a railroad was needed. On 2 December 1899, Railway Minister Heinrich von Wittek handed over the concession deed to enable the founding of the Zillerbahn on 26 December. Construction commenced almost immediately, and was completed to Mayr-hofen, 32km (20 miles) from Jenbach, on 31 July 1902. The line follows the course of the

RIGHT A vintage steam train runs up the Zillertal with 4-wheel passenger cars hauled by the 0-8-0 tender locomotive formerly belonging to the Bosnia-Herzegovinia State Railways.

Ziller river. This has led to washouts in various places in times of heavy rain, when the river bursts its banks. From 1902 the little railroad served the local communities, bringing much-needed supplies. Most trains were mixed, conveying freight as well as passenger cars.

BELOW *One of the Krauss (Linz) 0-6-2 tank locomotives about to leave Jenbach for a trip to Mayrhofen. This was a favorite type of locomotive to be found on most of the Austrian 760mm gauge railways.*

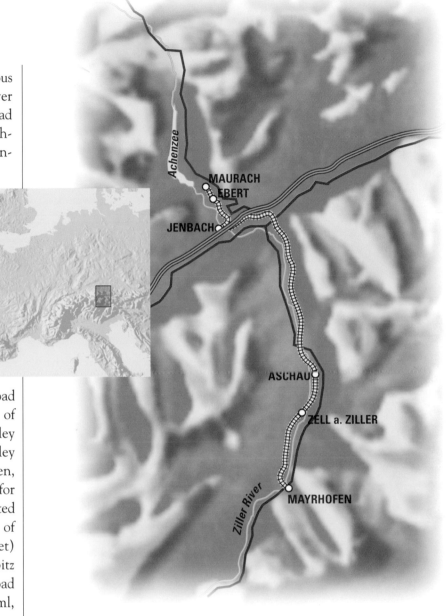

From Jenbach to Zell the valley is broad and shallow, passing through the villages of Fuegen, Ried and Aschau. At Zell the valley divides; the railroad follows the main valley through Ramsberg and Buehel to Mayrhofen, a favorite summer resort for British tourists for 100 years. Mayrhofen, the terminus, is situated on a wide plateau with four valleys, one of which has sides of nearly 3,350m (11,000 feet) high, topped by the Olpener and Ritterspitz glaciers. The other valley from Zell has a road that leads over the Gerloos Pass to Krimml, the terminus of another 760mm-gauge line to Zell-am-Zee, owned and operated by Austrian Federal Railways.

While the original line was, of course, operated by steam locomotives—and today six are in existence—the original No. 1 Raimund is now in the Landesmuseum/Zeughaus in Innsbruck. The other two, built for the original line in 1900–2 by Krauss in Linz, are still in operation. Three more were built between 1909 and 1930; the last came from the Bosnia-Herzegovina State Railroad. Vintage steam locomotives pull trains of vintage four-wheel coaches.

Most scheduled trains today are operated by

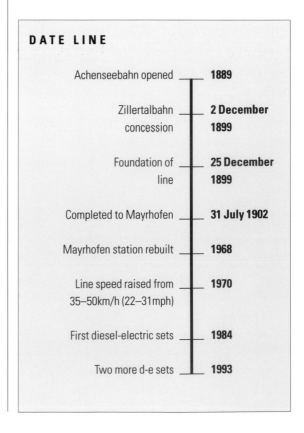

ABOVE *A small sample of the alpine scenery to be enjoyed from a Zillertalbahn train. This one is hauled by one of the Krauss 0-6-2 tank locomotives.*

modern diesel-electric railcar sets, of which there are five, while diesel locomotives operate the freight trains and do the shunting. Standard-gauge freight vehicles carrying various local products, usually timber, or supplies for the villages, often oil, are conveyed on purpose-built transporter wagons.

Trains are run throughout the year. From 1 May to the end of October, and during the Easter and Christmas holidays, two steam trains each way are included in the timetable, stopping at all stations and halts. The normal diesel train takes 57 minutes, while the steam train takes 1 hour and 40 minutes. The Zillertalbahn also runs the bus services. Special steam trains may be arranged with connection to bus tours from Mayrhofen.

In addition to the Zillertalbahn, there is another steam railroad running from Jenbach to the Achensee, a beautiful lake some 110m (360 feet) above Jenbach, to the north of the Inn valley. The level of the lake was artificially raised. The railroad and lake steamers are the property of the Tyrolean Waterworks Company. The Achenseebahn is a part rack, part adhesion line running 11km (6 miles) from Jenbach station, with a 6km (3½-mile) rack section first to Maurach, where the train reverses, and an adhesion line to the pier on the Achensee at Seespitz. This line preceded the Zillertalbahn and was opened in 1889. The four original steam locomotives still work the line, which is normally open only in the summer months.

DATE LINE	
Achenseebahn opened	**1889**
Zillertalbahn concession	**2 December 1899**
Foundation of line	**25 December 1899**
Completed to Mayrhofen	**31 July 1902**
Mayrhofen station rebuilt	**1968**
Line speed raised from 35–50km/h (22–31mph)	**1970**
First diesel-electric sets	**1984**
Two more d-e sets	**1993**

Three Valleys Steam Railroad

Chemin de Fer A Vapeur des Trois Vallées

B E L G I U M

LEFT *A scene at Tregnes station with on the left ex German 2-6-2 tank No 64.250 and on the right ex German 2-10-0 No 52.8200.*

USEFUL DATA

Headquarters Chemin de Fer à Vapeur des Trois Vallées, Chaussée de Givet, 49-51, B-5660 Mariembourg, Belgium.

Phone & Fax (32) 60 31 24 40.

Public Stations Mariembourg Depot, Olloy Sur Viroin, Treignes.

Timetables & Tickets Mariembourg. Reservations required for groups & special trains.

Public access by SNCB train from Charleroi. By car from RN 5 Charleroi-Couvin. Car park at Mariembourg.

Facilities Café & shops at Treignes & Mariembourg. Museum at Treignes. Locomotive depot at Mariembourg.

The Chemin de Fer à Vapeur des Trois Vallées, CFV3V, is an association that runs steam-hauled tourist trains over three scenic lines of the Belgian State Railroads (SNCB) in the picturesque Ardennes. Two of the lines run from Mariembourg, about 35km (22 miles) south of Charleroi, and the third runs along the valley of the Meuse from the city of Dinant. CFV3V was created in 1973 as a non-profit association. In 1976 they began to run a tourist operation on the former SNCB line, which joined Mariembourg with Vireux-sur-Meuse as far as Treignes, a distance of 14km (8 miles), along the valley of the Viroin, a tributary of the Meuse. The name "Three Valleys" is taken from the three rivers of the region: the Eau Blanche, the Eau Noire and the Viroin.

In 1985 CFV3V began to explore the possibilities of running tourist trains on another line, the 30km (18½-mile) line from Mariembourg west through Chimay to Momignies, close to the French border. This line goes on to join the French Railroads (SNCF) line from Hirson to Valenciennes and Lille. The cooperation of another operator, Transports de l'Entre Sambre et Meuse, de Chimay et des Ardennes (TEMCA), was needed. TEMCA uses the line to carry freight, mainly wood and stone, and in 1995 it was reserved exclusively for that traffic. In 1990, CFV3V began negotiations for tourist trains over the SNCB line along the Meuse from Dinant to Givet, a distance of 22km (13½ miles). This very scenic line was closed to passengers in 1988 and to freight in 1989.

For now, CFV3V operates only from Mariembourg to Treignes. They have a collection of steam and diesel locomotives, with some diesel railcars, obtained from SNCB, SNCF, Luxembourg Railroads (CFL) and German Railroads, both the Deutsche Bundesbahn (DB) and the former East German Deutsche Reichsbahn (DR). At present there are three steam locomotives, all of German origin, two main-line diesel locomotives and six diesel railcars, four of Belgian and two of French origin. There are also 20 passenger coaches

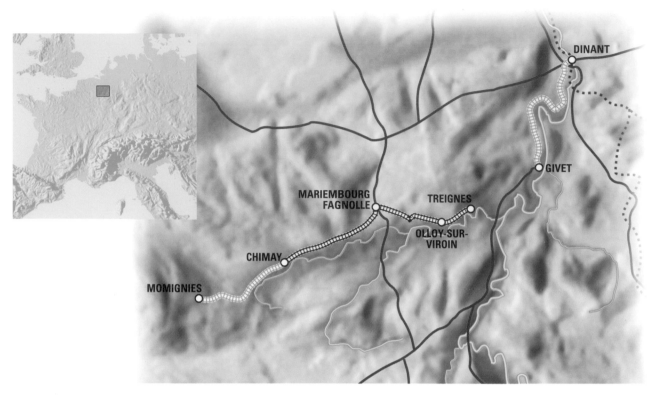

ABOVE *Former German class 52 No 8200 heads up a train of military vehicles out of Mariembourg.*

operate on most days, with extra steam trains on certain days. On one day in May and two in June there are special steam trains for school groups.

Mariembourg is 35km (22 miles) south of Charleroi (Brussels 50km [31 miles]) on Route Nationale 5 to Couvin. The Belgian Railroads branch operated by diesel traction to Couvin has a station at Mariembourg.

and some ten freight vehicles, the latter all used for work trains.

In 1994 a museum was set up at the station at Treignes. There is an exhibition hall of four 105m (345-foot) tracks, a works with two 30m (100-foot) tracks, a café and a shop. There is also a café and a shop at Mariembourg. Operation begins on 1 April and continues through to 31 October on Saturdays and Sundays, with steam trains at Easter and in the autumn most weekends to the end of October. There is an Autorail Festival (first weekend in June), when diesel trains run non-stop, and a Steam Festival (third weekend in September), when steam trains run non-stop. In the months of July and August, extra trains of diesel railcars

DATE LINE

CVF3V formed	**1973**
Mariembourg–Treignes opened	**1976**
Negotiations for Chimay–Momignies	**1985**
Dinant–Givet closed to passengers	**1988**
Dinant–Givet closed to freight	**1989**
Negotiations begun Dinant–Givet	**1990**

Jokioinen Museum Railroad

Jokioisten Museorantatic

F I N L A N D

USEFUL DATA

Headquarters

Museorautatieyhdistys ry, PL 1, FIN-31601, Jokioinen, Finland.

Phone (358) 433 3235.

Public Stations Jokioinen, Minkiö, Humppila.

Timetables from stations or by mail from Headquarters.

Tickets from stations. Special train reservations from Headquarters.

Public access

by Finnish State Railway to Humppila. By car to Mankiö or Jokioinen.

Facilities

Museum at Minkiö. Shop & refreshments at Jokioinen.

RIGHT *On the Jokioinen Museum Railway in Finland a train hauled by Tampela 2-8-2 tank locomotive No 5 is approaching the present Jokioinen terminus.*

The Jokioinen Museum Railroad is a 14km (8-mile) 750mm (2ft 5½in)-gauge line running between Humppila and Jokioinen in southwest Finland, part of a 23km (14½-mile) light railroad that originally extended from the main-line system at Humppila to Forssa.

The line was built in 1898 by the Jokioinen-Forrssa Railway Company, and opened for both passenger and freight traffic on 9 December 1898. It runs through a rural area and acted as a feeder to the main line at Humppila, supplying the villages and taking out their produce from the lakeland around Forssa. Traffic was always light, and on 31 August 1954, passenger services ceased, leaving a few freight trains to deal with the remaining traffic. The line struggled on for another 20 years, as there was usually enough traffic to carry a few broad (5-foot) gauge wagons on transporters.

In 1975 much of the track was lifted, but a group of enthusiasts, determined to preserve one of the remaining Finnish narrow-gauge lines, took steps to acquire as much as possible of what remained. On 25 June 1978, some 6km (3 miles) of line between Jokioinen and Minkiö had been restored, and trains began operating again. It was another 16 years before a further section could be restored, but in 1992, work began on the section between Minkiö and Humppila. On 5 May 1994, the main line was reached again at Humppila. The line is now operated by the Jokioinen Museum Railway Company. Their only plans at present are for a 1km (½ mile) extension at Jokioinen to take the line closer to the village. While the three main stations are at Humppila, Minkiö and Jokioinen, the former halt platforms at Kermala, Palomäki, Vuorela, Salminen Raemäki and Kirkkotie also remain.

ABOVE *In the Finnish
twilight a train returns to
Minkio hauled by 2-8-2
tank No 5.*

ABOVE *2-8-2 tank No
5 waits at Humppila for
any passengers off the
Finnish State Railway's*   *train visible in the
background.*

At Minkiö there is a unique collection of
material and rolling stock obtained from a
number of Finnish light railways. There is also
a shop selling railroad memorabilia. At
present, the Company owns 12 steam, 21
diesel and two electric locomotives, but only
two steam locomotives are in use: a 2-6-2 tank
built by Tubize in 1947, formerly Jokioinen
Railway No. 4, and a 2-8-2 tank built by
Tampella in 1917, formerly Wyvinkää-Karkkila
Railway No. 5. There are about 12 four-axle
passenger cars from various Finnish narrow-
gauge lines. There is a collection of 32 freight
vehicles all used for internal purposes, and

DATE LINE

Built by Jokioinen Rly Co.	**9 December 1898**
Closed to passengers	**31 August 1954**
Closed to all traffic	**31 March 1974**
Minkiö-Jokioinen reopened	**25 June 1978**
Relaying to Humppila started	**1992**
Minkiö reopened	**5 June 1994**

HUMPPILA
KERMALA
PALOMÄKI
VUORELA
MINKIÖ
SALMINEN
RAEMÄKI
KIRKKOTIE
JOKIOINEN

ABOVE *2-8-2 tank No 5 and newly restored 0-8-0 tender locomotive No 6 stand together at Minkio.*

three snowplows. There is also a large collection of stored or exhibited vehicles.

Trains are run on Sundays only from the beginning of June to the end of August, with two return trips from end to end of the line and one or two from Minkiö to Humppila. Extra trains operate in the high season between the end of June and the beginning of August. It is possible to arrange special trains in addition to the regular timetable.

Finnish State Railway trains from Turku and Tampere stop at Humppila, while Minkiö is the best spot for a visit by car. Access to all three main stations is from the Helsinki-Pori Route 2. Jokioinen is also accessible from the Turku-Hämeenlinna Route 10.

Baie de Somme Tourist Railroad

Chemin de Fer Touristique de la Baie de Somme

F R A N C E

RIGHT *Trains arriving at Noyelles-sur-Mer from Le Croty and Cayeux, the latter traversing the mixed gauge tracks of the SNCF. The locomotive on the right came from the Chemins de fer du Morbihan and that on the right from the Chemins de fer de l'Aisne.*

USEFUL DATA

Headquarters CFT Baie de Somme Gare, 80230 St Valery-sur-Somme, France.
Phone (33) 22 26 96 96.
Fax (33) 22 26 95 66.
Public Stations Le Crotoy, Morlay, Noyelles, St Valery Canal, St Valery Ville, St Valery Port, Routhiauville, Lanchères Pendé, Hurt, Cayeux-Brighton.
Timetables & Tickets from main stations. Reservations with Headquarters required for groups. Timetables by mail.
Le Petit Train de la Haute Somme Headquarters
APPEVA, PO Box 106, 80001 Amiens Cedex 1, France.
Phone (33) 22 44 55 40.
Fax (33) 22 44 04 99.
Public access
SNCF to Noyelles. By car from A16 and A28 & A40A to Noyelles.
Facilities
Shop at le Crotoy.

Little remains today of France's once large network of narrow-gauge railroads. Most of the small pieces remaining are now operated chiefly as tourist lines. The train line from Boulogne to Paris passes through Noyelles where, on the right or seaward side, is the 1m (3ft 3in) gauge terminus of the once much more extensive Chemin de Fer Touristique de la Baie de Somme. This little railroad has two arms, one running beside the Somme estuary to Le Crotoy, 9km (5.6 miles), and the other running west across the river to St Valery-sur-Somme, 6km (3.7 miles), and Cayeux-sur-Mer, 18km (11 miles) from Noyelles.

The Somme railways were laid down in 1887 by the Société Général des Chemins de Fer Economique. They then passed into the hands of the Chemins de Fer et Transports Automobiles (CFTA). Freight traffic went to the roads and passenger traffic, except for the summer months decreased; on 31 December 1972, the owners abandoned the line.

This was, however, not the end. The lines to Cayeux-Brighton had once carried heavy holiday and weekend traffic to the sea (winter traffic was light, and was usually worked by little four-wheel petrol or diesel railcars). Interest in the line was widespread, and an association was formed to preserve the two main branches. On 1 January 1973, they were taken over by L'association Chemin de Fer de la Baie de Somme to run as tourist lines from spring to autumn. Today only passengers are carried, but the line still serves two stations from Noyelles on the Le Crotoy line, and seven on the Cayeux-Brighton line. 27km (16 miles) are in use, and there are no plans at present for any extension.

In its original form, the heavy summer traffic was handled by steam locomotives, although toward the end, diesels made an appearance on a number of trains. Now steam is the main attraction, and the Association operates eight steam and five diesel

BELOW *A train between Noyelles and St Valery hauled by Buffaud 0-6-2 tank No 3714.*

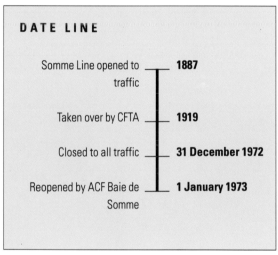

DATE LINE

Somme Line opened to traffic	**1887**
Taken over by CFTA	**1919**
Closed to all traffic	**31 December 1972**
Reopened by ACF Baie de Somme	**1 January 1973**

locomotives of various types. Some were owned by the original line and others have been acquired from other lines. Altogether there are 15 passenger vehicles of both French and Swiss origin.

Between Noyelles and Le Crotoy/St Valery, trains operate Sundays and holidays from mid-March to mid-November, with Tuesdays, Wednesdays, and Fridays added in July and August. Between Noyelles and Cayeux-Brighton, trains run on Saturdays, Sundays, and holidays in July and August.

While in the area, it is worth making a visit to another little line that runs from Froissy, about 18km (11 miles) northeast of Beauvais. This is a 60cm (23.625-inch)-gauge line, once part of a larger local system, called the Compagnie Générale des Voies Férrées d'Intérêt Local (VFIL). Just 7km (4½ miles) survives to Dompierre. Known as Le Petit Train de la Haute Somme, it has 10 steam and 18 diesel locomotives and is open on Sundays and holidays between May and September, with additional trains on Wednesdays and Saturdays from mid-July to end of August.

Chanteraines Railroad

Chemin de Fer des Chanteraines

F R A N C E

USEFUL DATA

Headquarters 46 Avenue Georges Pompidou, 92390 Villeneuve-la-Garenne, France.

Phone (1) 40 85 86 20.

Fax (1) 40 85 81 45.

Timetables from Headquarters.

Tickets from stations.

Group reservations from Headquarters: phone, fax or mail.

Public access

RER line C to Gennevilliers. RATP Metro lines 137, 138 A&B, 178, 238, 378. Bus 166. By car: A86, exit Villeneuve-la-Garenne and CD 9.

Facilities

Cards & souvenirs. Depot at La Ferme d'Enfants. Fast food shop at "La Rainette".

The Chemin de Fer des Chanteraines does not follow the normal pattern of preserved or tourist railroads. It is of comparatively recent origin, and was built as a narrow-gauge "work" railroad.

In 1981 a 60cm (23.625-inch)-gauge railroad was built by the Garden Department of the Council of the Départment of Hauts de Seine to serve the different sections of the Chanteraines Park at Villeneuve-la-Garenne, a suburb about 12km (7 miles) north of the center of Paris. The Park is in the loop of the River Seine and the railroad was used to move materials and personnel around the site. In 1984 the Chemin de Fer Chanteraines (CFC) club was formed to keep and run the railroad as a tourist attraction. Although owned by the Départment, the line has been extended and

ABOVE *Scenes from the little Chanteraines railroad in a public park at Villeneuve la Garenne, a modern suburb 7 miles north of Paris.*

adapted for passengers under the direction of the CFC committee.

The line now has a length of 4.5km (2 miles), and an additional 1km (0.6 miles) of sidings, loops, etc. It serves six stations, four of which are close to Metro (RATP) stations; one, Gennevilliers, has a connection with the RER (Réseau Express Régional) also. The line is single with passing loops, and runs from Epinay to Gennevilliers, with its operations center at La Ferme d'Enfants.

Although the original work railroad used diesel locomotives, the CFC has since

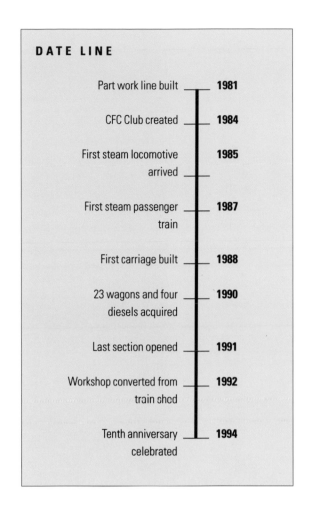

DATE LINE

Part work line built	**1981**
CFC Club created	**1984**
First steam locomotive arrived	**1985**
First steam passenger train	**1987**
First carriage built	**1988**
23 wagons and four diesels acquired	**1990**
Last section opened	**1991**
Workshop converted from train shed	**1992**
Tenth anniversary celebrated	**1994**

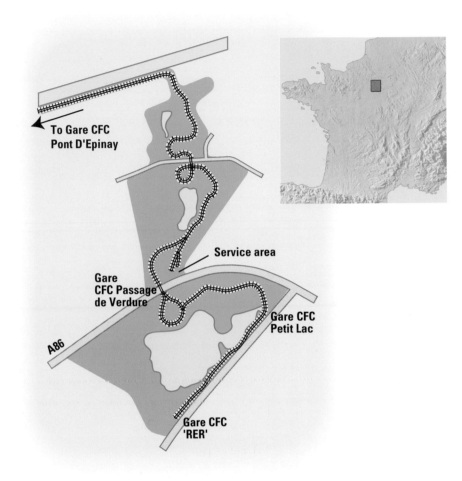

To Gare CFC
Pont D'Epinay

Service area

Gare
CFC Passage
de Verdure

Gare CFC
Petit Lac

A86

Gare CFC
'RER'

acquired some steam locomotives, and these are the major attraction. The oldest is a 0-4-0 tank locomotive built in 1905 by Orenstein & Koppel. There are two Decauville locomotives, an 0-4-0T of 1911 and an 0-6-0T of 1919. There are seven diesel locomotives, one built in 1928, four in 1948, and two (the originals) in 1981. The first steam locomotive arrived in 1985, but two years of restoration work were needed before it was able to run the first steam-hauled train. Since then carriages have been built, mostly of the open type, freight vehicles acquired, the original carriage shed converted to a workshop, and a true tourist attraction created.

There is no museum—the line is too new— but visitors are welcome at the shed area, where there is also a well-equipped workshop with mobile gantries and a good range of machine tools. There is no souvenir shop, but photographic cards are available for sale.

The railroad is easy to access, as the station at Pont d'Epinay is on Metro line 138 A & B, Pompidou on Metro line 137, Lac des Renier on Metro lines 178 & 378 and Gennevilliers on Metro lines 178 & 378 and RER line C. By car the Autoroute A86 exit for Villeneuve-la-Garenne is close, also route CD9.

Regular operation is March through November, with trains on Wednesdays and Saturdays every hour, and on Sundays with two or three trains each hour. There are a number of Gala days each year when as many as five trains may run each hour. Between November and March, trains run if the weather is good, usually on weekends.

Groups of 20 or more people visiting the railroad are advised to reserve ahead. Special group fares are available—steam trains cost a little more than diesel-operated trains! Otherwise tickets are obtainable from any of the stations.

French Railroad Museum

Musée Français du Chemin de Fer

F R A N C E

USEFUL DATA

Address 2 Rue Alfred de Glehn, F 68200 Mulhouse, France.

Phone (33) 89 42 25 67.

Fax (33) 89 42 41 82.

Reservations required for groups.

Public access

on Rue Alfred de Glehn. By rail to Mulhouse, bus 17 to museum. By car from A35 & A35. By air to Basle, then bus. Car park, bus park.

Facilities

Restaurant, shop, own "Halt" on Paris main line.

The French Railroad Museum at Mulhouse in eastern France claims to be "the most important railroad collection in continental Europe". A surface area of 30,000 square metres (323,000 sq ft) has been given over to this assembly of rolling stock, permanent-way equipment, signaling and structures. Locomotives include Stephenson's 2-2-2 No. 6 L'Aigle of 1846 for the Avignon and Marseille Railway, the 1884 Buddicome 2-2-2 No. 33 St Pierre, and examples of electric and diesel locomotives.

The need for a museum became clear in the late 1960s as French railroads entered a period of fundamental change, not only of motive power but also of operating methods, passenger and freight rolling stock and infrastructure. The aim was to record the contribution made by France to rail transport, from the invention of the multi-tube boiler of Marc Seguin to the high-speed trains of today.

A group calling themselves the French Association of Friends of the Railways (Association Française des Amis des Chemins de Fer) had the initiative to save a number of historic locomotives and to propose a permanent museum. Created in 1969, the Association of the Mulhouse French Railway Museum (Musée Français du Chemin de Fer de Mulhouse) obtained support from the public and from French Railroads (SNCF) for a museum to be in the town of Mulhouse. SNCF would undertake the restoration of preserved material in their works (except that in a very poor state), and the museum would be confined entirely to historic rolling stock from French Railroads and, in certain cases, the Wagons Lits company.

In July 1971 the association was able to open a temporary museum in an old roundhouse at the Mulhouse steam locomotive depot. This site drew a large number of visitors, and in 1976 the first stage in the construction of a proper exhibition site was completed. The

RIGHT *On entering the Mulhouse Museum the first locomotive one sees is "L'Aigle" built in 1846 by Robert Stephenson, Newcastle, for the Railroad between Avignon and Marseilles.*

second stage was finished in 1983 and today the museum draws a large number of visitors.

Steam locomotives represent the period from 1884 to 1949 and the last, the 232U1 of 1949, can be seen in motion on rollers. Among the later exhibits is the electric locomotive, No. 9004, which broke the world speed record in 1955 with a speed of 331km/hr (210mph)

The special coach built for Napoleon III is exhibited, as are various examples of those built for the luxury trains of the 1920s. The project is also supported by the RTP—the Paris Metro—and subway cars and other equipment are also included. These are all shown in the "Grand" exhibition hall, which

LEFT The Chapelon "Pacific" class 231.E of 1936 was a brilliant rebuild of a 1907–11 design and 48 of them went to the Northern Railway (Nord) of France where they did sterling work to the end of steam.

RIGHT The 232U1, the "swan song" of steam, embodied a number of advanced technical features and although capable of developing over 4000 ihp, no more were built. The exhibit is mounted on rollers and each hour it is run, complete with sound effects.

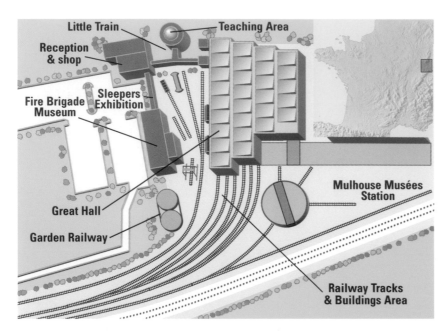

LEFT *One of Ettore Bugatti's distinctive railcars achieved a world speed record of 123 mph (196 km/hr) in 1937. There were a number of different versions and that exhibited is the "Presidential" type.*

also includes an art exhibit. Bugatti's famous railcar has a place, as does the special coach used by General de Gaulle. In the yard there are permanent-way and signaling equipment, interesting structures and other exhibits. One building is given over to a Fire Brigade Museum. There is, of course, a large indoor working model railroad, as well as an outdoor miniature railroad surrounding the lecture hall, and a garden railroad.

The entrance, reception and shop share a building with a restaurant, and there is ample parking space and room for buses. One other feature is a "Museum Halt" on the SNCF main line adjacent to the Museum.

The Museum is open year-round except Mondays, 25 and 26 December and 1 January, and on public and school holidays between 1 November and 28 or 29 February. Groups need to reserve space in the restaurant.

Mulhouse is on the main lines from Paris and Lille, Strasbourg to Basle. It can be reached by the A35 and A36 autoroutes and Basle Airport and by bus No. 17.

Rhine Tourist Railroad (CFTR)

Chemin de Fer Touristique du Rhin

FRANCE

RIGHT *141TB424 was earmarked for preservation and this was carried out jointly by SNCF and the Rhine Tourist Railway, CFTR.*

USEFUL DATA

Rhine Tourist Railway (CFTR) 16 Rue de Cordiers, F 68280 Andolsheim, France.

Phone 89 71 51 42 (evenings); 89 72 55 97 (weekends only).

Public Stations
Volgelsheim, Depot, Baltzenheim

Timetables & Tickets by phone or post from Headquarters. Tickets on sale from Volgelsheim, Baltzenheim.

Public access
There is no rail service on the SNCF lines. By car from Colmar, N415, or Freiburg (Germany), Mulhouse Boat from Sasbach (Germany).

Facilities
Reserved car park, food, depot.

The Rhine Tourist Railroad is a standard gauge line running alongside a private road from the Rhine port of Volgelsheim in the French département of Alsace north of the village of Baltzenheim.

On the orders of Bismarck, a line was opened on 5 January 1878 from Colmar to Brisach on the east side of the Rhine opposite Volgelsheim to reinforce communication between the provinces that had been taken back into the German Empire. By 1890 the line had already fallen into disuse, but in 1914 10 slow trains still ran in each direction. In the next 15 years traffic was reduced to two railcars in each direction excluding freight and military traffic.

In 1890 a new station was built with Austrian labor at Volgelsheim, then known as Neuf-Brisach. This was at the junction of the line into Germany and a secondary line between Colmar and a 21-km (13-mile-long) branch to Marckolsheim. As traffic fell off, the station was little used, and it was finally abandoned on 17 march 1969. Freight traffic continues to use the line between Colmar and Marckolsheim, constructed by SNCF in 1959–60 through the industrial zone close to the Port of Neuf-Brisach. The station was acquired by the municipality of Volgelsheim in 1987. The line into Germany also disappeared and the bridge was dismantled.

Earlier, in 1980, a group of railway enthusiasts formed an association to pursue two objectives: to protect the station from further vandalism and to create a tourist attraction by restoring a few miles of the railway line between Volgelsheim and Marckolsheim to be run under the banner of the Chemin de Fer Touristique du Rhin (CFTR). The association proposed that excursions should be run using old steam trains. Integration with the local community was decided in 1991.

Today the municipality rents the station to the CFTR as the departure point for vintage

ABOVE *Usually light trains are worked by one of the smaller tank locomotives. Here 0-4-0 tank No 4353 is on a train from Volgelsheim.*

steam trains along the branch line bordering the Rhine as far as Baltzenheim. The station has been carefully renovated and is fully protected by the association. The renovated station was inaugurated on 16 May 1993 and renamed Volgelsheim, and the inaugural train ran on 9 July 1993. Lines in the neighborhood date from 1839 (Mulhouse-Thann) and 1868 (Colmar-Munsterle).

In the first years the CFTR ran trains on Saturdays, Sundays, and public holidays on 16km (10 miles) of the branch, but later it was realised that a real tourist attraction was a combined train/boat trip, and arrangements were made for a connection at the northern limit of the line at Baltzenheim at the Sans-Souci pier. A round trip was offered from Volgelsheim or the pier close to the depot on the outskirts of Volgelsheim with a visit to Marckolsheim and return by boat to the pier near the depot at Port Rhénan and train to Volgelsheim.

There are four 0-4-0 and two 0-6-0 steam tank locomotives, a number of diesels, including one A1A-A1A 62000 class Baldwin used on special trains, and one diesel railcar. Coaches are a mixture of four- and six-wheelers; the four-wheelers are mainly Austrian dating from the 1920s and the bogie vehicles are ex-Swiss Federal Railways (CFF) built between 1947 and 1950 for secondary lines.

The depot is in the outskirts of Volgelsheim at Port Rhénan where renovation and normal maintenance work is undertaken.

Trains are run each weekend from Whitsun to the second weekend in September and on fête days and public holidays. Access is by car to Volgelsheim, which is on the N415 from Colmar to Freiburg. When 2 kilometres (1.2 miles) from the Neuf-Brisach junction, turn left onto the D52. The depot-museum is about 1 kilometre (0.6 miles) north on the turning signposted Port Rhénan. Volgelsheim is 18km (11 miles) east of Colmar.

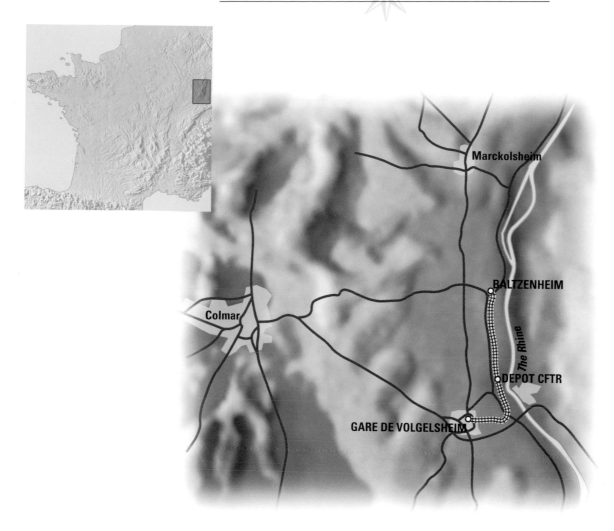

ABOVE *One of the two 0-6-0 tanks, this one is No 030TB130 which was built by Graffenstaden for the* *Alsace & Lorraine Railway in 1900 and is used between Volgelsheim and Marckolsheim.*

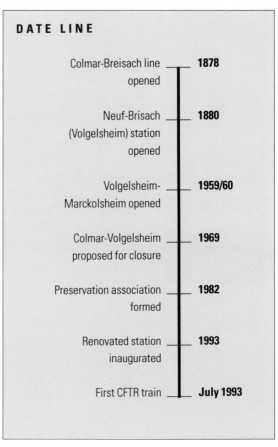

DATE LINE

Colmar-Breisach line opened	**1878**
Neuf-Brisach (Volgelsheim) station opened	**1880**
Volgelsheim-Marckolsheim opened	**1959/60**
Colmar-Volgelsheim proposed for closure	**1969**
Preservation association formed	**1982**
Renovated station inaugurated	**1993**
First CFTR train	**July 1993**

Vivarais Railroad

Chemin de Fer du Vivarais

FRANCE

USEFUL DATA

Headquarters CFTM, 2 Quai Jean Moulin, F69001 Lyon, France.

Phone (33) 78 28 83 34.

Fax (33) 72 00 97 67.

Main Stations Tournon, Boucieu-le Roi, Lamastre.

Other Stations Pont de Duzon, Colombier-le-Vieux.

Timetables from Headquarters or main stations.

Tickets from main stations, Headquarters, on train.

Public access by train from Lyon or Valence, or by local buses

Facilities Shop at Lamastre. Refreshments available, also Boucieu-le-Roi. Depot at Tournon—visits by arrangement. Good restaurants in Tournon and Lamastre.

LEFT *A train from Tournon to Lamastre hauled by one of the Mallet tanks rounding the curves which hug the almost sheer sides of the Doux Gorge.*

The Chemin de Fer du Vivarais or Vivarais Railway, which is operated by CFTM (Chemins de Fer Touristique et de Montagne), today runs for 33km (20 miles) from the Rhône Valley town of Tournon up the valley of the River Doux, through the Gorges to Lamastre, Ardèche. The whole region is very picturesque and the trip is highly recommended.

The line was once part of a much more extensive 1m (3ft 3in) gauge system owned by the Société des Chemins de Fer Départemen-taux (CFD) extending beyond Lamastre to the focal point of the system at Le Cheylard, built in 1891. From there it continued north to join a branch of the SNCF at Dunières. 37km (23 miles) of track was operated from Dunières to St Agrève as a tourist line but this section has been out of use for some time. However, it is now possible that this line may be reopened by the CFTM in July 1996 using steam locomotives. The other section from Le Cheylard down the Vallée de l'Eyrieux to the

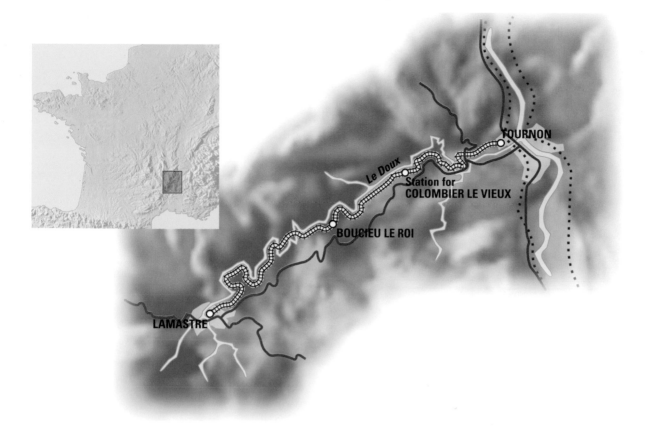

Rhône at La Voulte-sur-Rhône was unfortunately dismantled in 1968.

Whilst the line to Lamastre ceased to operate under CFD control on 30 October 1968, a body of enthusiasts saw its value as a tourist line and were able to acquire an interest. The line reopened in June 1969.

The headquarters, main depot and workshops of the CFTM are at Tournon, just across the Rhône from the famous Tain l'Hérmitage vineyards. Two SNCF lines run down the Rhône from Lyon; the passenger trains use the line on the left bank so one has to cross the river to reach the CFTA terminus.

Leaving Tournon the line uses the SNCF (French Railways) line on multi-gauge, three-rail track for 2km (1.2 miles) then turns west up the Doux. It is soon climbing into the narrow gorge where it runs on a ledge with a sheer drop to the rapids many feet below. The rapids rise almost to the same level as the train in some sections. Then the country widens out at Boucieu-le-Roi where the station allows trains to pass.

Steam and diesel traction are employed with a mix of steam locomotives and diesel railcars. There are six serviceable steam locomotives with two held in reserve, three diesel locomotives and four diesel-mechanical bogie railcars, plus some trailers. A variety of passenger cars are used, including bogie vehicles from the Vivarias, Brittany, Sarthe, and Switzerland, plus eight four-wheelers as well as three railcar trailers.

Some 50 freight vehicles are available and freight trains are operated from time to time but less now than formerly. Only diesel locomotives are employed for these. There is no museum but a shop is situated in Lamastre

ABOVE 0-6-6-0 Mallet No 404 waits at Boucieu-le-Roi, Ardeche while passengers take refreshments.

BELOW *One of the little Billard railcars used when traffic is light or when required for hire by special parties.*

ABOVE *An unusual "Tram" locomotive with a driving cab at each end avoiding the need for turning at each end of a journey. Known as a "Pinguely" it was built for the Lyon-St. Marcellin railway.*

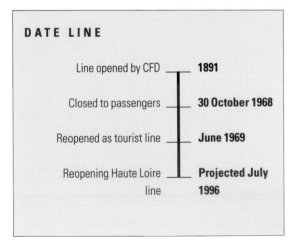

DATE LINE

Line opened by CFD	**1891**
Closed to passengers	**30 October 1968**
Reopened as tourist line	**June 1969**
Reopening Haute Loire line	**Projected July 1996**

station for the sale of souvenirs. Lamastre is also famous for its cuisine.

The operating season is normally from Easter to the end of October and differing schedules apply depending on the time of year. In summer there is always at least one daily steam departure from Tournon at 10.00.

There are five intermediate stops with one pass. The journey usually takes about two hours allowing ample time for lunch and a look at Lamastre.

Public access is best achieved by SNCF from Lyon or Valence to Tain-Tournon on the main line from Lyon to Marseilles and then by bus. By road, access may be obtained from Autoroute A7 (Lyon-Marseilles) taking the Tain exit, or by National roads 7 or 86 between Lyon and the South.

The same company also operates a 600mm (2ft) gauge line in Isère, 60km (7 miles) east of Lyon. The Chemin de Fer du Haute Rhône, as it is called, is about 4km (2½ miles) long and runs from Mantalieu-Vallée Bleue along the Rhône to Pont de Sault-Brénaz. It operates one steam locomotive and three diesel locomotives with an interesting collection of four-wheel passenger cars. The line is well worth a visit and details can be obtained either from Tournon or from CFTM headquarters in Lyon.

Harz Narrow-Gauge Railroads

Harzer Schmalspurbahnen

G E R M A N Y

USEFUL DATA

Headquarters Harzer Schmalspurbahnen GmbH, Forkestrasse 17, 38855 Wernigerode, Germany.

Phone (49) 3943 32074.

Fax (49) 3943 32107.

Main Stations

Wernigerode, Nordhausen Nord, Gernrode/Harz. 31 other stations and halts.

Timetables by mail, phone, or fax from Headquarters.

Tickets reservations from Headquarters. Normal travel from ticket offices.

Public access

by train from main centers. By road—check with automobile organizations.

The Harz mountains lie in the northern part of Germany, south of a line joining Magdeburg and Hannover. Before the reunification of Germany, the border between East and West ran just to the east of the summit of the highest mountain, the Brocken, 1,142m (3,760 feet) above sea level. To help exploit the mineral wealth, and provide connections with the main-line railroads to the north, south and east of the area, a system of narrow (1-metre, 3ft 3in)-gauge railroads was developed, beginning in 1897, with a total of 132km (82 miles) of line: the Harzer Schmalspurbahnen.

One route runs roughly north to south across the mountains from Nordhausen, on the Kassel-Leipzig line, to Wernigerode on the Hannover-Magdeburg line. Another runs from Eisfelder Talmühle to Gernrode/Harz on the Braunschweig-Halle-Leipzig line, with branches to Hasselfelde and Harzgerode. Another line runs from the Wernigerode-Nordhausen line at Drei-Annen-Hohne to a station just below the summit of the Brocken at 1,125m (3,700 feet).

In the former East Germany, the Harz Narrow-Gauge Railroads came under the control of the Transport Ministry. Since reunification they have been privatized and, while under one management, are run as three lines: the Harzquerbahn, the north-to-south line; the Selketalbahn, the west-to-east branch; and the Brockenbahn—all under the initials HSB.

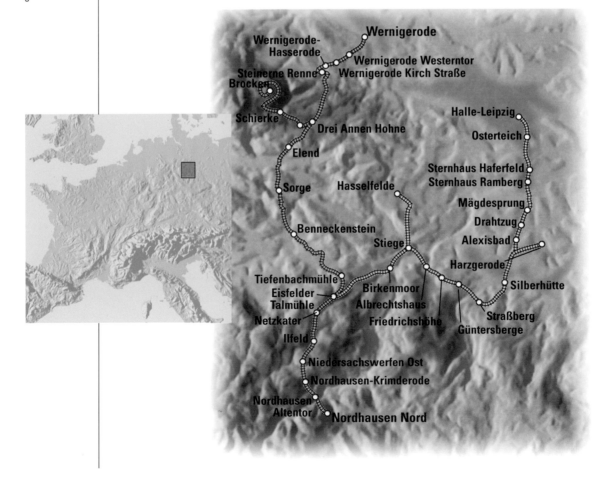

ABOVE AND TOP RIGHT *The Harz Mountain railways use some of the largest tank locomotives of any narrow gauge railway. Here at the Weringerode depot in June 1992 are two of the large 2-10-2 tanks.*

The Harzquerbahn is 60km (37 miles) from end to end. Between Drei-Annen-Hohne and Steinerne Renne, the next station to the north, there are 72 sharp curves, some having a 60m (200-foot) radius, while the maximum gradient is 4.0% (1 in 25). The scenery is superb, varying from open forest to mountain valleys. The longest tunnel is 70m (230 feet).

The Selketalbahn, 52km (32 miles) long, is romantic, and crosses mainly forest country with many small lakes and a typical Harz charm. Near Alexisbad, the traveler can see the rare sight of two steam trains on parallel tracks, one slightly higher than the other.

The Brockenbahn, as its title suggests, is the mountain line, climbing partly by adhesion and partly on rack to the station close to the summit of the Brocken—the highest point reached on any narrow-gauge line in Germany other than pure rack-mountain railroads. This task requires steam locomotives capable of

developing around 700hp. The area is popular for winter sports.

When in north Germany, a visit to these little railroads is a must! They are still operated mainly by steam locomotives; there are eight large modern tank locomotives and 17 vintage steam locomotives of 50 years old or more. There are also 10 diesel locomotives and a few diesel railcars. Special trains can seat up to 250 people, a vintage train 150, while a diesel railcar will take 25. Special trains can be arranged through the headquarters of the HSB at Wernigerode.

The three main centers are Wernigerode, the northern terminus, where the HSB have their headquarters, Nordhausen Nord in the south, and Gernrode/Harz in the east of the system. All three can be reached by German railroads from main centers such as Hannover, Halle and Leipzig. Main roads come close to all three.

Twente Steam Museum Railroad

De Twentse Stoomtrein

N E T H E R L A N D S

The region of Twente lies in the eastern Netherlands provinces of Overijsel and Gelderland. Its western part reaches as far as the river Ijsel and its eastern border is the frontier with Germany. The region has vast stretches of sandy plains, which rise in the east to 85m (280 feet) above sea level. One local craft developed into a thriving textile industry, with cotton processing, spinning, and weaving; the main centers are the towns of Hengelo, Almelo and Oldenzaal. Hengelo is close to the Twente Steam Museum Railroad, MBS (Museum Buurtspoorweg), which has one terminus about 7km (4 miles) south of Hengelo.

The first railroads in the area opened around 1865, and connections to the German railroads followed in 1875. The more remote areas developed a network of light railroads supported by local industry. The Geldersch-Overijsselsche Secondary Railroad Company (GOLS) was one of these, and opened various lines in the area between 1884 and 1910. The main purpose was to transport coal from Germany for the growing textile industry more cheaply than by the main-line railroad.

A line opened between Hengelo and Winterswijk in 1884, and was extended in 1885 to Enschede and Zevenaar, with a branch from Neede to Doetchinchem. It was operated by HIJSM, a main line of the old Dutch Iron Company of 1839, which was later absorbed by the national railroad company, Nederlandse Spoorwegen. In the Twente area, passenger traffic never flourished—the area was too sparsely populated—and passenger

USEFUL DATA

Headquarters Museum Buurtspoorweg, Stationsstraat 3, NL-7481 JA Haaksbergen, Netherlands.

Phone (31) 53 57 21516.

Fax (31) 53 57 41196.

Public Stations
Haaksbergen, Boekelo.

Timetables from Headquarters.

Tickets from Haaksbergen ticket office.

Public access
by rail to Enschede or Hengelo, then by bus to Haaksbergen. By car on N18 from Enschede. From Arnhem take A12 east, then A18 to Varsseveld & N18 to Haaksbergen. Car parks.

Facilities
Light refreshments. Museum & shop at Haaksbergen.

LEFT *The "red" steam tram locomotive No. 2 in the running shed at night.*

ABOVE *0-6-0 tank No 5, built by Henschel, on the turntable at Boekelo.*

services were withdrawn in 1937. There was a slight revival in 1944 when workmen's trains were re-instituted, but this did not last.

Gradually all the local lines, then owned by the NS, were closed. During World War II many lines were destroyed. Freight traffic gradually slipped away. Encouraged by the success of the TALYLLYN RAILWAY in north Wales, Museum Buurtspoorweg (MBS) was formed in 1967 as a voluntary foundation, with the aim of creating and maintaining a "live" railroad museum. MBS planned to obtain historical railroad material and restore it, as far as possible, to its original state. They wanted to set up a tourist operation to exhibit and run the restored material, and the line between Enschede and Haaksbergen provided a good opportunity.

A tourist operation was started in 1971, when the line was still connected with the state system, and passenger trains began to run again in 1972. Unfortunately by 1975 roads were dominant again; the building of the A35 highway curtailed operations to the 7.5km (4.7-mile) section between Boekelo and Haaksbergen, and isolated them from the state railroad system.

Nevertheless the little railroad has flourished. It is operated during the summer season, and serves as a permanent reminder of the original network. MBS bought the line from NS in 1989, making it the second independent railroad company in the Netherlands with its own concession.

MBS is run entirely by volunteers. The quality of the restoration work is admirable. During the rapid modernization that followed World War II, much that might have been of interest was scrapped; rolling stock and other material that is representative of earlier times was obtained from Dutch, German, and Belgian sources. Haaksbergen, where the station dates from 1884, is the headquarters. It contains the locomotive shed and workshops; there are plans to enlarge the latter. Boekelo, now the northern terminus, has a carriage shed, a well-restored turntable and many other items. There is an intermediate halt, "Hotel Boekelo," once a halt for the local salt works. MBS plans to re-establish a connection with the main-line railroad intercity station in Hengelo, which will involve bridging the A35 and the Twente canal.

At present there are four working steam

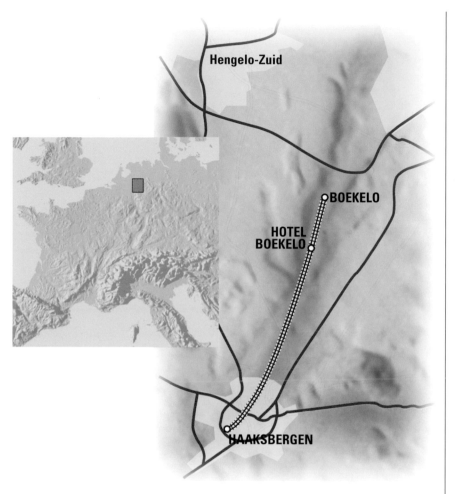

Hengelo-Zuid

BOEKELO

HOTEL
BOEKELO

HAAKSBERGEN

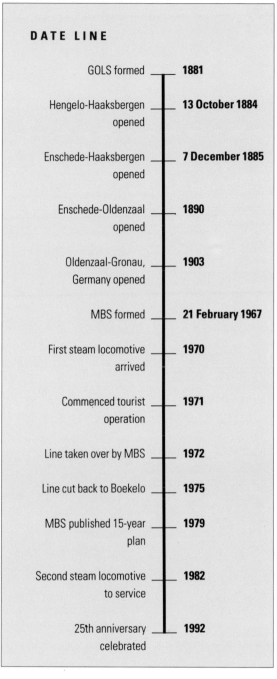

DATE LINE

GOLS formed	**1881**
Hengelo-Haaksbergen opened	**13 October 1884**
Enschede-Haaksbergen opened	**7 December 1885**
Enschede-Oldenzaal opened	**1890**
Oldenzaal-Gronau, Germany opened	**1903**
MBS formed	**21 February 1967**
First steam locomotive arrived	**1970**
Commenced tourist operation	**1971**
Line taken over by MBS	**1972**
Line cut back to Boekelo	**1975**
MBS published 15-year plan	**1979**
Second steam locomotive to service	**1982**
25th anniversary celebrated	**1992**

locomotives and two others on exhibition, two diesel-electric and four other diesel locomotives. There is a vintage gasoline railbus and another with a diesel engine. The nine coaches in use came mainly from Germany and Belgium, and are 4- and 6-wheel carriages. There are also 5 luggage vans and 11 freight cars.

There is a museum at Haaksbergen station housed in the goods shed, accessible from the ticket hall and free of charge to passengers (there is a small admission fee for other visitors). This museum deals with local transport and distribution. Haaksbergen station also has a shop and snack bar.

Trains are run on weekends from May to the end of September; this may be extended in the future. Trains also run in July and August on Wednesdays, Thursdays and public holidays, with a special school holiday event in October. Reservations are recommended for groups, especially for cycling groups. Help can be given to disabled passengers with advance notice. Steam or diesel specials can be arranged by contact with Headquarters.

Haaksbergen may be reached by taking Netherlands Railroads from principal towns to Enschede, then by bus to Haaksbergen. Haaksbergen is on the N18 and is just over 15km (9 miles) south-west of Enschede, or 76km (47 miles) from Arnhem, by the A12 and A18 to Varsseveld and then the N18.

Veluwsche Steam Railroad

Veluwsche Stoomtrein Maatschappij

NETHERLANDS

USEFUL DATA

Headquarters Dorpstraat 140, 7361 AZ Beekbergen, Netherlands.

Phone (31) 5766 1989.

Main Stations Apeldoorn, Dieren.

Other Stations Beekbergen, Immenbergweg, Loenen, Eerbeek.

Timetables, Tickets, Reservations VVV Apeldoorn, Postbus 1142, 7301 BJ Apeldoorn, Netherlands.

Phone (31) 55 788837.

Fax (31) 55 211290.

Public access by train or car to Apeldoorn or Dieren. Car parks.

Facilities Refreshment car & shop on most trains. Depot & extensive sidings at Beekbergen.

RIGHT Apeldoorn is the principal connection to the Netherlands State Railway system. No 8139 is seen leaving with a train for Dieren.

The Veluwsche Steam Railway Company (VSM-steamtrain) operates trains for railroad enthusiasts over a branch line still owned by the Netherlands Railways, between Apeldoorn and Dieren in the eastern part of the country. The Veluwe is an extensive sandy area with a thriving tourist industry, a special attraction being the Hogue Veluwe, the National Park to the north of Arnhem. The Apeldoorn-Dieren line runs along the eastern boundary of the National Park.

The line was built originally by the Royal Netherlands Local Railroad Company (KNLS), and was first opened to traffic on 2 July 1887. Apeldoorn is an ancient town and is even now the center of five lines, one of which is the main line from Amsterdam to the border town of Hengelo and Osnabrück, Germany.

The line to Dieren connected with another main line through Arnhem, also to Hengelo, and carried light passenger and freight traffic. It passed successively into the ownership of the Holland Iron Railroad Company (HSM) and later to Netherlands Railroads, who own the track and right-of-way now. As the other line connecting Arnhem with Apeldoorn also served two other small towns, this was of greater importance.

With ever-increasing automobile traffic, the intermediate villages were better served by buses, and the 22km (14 mile) link from Dieren lost its passenger traffic in 1950. Freight traffic continued until 1972, when it was withdrawn, except for 4km (2½ miles) at the Apeldoorn end.

Enthusiasm for railways is high in the Netherlands, and a group saw the opportunity to make use of the line for running preserved steam and diesel locomotives on tourist passenger trains. Agreement was reached with Netherlands Railroads, and steam trains began to operate between Apeldoorn and Dieren in 1975.

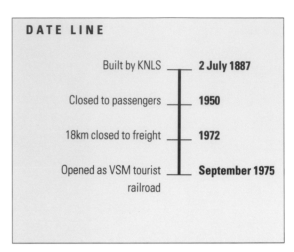

DATE LINE

Built by KNLS	**2 July 1887**
Closed to passengers	**1950**
18km closed to freight	**1972**
Opened as VSM tourist railroad	**September 1975**

Locomotives and rolling stock have been acquired from a number of European railroads. The steam locomotives, of which there are 11, are mainly from the Deutsche Bundesbahn and the former Deutsche Reichsbahn, with one from former Czechoslovakia, while there are six diesel locomotives from the Netherlands and one from the former DR. Passenger rolling stock has been obtained from Austrian Federal Railroads Deutsche Reichsbahn and of course the Netherlands. There are also some dozen freight vehicles, mainly of Netherlands origin.

As the title implies, steam train operation is the main activity, although diesel locomotives are used at certain times. Trains are operated from April to mid-July at weekends only, then from mid-July until the end of August on Mondays to Fridays also, reverting to weekends again until end of October. In the high season a combined rail-riverboat-rail trip can be made by NS diesel train between Apeldoorn and Zutphen, boat on the River Ijsel to Dieren, and VSM steam train back to Apeldoorn or vice versa. These trips must be reserved in advance. A number of special events are held

each year, and it is necessary to enquire from VSM early in each season for details of these. Charter trains can be arranged for special visits or other occasions. National Steam Day is in May, and the 20th anniversary of the line was celebrated on 2 September 1995. There are no plans for any extensions, but a museum is planned for the future.

Apeldoorn or Dieren are best reached by Netherlands Railroads, which run at regular half-hour intervals throughout every day.

ABOVE *Former Deutsche Bundesbahn class 23 2-6-2 No 071 on a train near Eerbeek.*

Blonay-Chamby Museum Railroad

Chemin de Fer-Musée Blonay-Chamby

S W I T Z E R L A N D

USEFUL DATA

Headquarters PO Box 366, CH-1001, Lausanne, Switzerland.

Phone (41) 21 943 21 21.

Information/Reservations CP63, CH-1138 Villars sous Yens, Switzerland.

Phone/Fax (41) 21 943 21 21.

Public Stations Blonay, Chamby. Other stops: Chantemerle, Cornaux.

Timetables & Tickets see above.

Public access
SBB/CFF train, then:
Train: from Vevey by CEV to Blonay; from Montreux by MOB to Chamby.
by car from N9: for Blonay exit Vevey, then St Legier-Blonay. For Chamby exit Montreux, then Fontanivent-Les Avants.

Facilities
Museum and depot at Chaulin, with shop and refreshments.

RIGHT *Five steam locomotives and a train of vintage rolling stock make a spectacular sight as they cross the Baye de Clarens Viaduct.*

ABOVE *Former Brig-Furka-Disentis (BFD) HG3/4 2-6-0 tank locomotive No. 3 and train cross the road after leaving Cornaux on 15 October 1989.*

The Blonay-Chamby Museum Railroad is an association of railroad enthusiasts. It functions on a totally voluntary basis, its aim being to conserve, restore and run historical narrow-gauge railroad equipment.

A link was built in 1912 between Blonay and Chamby, above the resorts of Vevey and Montreux, to connect two previously independent 1m-(3ft 3in) gauge railroads, the Vevey Electric Railroad (CEV) and the Montreux-Oberland-Bernois (MOB). The MOB connects the Lake of Geneva region with the Bernese Oberland. Originally a line was built from Blonay to Les Pleiades. This was an electric rack railroad opened in 1911–13. The line climbs to an altitude of 1,360m (4,461 feet) with a maximum gradient of 20% (1 in 5). In 1950 it was absorbed into the Vevey Electric Railroad, which gave direct access between Vevey and Les Pleiades, and the line voltage was increased from 750 to 900 volts DC.

The Montreux-Oberland-Bernois Railroad was opened in stages between Montreux and Zweisimmen between 1901 and 1905, and to Lenk in 1912. A connecting link was built between Blonay and the village of Chamby on the MOB, giving access from Montreux to Les Pleiades. The distance from Montreux to Lenk is 75.2km (46.7 miles). Electric traction was used from the beginning.

In 1955, MOB and CEV merged and also took over another rack railroad, the 800mm-gauge (31½ inch) Chemins de Fer des Rochers de Naye. At the same time, traffic using the Blonay-Chamby link diminished, and the operation was suspended for economic reasons, the last train running in 1966. The track and right-of-way were retained, however, as the Swiss Transport Museum at Lucerne was interested in it as a possible line on which to run trains of historical interest. The project was abandoned due to difficulties of access and administration.

In 1968, a group of railroad enthusiasts took up the idea, and after a time formed the Blonay-Chamby Museum Railroad Association. Not much real deterioration had occurred, but work had to be done by a team of volunteers to meet the standards required by the Swiss Federal Transport Office, who, when satisfied, granted a concession to run historical trains, the first concession of this type in Switzerland.

The Association began building workshops and the Chaulin Museum at the Chamby end of the line. This took thousands of hours of work by volunteers, and thousands more have been spent on renovating locomotives and rolling stock, much of it in a pretty delapidated state and requiring complete overhaul—not to mention keeping the track in good order.

The Museum Railroad now runs trains on Saturday afternoons and Sundays from mid-May to the end of October. A mixed service of steam and electric trains is run. Though short, the line has wonderful views over Montreux

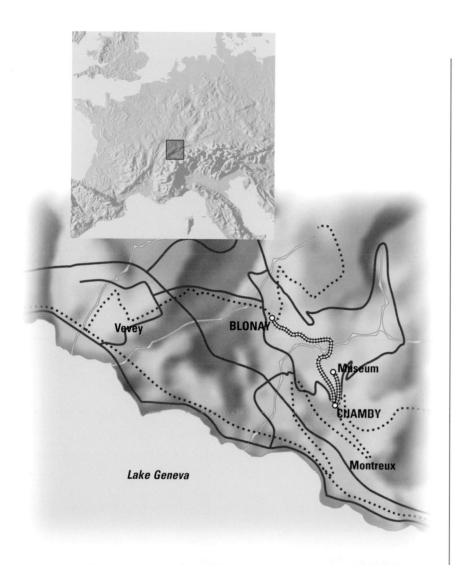

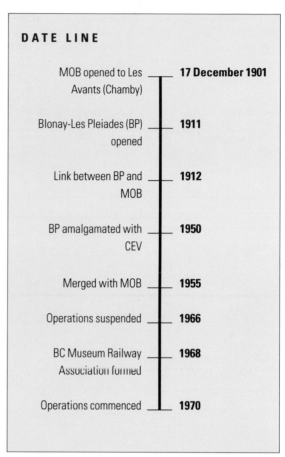

DATE LINE

MOB opened to Les Avants (Chamby)	**17 December 1901**
Blonay-Les Pleiades (BP) opened	**1911**
Link between BP and MOB	**1912**
BP amalgamated with CEV	**1950**
Merged with MOB	**1955**
Operations suspended	**1966**
BC Museum Railway Association formed	**1968**
Operations commenced	**1970**

ABOVE *Former Geneva tram car of 1920 vintage and other tramway auxiliary vehicles outside Chaulin depot.*

and the Lake of Geneva, running at an elevation of between 620 and 750m (2,034 and 2,460 feet). There is a 78m (256-foot) six-arch viaduct over the Baye de Clarens and a short tunnel below Cornaux.

Normally trains run from Blonay to Chamby, and then in and out of the Chaulin Museum. On Sunday afternoons, there are additional trips from Chamby to the Museum and back again for visitors arriving by car. Special trains, outside scheduled times, can be booked for groups, weddings, and other special occasions. Some special excursions are run from Chamby over the MOB line to Montbovon and then on to the Gruyère Railway (GFM). Rolling stock consists of 11 steam locomotives from Switzerland, France, Germany, Spain, and Italy, three electric locomotives (Swiss), five electric motor-coaches (Swiss), seven electric tram cars and 13 assorted passenger cars. The line is electrified throughout at 900V DC and power is supplied by the MOB, or in emergency by CEV.

SOUTHERN HEMISPHERE

Pichi Richi Railway

S O U T H   A U S T R A L I A

USEFUL DATA

Headquarters Pichi Richi Railway, Railway Station, Railway Terrace, Quorn, South Australia 5433.

Phone (61) 8 296 6352.

Fax (43) 5244 398339.

Public Station Quorn. Other stations at Summit, Pichi Richi, Woolshed Flat. Trains will set down at these places only.

Timetables & Tickets

Pichi Richi Rly Booking Officer, 6 First Street, Ororoo, South Australia 5431.

Fax (61) 86 581109.

Or BASS-SA, 131 246 in S Australia, 008 888 327 Interstate.

Private Hire/Charter

Traffic Superintendent, 20 Currawong Crescent, Modbury Heights, South Australia 5092.

Phone (61) 8 264 7439 (A/Hrs).

Public access

Train to Port Augusta. Bus or rental car to Quorn. Bus from Adelaide or private car to Quorn.

Note Port Augusta may be reached by air from Adelaide—Augusta Airways, phone 086 423 100 or 08 234 3000. Car from Adelaide via Highway One. Stateliner Bus, phone 08 415 5555.

Facilities

Museum & workshop, guided tours, souvenir/book shop at Quorn station, refreshments at Woolshed Flat & in Quorn.

The railroad over the Pichi Richi Pass was opened in 1879. It is the last remnant of the 3ft 6in-gauge (1,067mm) Great Northern Railway originally planned to link Port Augusta, South Australia, Alice Springs and Darwin in the Northern Territory with Adelaide. Later it formed a vital link in Sir John Forrest's Great Western Railway across the Nullabor Plain to Kalgoorlie and Perth, Western Australia.

The first section of the line was opened to Quorn on 15 December 1879, and the line was pushed to Oonadatta, where for many years the "Great Northern Express" terminated. The line was completed to Alice Springs in 1929. In 1911, control of the Northern Territory was handed over to the Commonwealth Government (central government of Australia). They took over the railroads on 1 January 1911, but the lines were still operated by

ABOVE *Pichi Richi steam railcar "The Coffee Pot" built in* *Leeds, England by Kitson and Company in 1909.*

South Australian Railways until 1 January 1926. A 3ft 6in-gauge line was started from Darwin but for many years did not project further south than Birdum, from which the Stuart Highway led to Alice Springs.

At Quorn in 1923, the "Great Northern Express" began to be called "The Afghan Express" (later just the "Ghan"), after the Afghan camel-traders who pioneered a supply line across the arid territory of the Great Victoria and Simpson Deserts.

In time, sections of the original line were either bypassed or, later, converted to standard gauge. In fact, the orders for two classes of diesel-electric locomotives supplied in 1954

and 1965–7 specified one set of standard-gauge bogies so that, if necessary, they could be used on Commonwealth Railways standard-gauge lines. Later still, a new standard-gauge line was built between Tarcoola and Alice Springs.

The line between Port Augusta and Quorn was closed to all traffic on 14 January 1957, but the track and right-of-way remained. Quorn was the junction of three lines. On the one to Peterborough, Terowie and Adelaide, the track still exists as far as Bruce but is not used. The original Quorn-Hawker-Alice Springs 3ft 6in-gauge line now has only 4km (2½ miles) remaining. The Quorn-Port Augusta line is operated only to Woolshed-Flat, 16.5km (10¼ miles). There are plans to extend to Portre Augusta.

Following closure of the line in 1957, things remained dormant for a time. Then the Pichi Richi Preservation Society Inc. was formed, with plans to restore at least part of one of the historic 3ft 6in-gauge lines of the former Great Northern/Commonwealth Railways. On 22 July 1973 the line reopened as a tourist operation. The line over the Pichi Richi Pass is particularly scenic, with a steep climb to the summit of the line 401m (1,322 feet) above sea level. From the summit, the line winds through the pass to the derelict town of Pichi Richi, then down over the S-bend bridge to Woolshed Flat, the terminus of the line until the proposed 23.5km (14½-mile) extension to Port Augusta can be completed.

There is a wide and interesting collection of motive power and rolling stock, including an ex-South Australian Railway (SAR) 4-8-0 built in South Australia in 1909; two 4-8-2s built in England by Beyer Peacock as late as 1951; one 955hp "NSU" class diesel-electric built in Birmingham, England in 1954; and one 1,400hp "NT" class of British design built in Australia by Tulloch of Rhodes, Sydney, in

1968. Perhaps one of the most unusual items is a self-contained steam rail car (rail motor) built by Kitson of Leeds, England, in 1909. Known as "The Coffee Pot," this may be rented for an exclusive group of 22 passengers for a run to Woolshed Flat. There is also a Brill diesel railcar, designed in the USA and built in 1926.

The 10 passenger cars all came from the SAR or Commonwealth Railways, and were built in Australia. These are mainly wood-bodied vehicles like those that would have been used on the "Ghan" and other expresses,

ABOVE *A spectacular sight as W class 4-8-2 No 934, built in England by Beyer Peacock in Manchester for the former Western Australian Government Railways, storms up to the summit.*

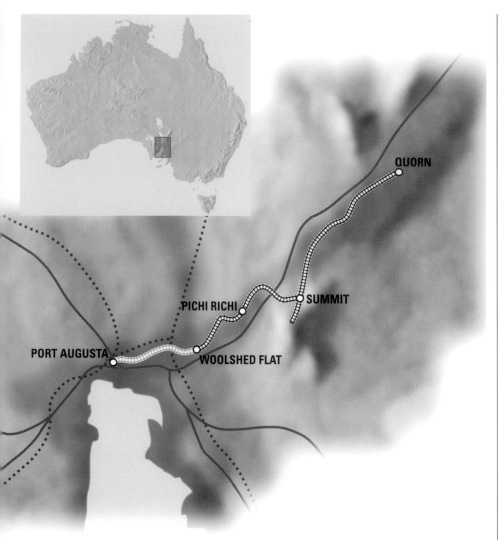

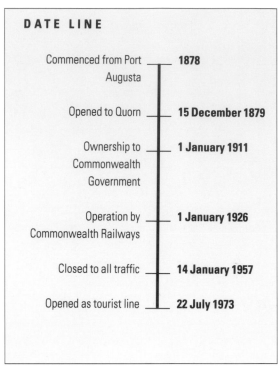

DATE LINE

Commenced from Port Augusta	**1878**
Opened to Quorn	**15 December 1879**
Ownership to Commonwealth Government	**1 January 1911**
Operation by Commonwealth Railways	**1 January 1926**
Closed to all traffic	**14 January 1957**
Opened as tourist line	**22 July 1973**

ABOVE *Replenishing the water supply of "The Coffee Pot".*

and include the former SAR Commissioner's private car, "Flinders". This may also be rented in advance by a group of up to 16 people, and attached to scheduled trains.

At Quorn, the operational headquarters of the Pichi Richi, is the Railway Workshop-Museum, which is open to visitors. Guided tours take visitors through over a century of railway heritage. Work is in progress on the restoration of locomotives and rolling stock, one of which is a steam 2-6-0 built by Beyer Peacock of Manchester in 1879.

Trains are operated on the second and fourth Sunday in each month from March to the end of November. Extra trains are scheduled to suit school vacations and public holidays. From mid-August to mid-October, trains run every Saturday and Sunday. The round trip is normally about 2 hours.

At Woolshed Flat, refreshments are served from a vintage dining car, "Light," which has an operating wood stove. The area has many other attractions: important for railroad enthusiasts is "Steamtown" at Peterborough. Other South Australia railroad attractions are the Port Dock Railway Museum, St Kilda Tramway Museum, Steamranger (broad gauge) & Goolwa "Cockle" train.

Quorn may be reached from Adelaide by bus on four days each week. Rail passengers on the trans-Australia can stop at Port Augusta and travel either by bus or rental car to Quorn, 43km (27 miles).

Reservations are necessary only for groups or to rent special trains, the "Coffee Pot" or the Brill diesel car, "Barwell Bull". The reservation office is Bass-SA, who have a Dial-n-Charge service: phone 131 246 from South Australia, or Interstate (Free call) 008 888 327. Tickets may be reserved by writing.

Puffing Billy

VICTORIA, AUSTRALIA

USEFUL DATA

Headquarters Puffing Billy Railway, PO Box 451, Belgrave 3160, Victoria, Australia.

Phone (61) 3 9754 6800.

Fax (61) 3 9754 2513.

Main Stations Belgrave, Menzies Creek, Emerald, Lakeside.

Other Stations Selby, Clematis Nobelius Siding, Nobelius.

Timetables by phone or mail from Headquarters.

Tickets from main stations.

Reservations required for Luncheon Train and Night Train with pre-payment. Also required for groups of 20 or more.

Public access

Train from Melbourne. Road from Melbourne, Melway map 75.

Facilities

Steam Museum at Menzies Creek. Refreshments: Belgrave, Menzies Creek & Lakeside; Emerald weekends. Souvenirs: Belgrave & Lakeside. Menzies Creek, limited range.

RIGHT *An "NA" class 2-6-2 tank of Baldwin design but built in Australia by Victorian Railways and still the staple motive power on this real gem of a preserved railway.*

The "Puffing Billy Railway" is a 2ft 6in-gauge (762mm) line in the state of Victoria, Australia 42km (26 miles) by rail from Melbourne, in the Dandenong Ranges. It runs from Belgrave at an altitude of 228m (747 feet), and follows a sinuous route through scenic forest and farmland country to Emerald Lake (Lakeside), a distance of 13.3km (8¼ miles).

The "Puffing Billy" runs over part of what was once a 30km (18½-mile) line between Upper Ferntree Gulley and Gembrook. The original line was one of four low-cost narrow-gauge lines built at the beginning of the 20th century to open up remote areas of the state of Victoria for settlements. It was built by the Victorian Government Railways and the gauge of 2ft 6in was chosen, as with many other narrow-gauge railways, for economy of construction. The line was approved by Act of Parliament, and work commenced in August 1899, progressing so rapidly that the line was opened for traffic on 18 December 1900.

Because it was near the city of Melbourne, the line soon became well known as a scenic attraction. For two generations it served the community as a source of pleasure to picnic groups and as a carrier for farmers and timber cutters. With the coming of the automobile, traffic gradually declined and operating losses mounted—but on 30 April 1953 a landslide blocked the track, which finally sealed its fate, and the line was closed to all traffic.

There had always been considerable public interest in the Gembrook line, and following closure, the "Puffing Billy Preservation

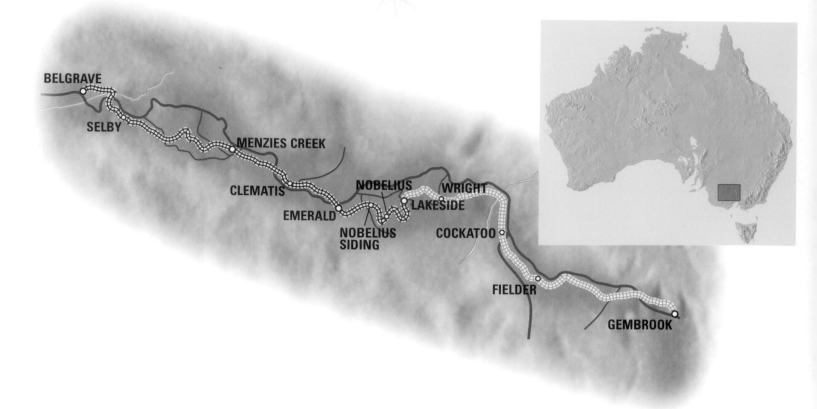

Society" was set up. This voluntary group ensured the survival of the trains until 1958, on the only operable section of the line, between Upper Ferntree Gully and Belgrave. It was then taken over by Victorian Railways, for 5ft 3in-gauge (1,600mm) electric trains between Melbourne and Belgrave.

The Society decided the remaining part of the line could be restored, and with the blessing of the Victorian Railways and help from the Citizens Military Forces, work was commenced. The first obstacle, the large landslide, was eventually bypassed. Trains were returned to the line on 1 October 1962 between Belgrave and Menzies Park, a distance of 4.8km (3 miles). It took three years to rebuild the line between Menzies Park and Emerald, a distance of 3.6km (2¼ miles), and this was reopened in 1965. The final 3.6km (2¼ miles) to Lakeside were restored in 1975.

By Act of Parliament, the Emerald Tourist Railway Board was able to assume ownership and control of the railroad from Victorian Railways on 1 October 1977. Since then, the railroad has restored locomotives and rolling stock, and has gradually increased its operations to become one of the major railroad attractions in the state of Victoria.

There are plans to extend operations over the whole of the remaining 10.5km (6½ miles)

to Gembrook, the original terminus. Work is in progress on this extension; the aim is to have it operating before the end of 1998, in good time to celebrate the line's centennial.

The line is still owned by the emerald Tourist Railway Board, which consists of members of the Preservation Society Executive Committee with appointees of the Ministry of Transport and the Ministry of Tourism. Today the track, stations and trains are in as good shape as they ever were. Headquarters of the Railway are at Belgrave, where an entirely new station was built by Society volunteers between 1958 and 1962. Locomotive workshops were completed in 1975, with extensive servicing and repair facilities.

Having left Belgrave, the route passes close to the Sherbrook Forest, crossing an 85m (280 foot) long, 13m (42 foot) high trestle bridge over Monbulk Creek and the main road. This is the lowest point on the line. The first station (trains do not normally stop here) is at Selby; it was opened in 1904 and named after an early landowner. The landslide of 1953 occurred just beyond here, and the line now uses a new formation to bypass the area.

By Menzies Creek, the first stop, the train has climbed 74m (243 feet) from the lowest point. Before reaching the station there is a view across to Port Phillip Bay. Adjacent to

RIGHT *Two "NA" class 2-6-2 tanks working hard as they cross the new long curved trestle.*

feet) the highest point on the line.

Gold was discovered at Emerald in 1858, and the township grew up near the workings. When gold was used up, the town became an agricultural center. Here are the Railway's carriage repair workshops, where the restoration of passenger and freight vehicles is undertaken. A little further on is Nobelius Siding, named after the Nobelius & Co estates, from where seedlings and plants were once sent by rail to all parts of Australia and the world. Nobelius station follows, originally set in a magnificent garden which there are plans to restore. The terminus is at Lakeside (Emerald Lake), at an altitude of 242m (795 feet).

Trains are worked by four of six 2-6-2 NA class tank locomotives. These were built by Victorian Railways to a Baldwin (USA) design between 1902 and 1912. Three other steam locomotives are used from time to time, and one diesel shunting locomotive. Under restoration is a 2-6-0+0-6-2 G42 class Garratt locomotive built by Beyer Peacock, Manchester, in 1926, originally used on one of the sister lines, the Moe and Walhalla in the Baw Ranges. Passengers ride in 36 vehicles all built by Victorian Railways, some of them open cars.

Trains run throughout the year, with three, four, or five departures each day depending on the time of year. There are no trains on Christmas Day. In times of very dry weather, steam locomotives may have to be replaced by diesel, but normally all trains are steam operated. At certain times there are special events with their own timetables. There are "Santa Specials" on three Sundays in December. One popular feature is the Dinner Train.

Belgrave may be reached from Melbourne Flinders Street station direct by electric train. By car, Belgrave is 45km (25 miles) from Melbourne and is on Melway map 75, reference G9. Alternatively, go to Clematis and turn left for Menzies Creek or right for Emerald. There is no parking area or road access to "Puffing Billy" Station at Belgrave. Park in the 'Met' car park near the suburban railway station, and follow the walkway under the main road bridge, or park in the Bayview Road parking area.

ABOVE An "NA" class with a well-loaded train leaving a thickly wooded area with many youngsters clearly enjoying the ride.

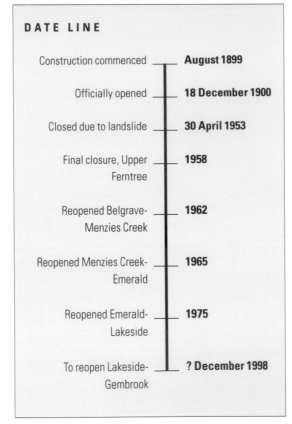

DATE LINE

Construction commenced	**August 1899**
Officially opened	**18 December 1900**
Closed due to landslide	**30 April 1953**
Final closure, Upper Ferntree	**1958**
Reopened Belgrave-Menzies Creek	**1962**
Reopened Menzies Creek-Emerald	**1965**
Reopened Emerald-Lakeside	**1975**
To reopen Lakeside-Gembrook	**? December 1998**

the station is the Steam Museum, which houses a unique collection of steam locomotives from Australia and overseas, together with rolling stock and steam machinery. Menzies Creek is the half-way point. Beyond it there are magnificent views on the "low" side of the track. The next station is Clematis, formerly called Paradise, and from here the line rises at its steepest, with a gradient of 3.3% (1 in 30), to Emerald, at 318m (1,045

Steamtown

S O U T H   A U S T R A L I A

USEFUL DATA

Headquarters Steamtown, PO Box 133, Peterborough, SA 5422, Australia.

Phone (61) 86 512759. Reservations: (61) 85 221394. Peterborough Corpn: (61) 86 512106. SA Tourism: (61) 08 2121505.

Stations Peterborough, Eurelia, Orrorro.

Public access by private car, hired car or bus from Adelaide or Port Augusta.

Facilities Museum in railway workshops. Refreshments on trains including souvenirs and books.

Reservations strongly recommended!

LEFT *A well-patronized train hauled by "W" class 4-8-2 No 901 makes good speed on one of the specials sponsored by "Steamtown".*

ABOVE "W" class 901 seems to have reached the end of the line!

Steamtown was formed in 1977 to operate a working steam railway museum on a section of narrow (3ft 6in, 1,067mm) gauge line between Peterborough and Quorn, South Australia. Peterborough (Petersburg until 1917) is a town of 2,600 inhabitants situated 243km (151 miles) due north of Adelaide. Its roots lay in agriculture; it was founded in 1875 and its first building was erected in 1879. The railway followed on 17 January 1881, the line running from Adelaide via Jamestown.

The railway system grew rapidly with lines connecting Peterborough to Towerie and the New South Wales border, so that Peterborough became a center of lines to Port Pirie, Port Augusta, Adelaide and the Silverton Mines. The town developed rapidly, largely due to the railway which provided its lifeblood for the next 110 years.

Sitting astride the backbone of the South Australian Railway system, narrow gauge lines went north to Quorn where they connected with the Commonwealth Railways line to Alice Springs. At Towerie to the south they connected with the broad gauge (5ft 3in, 1,600mm) line to Adelaide. Peterborough was the divisional headquarters of the South

Australian Railways with a major locomotive depot and workshops.

In January 1970 a new standard (4ft 8½in, 1,435mm) gauge line was brought into operation to Broken Hill, and the line to Towerie was converted to broad gauge making Peterborough a three gauge railway center. The locomotive roundhouse remains as a symbol of the steam era and is now listed by the Australian National Heritage. From 1970 the workforce was gradually reduced as work was transferred to other railway centers. The town now relies on other industries for its survival. In 1977 a group of enthusiasts founded The Steamtown Peterborough Preservation Society Inc. with a view to preserving an operating museum on a section of track on the narrow gauge Peterborough-Quorn line and to run steam-hauled trains on it.

Train-running operations began on 1 April 1981 with trains to and from Eurelia, a distance of 56km (35 miles) along the line to Port Augusta. Now trains operate during the winter months, on public holiday weekends and some school holidays, between Peterborough and Orroroo, the junction of the Port Augusta and Hawker and Alice Springs lines,

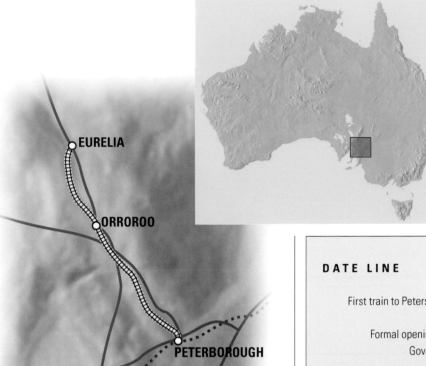

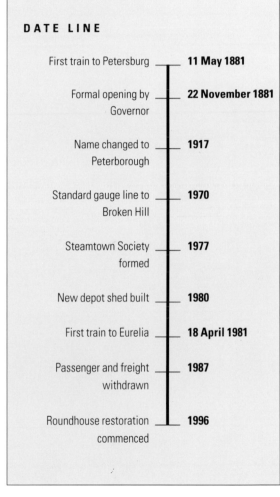

DATE LINE

First train to Petersburg	**11 May 1881**
Formal opening by Governor	**22 November 1881**
Name changed to Peterborough	**1917**
Standard gauge line to Broken Hill	**1970**
Steamtown Society formed	**1977**
New depot shed built	**1980**
First train to Eurelia	**18 April 1981**
Passenger and freight withdrawn	**1987**
Roundhouse restoration commenced	**1996**

a round trip of 71km (44 miles), or to Eurelia 113km (70 miles) away. The journey takes five and seven hours respectively. Steam trains cannot be run in the summer months as there is a total fire ban because of the risk of bush fires between October and March.

Special features are the steam-hauled trains comprising former Commonwealth Railways wood-body carriages built between 1917 and 1928 for the standard gauge Trans-Australia railway. These vehicles are some of those which were transferred to narrow gauge bogies for use on the Alice Springs "Ghan" train. The Society owns four steam locomotives and four diesels, 17 passenger coaches and a variety of freight vehicles. All operations are based on the Peterborough roundhouse. Steam is the normal motive power but one diesel locomotive of the former Commonwealth Railways is available for use in emergency.

The roundhouse and workshops have been transferred from National Railways to the Department of Environment and National Resources under leasing arrangements negotiated with Steamtown and the Corporation of Peterborough. Steamtown is currently (1996) restoring the workshops, presently used as the

museum, to enable their full use as part of Steamtown's operations. Steamtown is run by a small band of volunteers and is a self-supporting non-profit organization.

Access to Peterborough is now only possible by road, either by private car or by bus. There is normally only one train departure each day at either 10.00 or 11.00am. Tickets may be available on the day but booking in advance is strongly recommended. Reserved seats must be paid in full prior to travel.

Bay of Islands Vintage Railway

N O R T H   I S L A N D ,   N E W   Z E A L A N D

USEFUL DATA

Headquarters Bay of
Islands Railway, Railway
Station, 102, Gillies Street,
Kawakawa, Bay of Islands,
North Island, New Zealand.

Phone (64) 9 404 0684.
(After hours: (64) 9 404
0450).

Fax (64) 9 404 0291.

**Timetables &
Reservations** from
Headquarters.

Tickets Kawakawa Station.

Public access
by bus or car from Auckland
(about 193km, 120 miles).

Facilities
Shop at Kawakawa & on
train.

The Bay of Islands Vintage Railway is a non-profit organization run by the Taumerere Northland Rail Trust and the Opua-Kawakawa Railway Preservation Society Inc. The Trust owns the tracks and leases the 13.8km (8½-mile) right-of-way, and the Kawakawa Station building, from New Zealand Rail Limited. The Preservation Society owns the locomotives, rolling stock and all other equipment necessary to run the Railway. Operations are directed by the Joint Venture Committee of three representatives from each organization.

The line runs on what was part of the northern extremity of the NZR system, and has now been isolated from it with the recent removal of the track between Kawakawa and Moerewa. Nevertheless, the railroad thrives with the continued support of the NZR.

The Bay of Islands Coal Company built the railroad in 1868 to standard gauge (4ft 8½in, 1,435mm), to convey coal from mines in Kawakawa to the navigable river at Taumarere, where the coal was transferred to barges and later to ships further down-river. In 1884 the line was extended to Opua, so that coal could be transferred direct to vessels, eliminating the barge journey.

The first coal train ran to Taumarere on 28 January 1871, and the first passenger train on 4 December in the same year; this was the first passenger train service on the North Island. New Zealand Railways had adopted the 3ft 6in (1,067mm) gauge in 1870, and an Act of the central government stipulated that all lines should be constructed to that gauge. Between 1885 and 1908 all other former private lines were converted to 3ft 6in gauge, including the Bay of Islands line.

NZR withdrew regular passenger trains in 1976, and freight in 1980. A few special tourist trains continued to run to this scenic area of the North Island, until on 28

RIGHT *1927 built Peckett (Bristol UK) 4-4-0 "Gabriel" makes a special photographic stop en route to Opua with a train of former NZR suburban cars.*

OPUS

Bay of Islands

KAWAKAWA

NORTHLAND

December 1985 the line reopened as a tourist line. Things deteriorated, however, and a Preservation Society was formed in 1987 to help preserve and operate the line.

In late 1988, NZR gave notice that because the line was run-down and not in regular use, they planned to close it and to lift the tracks for use elsewhere. After some months of negotiation by concerned local citizens and the Preservation Society, a temporary lease was granted. The first train ran on 16 December 1989; this proved successful, and negotiations continued with NZR, leading to the purchase of the track. A lease arrangement was concluded on 18 September 1993.

There are two British-built steam locomotives and four diesel locomotives operating the line between Kawakawa and Opua. There are six passenger cars, including four former-NZR 1934–8 vintage suburban cars and two ex-main-line 1927 wood-body cars. The line

RIGHT *A Peckett 4-4-0 tank crosses Taumarere Bridge in what appears to be very inclement weather.*

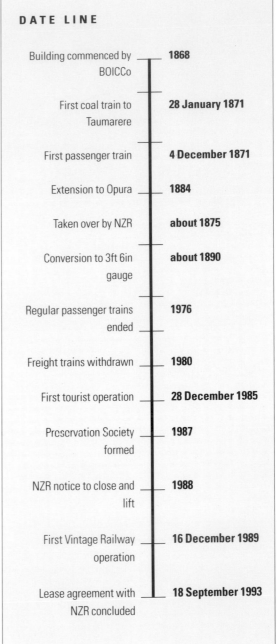

DATE LINE

Building commenced by BOICCo	**1868**
First coal train to Taumarere	**28 January 1871**
First passenger train	**4 December 1871**
Extension to Opura	**1884**
Taken over by NZR	**about 1875**
Conversion to 3ft 6in gauge	**about 1890**
Regular passenger trains ended	**1976**
Freight trains withdrawn	**1980**
First tourist operation	**28 December 1985**
Preservation Society formed	**1987**
NZR notice to close and lift	**1988**
First Vintage Railway operation	**16 December 1989**
Lease agreement with NZR concluded	**18 September 1993**

TOP *On those occasions when a steam locomotive is unavailable or cannot be used recourse is made to diesels.*

ABOVE *On fine days an "open" car is included in the formation of trains and such a train is about to leave Kawa Kawa behind a 1958 0-4-0 Price diesel-mechanical "Star".*

also owns 12 freight vehicles. The journey takes 45 minutes each way.

At present, only the stations at each end of the line are open, but at Taumarere the site of the former station is still visible, and there are plans to recover (from a farm nearby) and restore the old station building. An old church building was recently donated, and there are plans to use it as a museum. There is a shop in Kawakawa station, and souvenirs are sold on the train.

Today the line operates tourist passenger trains year-round. Between late April and mid-December there are two trains each day from Sunday to Tuesday, except during the "maintenance periods," which are mid-July to

mid-August and the week before and including Christmas Day. During school vacations, trains run every day; in the "high season" from Christmas to the end of April, there are three trains every day.

Special trains may be run. Reservations are required for parties of 40 or more; otherwise tickets may be purchased at Kawakawa station.

Taieri Gorge Railway

S O U T H I S L A N D , N E W Z E A L A N D

USEFUL DATA

Headquarters Taieri Gorge
Railway, Dunedin Railway
Station, PO Box 140,
Dunedin, New Zealand.

Phone (64) 3 477 4449.

Fax (64) 3 477 4953.

Public Station Dunedin.

Other Stops Hundon,
Pukerangi, Middlemarch.

Timetables by mail or
phone request from
Headquarters.

Tickets from Dunedin
Railway Station—reserve
early! Special trips, groups,
etc: inquire at Headquarters.

Public access
NZ Rail to Dunedin. Roads
from Christchurch &
Invercargill. Wheelchair
access by reservation.

Facilities
Snack bar, light
refreshments, wines, hot &
cold drinks, pre-order meals.
Museum & craft shops at
Middlemarch.

LEFT *An ex-NZR
EMD diesel electric is the
motive power for this
train threading its way
through the rocky
territory between
Dunedin and Pukerangi.*

The Taieri Gorge Railway follows the gold-bearing Taieri River in New Zealand's South Island. The river rises in the district of Otago, flows north for a while, then turns south to reach the sea about 32km (20 miles) south of Dunedin, carving out a spectacular valley and gorges on its way.

Between 1879 and 1891, a 3ft 6in-gauge (1,067mm) railroad was built from Dunedin, capital of the Otago, by the Otago Central Railway, running into the Dunstan Mountains as far as Cromwell on the Clutha river. It was built primarily to transport the products of the mines and forests to the sea. It used the course of the Taieri river and its tributaries, but even so, the civil engineering work was considerable: there a number of tunnels and some splendid viaducts.

Taieri Gorge Railways is a trust that has operated trains throughout the South Island since 1978. Regular tourist runs from Dunedin to Pukerangi, 58km (36 miles), and Middlemarch, 77km (48 miles), have been operated since 1987. There is usually one train each afternoon. The full return journey takes 5½ hours.

The journey has been compared to the DURANGO & SILVERTON trip in Colorado, USA.

The route follows the main line 12km (7½ miles) south to Wingatui Junction, then turns north through two tunnels to Salisbury, on the edge of the Mount Allan Forest. After a short ride to Taioma, the train emerges from the Mullocky tunnel to cross the Taieri River by the high Wingatui Viaduct, a steel trestle with eight spans, and goes on to Parera.

Still with the Mount Allan forest on the right, the train snakes along the mountainside and through another tunnel, and arrives at Mount Allan station. The line continues through Christmas Creek, Hindon, Deep Stream, Flat Stream and The Reefs, and finally arrives at Pukerangi, approximately 2 hours from the start. The railroad reaches its highest altitude at Pukerangi, the head of the gorge, 250m (822 feet) above sea-level. The landscape is distinguished by unique rock formations, which provide refuge for lizards, birds, and other wildlife—in Maori "Pukerangi" means "Hill of Heaven". From here the line crosses undulating territory for 19km (12 miles) to Middlemarch. This is the last township to retain its link with the Otago Central Railway. There are historic farm homesteads to visit, a well-kept museum and craft shops.

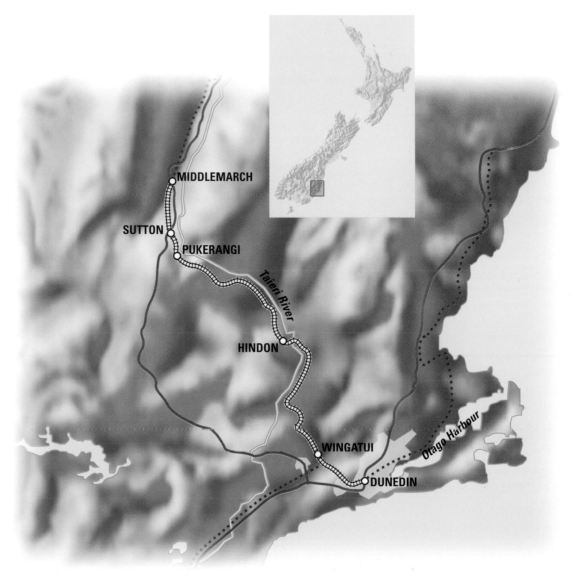

Trains are run in conjunction with Pacific Tourways' daily bus tour to and from Queenstown. Travelers may stop over for a few days at any point. Trains are hauled by New Zealand Railways' diesel locomotives and include both modern, panoramic air-conditioned coaches and restored 1920s vintage coaches. All trains serve refreshments: light food, wines, ales, and hot or cold beverages. Groups may pre-order set-menu meals to be served on board. Every train has wheelchair access to one carriage and restroom, but advance reservation is necessary.

Trains run throughout the year, but not every day, between May and August. From the beginning of September there is a daily train to Pukerangi; this is extended to Middlemarch on Saturdays from October to the second weekend in March. There are two daily trains on certain days in December and January.

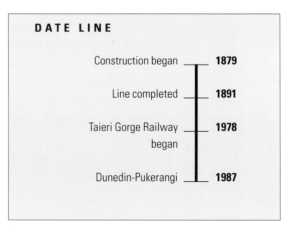

DATE LINE	
Construction began	**1879**
Line completed	**1891**
Taieri Gorge Railway began	**1978**
Dunedin-Pukerangi	**1987**

Special extra trains can be arranged for guaranteed groups.

The train is known as "The Taieri Gorge Limited" and departs from the Dunedin Railway Station in the city center. Dunedin is on the main line from Christchurch, from which there is also a good road. Christchurch has air connection to North Island, Australia, etc.

Outeniqualand Preserved Railway

C A P E   P R O V I N C E ,   S O U T H   A F R I C A

USEFUL DATA

Headquarters Heritage Foundation of Transnet Limited, PO Box 850, George 6530, Republic of South Africa.

Phone (27) 441 73 8288, Knysna 2 1361.

Fax (27) 441 73 8286.

Main Stations George, Knysna.

Other Stations Wilderness, Duiwerivier, Rocketed, Sedgefield, Ruigtevlei, Goukamma, Keytersnek.

Timetables & Tickets from Headquarters or main stations. Reservations recommended.

Public access
by air to George. Bus from Cape Town, Port Elizabeth or Gauteng.

Facilities
Souvenir shop & coffee shop at Knysna. Refreshments on trains.

RIGHT A mixed train crosses the spectacular Kaaimans River bridge hauled by a class 24 2-8-4 locomotive, built in Glasgow in 1949.

The Outeniqua Choo-Tjoe is South Africa's only remaining scheduled mixed steam train service. It operates on the Outeniqualand Preserved Railway between George and Knysna, on the south coast of South Africa, almost mid-way between Port Elizabeth and Cape Town. George and Knysna are in the heart of the well-known Garden Route, the area of Cape Province renowned for its wild flowers, fruit, and lush green valleys.

This piece of 3ft 6in-gauge (1,067mm) railroad was built by South African Railways and Harbors. It opened on 27 February 1928 between George and Ruigteval, and went on to Knysna on 27 October the same year, on which day the opening ceremony was performed. The line was closed only for a brief period between 15 November and 10 December 1928 to allow commissioning of the new bridge over the Kaaimans River; otherwise it has operated continuously to the present day.

South African Railways have undergone two changes of identity. On 1 April 1981 the company became South African Transport Services, and on 1 April 1991 it became Spoornet (Railways), the business unit of Transnet, who operated the George-Knysna line until it was handed over to Transnet Museum (now Transnet Heritage Foundation), the present operators, on 1 April 1993.

The 67km (42-mile) journey from George, on the Cape Town to Port Elizabeth, is described as an animated art exhibit. The line winds down rapidly to the sea, past fern-covered hills and deep gullies studded with wild flowers. The Indian Ocean is first glimpsed at Victoria Bay. From there the railroad follows the shore line on a cliff face, before crossing the mouth of the Kaaimans River on the curved bridge.

As the train emerges from the final tunnel, the scene opens up to include the golden beaches and enticing woodlands of the "Wilderness". From there the line crosses an

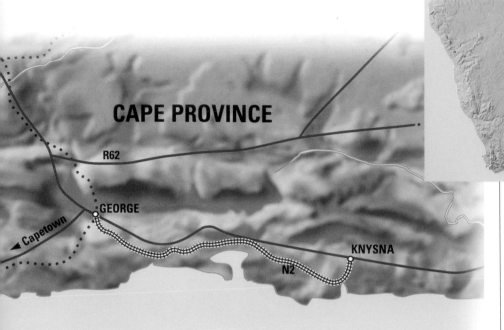

CAPE PROVINCE

R62

GEORGE

← Capetown

KNYSNA

N2

DATE LINE

Opened George to Ruigtevlei — **27 February 1928**

Opened to Knysna — **27 October 1928**

South African Transport Services from — **1 April 1981**

Transnet-Spoornet (railways) — **1 April 1991**

Handed to Transnet Museum — **1 April 1993**

area with many lakes, where thousands of wild birds may be seen. The Goukamma valley offers a scene of rural tranquility. Wooded hills surround a lush green valley of farmland, crossed by a placid stream from which the valley takes its name. This is followed by a climb through forested land to Keytersnek, when the view of Knysna and its lagoon unfolds. Here elephants may sometimes be seen.

There are nine stations, and both passenger and freight trains are operated, with steam locomotives on the scheduled trains. Freight trains are mainly through-trains from the main line, and traffic is carried in Spoornet wagons. Heavy goods trains are sometimes worked by 32 class diesel-electric locomotives.

The locomotive depot servicing the line is at Voorbaai, near Mossel Bay, about 48km (30 miles) west of George. There is an allocation of 18 steam locomotives, of which eight are worked daily, seven are preserved—two of these are Garratts—and three more are GMA class Garratts, rarely used on the line. The regularly-worked locomotives are two 19D class 4-8-2s built in 1937, and six 24 class 2-8-4s built in 1948, all by the North British Locomotive Company in Glasgow, Scotland.

Some of the 16 passenger carriages are wood vehicles, and some steel. Three of the wood-body vehicles date from 1903–9, but the majority of the rest are from the 1933–50 era. Eight have been restored as recently as 1995. Plans for Knysna station include a museum exhibition hall. There is a souvenir store and a coffee shop at Knysna, and refreshments are available on the trains.

Trains are operated throughout the year, except Sundays and certain holidays. There is one morning and one afternoon departure each way. Morning trains cross at Sedgefield and afternoon trains at Goukamma. A single journey takes around 2½ hours.

Access is best by air, to George Airport from all major South African airports. There are long-distance buses from Cape Town, Port Elizabeth and Gauteng. Both George and Knysna are on the main highway that joins Cape Town with Port Elizabeth.

Port Shepstone & Alfred County Railway

N A T A L , S O U T H A F R I C A

USEFUL DATA

Headquarters Banana Express, PO Box 572, Port Shepstone 4240, Republic of South Africa.

Public Stations Port Shepstone, Izotsha, Paddock.

Timetables & Tickets Banana Express Booking Office, PO Box 572, Port Shepstone, Republic of South Africa.

Phone (27) 391 205 30.

Public access by bus or car from Durban.

Facilities Shop & refreshments on Banana Express.

LEFT *A far cry from the Festiniog double Fairlies this 2 foot gauge Beyer Garratt heads a freight train through bush country of the upper part of the line.*

This 2-foot-gauge (610mm) railway has been partly open to tourist traffic since June 1987, when 13km (8 miles) from Port Shepstone to Izotsha was restored to passengers. A further 27km (10¼ miles) was opened to Paddock on 4 December 1988, and 82km (51 miles) to Harding reopened to freight traffic from March 1988.

Port Shepstone lies on the Indian Ocean, at the end of an electrified line of South African Railways 3ft 6in-gauge (1,067mm) system, a little over 100km (63 miles) south down the coast from Durban. The original line was surveyed in 1902 and construction for Natal Government Railways began in 1907 on 3ft 6in gauge, building inland towards the Drakensberg mountains as an extension of the line from Durban. Only the first 7km (4½ miles) were laid to 3ft 6in gauge, which was then converted to 2-foot gauge. The line reached Paddock, 40km (25 miles) from Port Shepstone, in September 1911, when it was taken over by South African Railways following the incorporation of Natal into the Union in 1910. It reached Harding, 122km (76 miles) northeast of Port Shepstone, in 1917.

The original line was built mainly to bring agricultural products to the coast, chiefly fruit and sugar beet, which were either shipped out from Port Shepstone or sent north by rail via Durban to other parts. The line climbed into the hills on fairly steep gradients and with much curvature. As train loads became heavier, the most powerful and flexible loco-

motives, Beyer Garratts, were employed, as on other South African narrow-gauge lines.

Following the growth of motor transport, passenger traffic was discontinued in 1963. The line was sold by South African Railways & Harbours in 1982, but the new owners continued with freight traffic until October 1986. The present owners are the Port Shepstone and Alfred County Railway Company Limited—a public company with about 600 shareholders, all railroad enthusiasts!

The new owners set about restoring the railroad, and limited passenger traffic recommenced in 1987, first to Izotsha, then five months later to Paddock. Freight was restored over the whole line in 1988. Passenger trains are operated to Izotsha, Bohela, Renken, Plains, and Paddock; other stations on the freight line are Izingolweni, Nqabeni, Gindrah, Bongwana, Hluku, Wetherby, and Harding.

Traffic is operated by both steam and diesel locomotives year-round. Three of the steam locomotives are ex-SAR Garratts. There are two diesel-electric locomotives, 12 passenger cars and about 180 freight vehicles. There is no museum, but the "Banana Express" has a shop on board. Reservations are necessary for the "Banana Express".

The headquarters of the line are at Port Shepstone. Best access is by car or bus from Durban (about 110km, 68 miles).

ABOVE *An Alfred County Railway (ACR) 2 foot gauge Garratt in its new smart red livery prepares to take a mixed train down to the coast.*

NATAL

Mzimkulu

HARDING

PADDOCK

PLAINS RENKEN

BOMELA

IZOTSHA

PORT SHEPSTONE

ABOVE *An ACR Garratt waits to depart from Port Shepstone* *with the "Banana Express" for the long uphill drag to Paddock.*

DATE LINE

Original survey	**1902**
Construction commenced	**1907**
Completed to Paddock	**September 1911**
Taken over by S. African Railways	**1911**
Completed to Harding	**1917**
Passenger traffic discontinued	**1963**
Sold by S. African Railways	**1982**
Freight traffic discontinued	**October 1986**
Passenger trains to Izotsha	**1987**
Freight trains to Harding	**1988**

Index

Acknowledgments

The publishers and the author wish to thank all the museums and railroads who helped in the compilation of this book, and the following railroads, archives and photographers who supplied the photographs. Pictures are here identified by their page numbers.

2: Les MacDonald/Conway Scenic Railroad. 6: Musée Français du Chemin de Fer Mulhouse. 7: J. David Conrad/Valley Railroad. 8–9: Jim Winkley. 10, 11: J. Michael Jackson. 12: Royal Hudson Steam Train. 13, 14, 15: Mike White. 16: Michael Anderson/WP & YR. 17: E. A. Hegg, University of Washington/WP & YR. 18: Dedman's Photo Shop/WP & YR. 19: Al Richmond/Grand Canyon Railway. 21: Grand Canyon Railway. 22, 24, 25, 26: Jim Winkley. 28 (top left): Denver Public Library, Western Collection. 28: Jim Winkley. 29, 30, 31: Shoreline Trolley Museum. 32, 33: J. David Conrad/Valley Railroad. 34: J. Devitt/S. Brackley. 35: J. Devitt. 36 (top): Illinois Railway Museum. 36 (center): J. Devitt. 37, 38: Illinois Railway Museum. 39: John Hillman/Indiana Scenic Images/Whitewater Valley Railroad. 40: Lonnie W. Neimeister. 41, 44: Boone & Scenic Valley Railroad. 45, 46: Western Maryland Scenic Railroad. 49: Leo Paro/Huckleberry Railroad. 51: Janna Myracle/St. Louis Iron Mountain and Southern Railway. 52, 53 (left and right): St. Louis Iron Mountain and Southern Railway. 54: Les MacDonald/Conway Scenic Railroad. 56: Jim Winkley. 58: Cumbres & Toltec Scenic Railroad. 59 (top): Mike Taylor. 59 (bottom left and right): Cumbres & Toltec Scenic Railroad. 60: J. W. Swanberg/East Broad Top Railroad. 63 (both): Knox & Kane Railroad. 64, 65, 66: NPS Photo. 67, 69, 70 (top): Jim Winkley. 70 (bottom): William Moedinger/Strasburg Rail Road. 71, 72, 73: Texas State Railroad. 74, 75: Jim Winkley. 76–7, 78, 79: MidContinent Railway. 80–1: K. J. C. Jackson. 82: The Bluebell Railway. 83: Peter Herring. 84: The Bluebell Railway. 85, 86 (both top): Peter Herring. 86 (bottom): The Bluebell Railway. 87, 88: Peter Herring. 90, 91, 92, 93, 94: John A. East/Great Central Railway. 95, 96 (both), 97: K. J. C. Jackson. 98: North Yorkshire Moors Railway. 99, 100: North Yorkshire Moors Railway. 101, 102: Peter Herring. 104, 105, 106, 107, 108: Graham John Maple. 109, 110: Clonmacnoise & West Offaly Railway. 111: Paul Blowfield/Isle of Man Railway. 112: Isle of Man Railway. 113: Paul Blowfield/Isle of Man Railway. 114: Manx Museum. 115 (top): Isle of Man Railways. 115 (bottom): K. J. C. Jackson. 116, 117, 118, 119: Paul Blowfield/Isle of Man Railways. 120: K. J. C. Jackson. 121, 122: Alan Barnes. 124, 125, 126, 127 (both): Ffestiniog Railway. 128–9, 130, 131: K. J. C. Jackson. 132–3: Antti Roivainen/Jokioinen Museum. 134: Zillertalbahn. 135: Jim Winkley. 136: Zillertalbahn. 137, 138: Christian Dosogne/Chemin de Fer des Trois Vallées. 139, 140 (top): Jorha Attila/Jokioinen Museum. 140 (bottom): Antti Roivainen/Jokioinen Museum. 141: Jorha Attila/Jokioinen Museum. 142, 143: éditions MAGE. 144: M. Dubuis/Chemin de Fer des Chanteraines. 146: SNCF/Musée Français du Chemin de Fer Mulhouse. 147: Musée Français du Chemin de Fer Mulhouse/Pfister Editions. 147 (bottom): SNCF/Musée Français du Chemin de Fer. 148: Musée Français du Chemin de Fer. 149, 150, 151: Chemin de Fer Touristique et de Montagne. 156: J. Devitt. 157, 158: L. J. Kooy. 160–1: Hans Ouwerkerk/Veluwsche Steam Railroad. 162: Veluwsche Steam Railroad. 163, 164, 165: Chemin de Fer-Musée Blonay-Chamby. 166–7: Tourism Victoria. 168, 169, 170: Nic Doncaster/Eyre Railway Photographics. 171: Tourism Victoria. 173, 174: Puffing Billy Railway. 175, 176 (both): Nic Doncaster/Eyre Railway Photographics. 178, 179, 180 (both): Bay of Islands Vintage Railway. 181, 182: Taieri Gorge Railway. 184–5, 187, 188, 189: Keith Lawrence.